MW01090129

"A life of reading takes a lot of planning—and a lot of thinking about what to read. That's why Christopher Scalia's smart guide to novels is so useful with its surprising but persuasive suggestions. It may point you to your next great book. But you should start by reading this great book."

—**John J. Miller**, director of the Dow Journalism Program at Hillsdale College

13 Novels Conservatives Will Love

(BUT PROBABLY HAVEN'T READ)

Christopher J. Scalia

Since 1947
REGNERY
An Imprint of Skyhorse Publishing, Inc.

Regnery books may be purchased in bulk at special discounts for sales promotion, corporate gifts, fund-raising, or educational purposes. Special editions can also be created to specifications. For details, contact the Special Sales Department, Regnery, 307 West 36th Street, 11th Floor, New York, NY 10018 or info@skyhorsepublishing.com.

Regnery® is an imprint of Skyhorse Publishing, Inc.®, a Delaware corporation.

Visit our website at www.regnery.com.
Please follow our publisher Tony Lyons on Instagram @tonylyonsisuncertain.

10 9 8 7 6 5 4 3 2 1

Library of Congress Cataloging-in-Publication Data is available on file.

Cover design by David Ter-Avanesyan
Cover photograph by James O'Gara

Print ISBN: 978-1-5107-8239-6
eBook ISBN: 978-1-5107-8240-2

Printed in the United States of America

For Adele
Every day we write the book.

Contents

Introduction

This book is an introduction to many great stories, so I'll introduce it with a true story of my own. More years ago than I care to count, when I was studying English literature in graduate school, I found a used copy of the American philosopher Russell Kirk's *The Portable Conservative Reader* at the university bookstore. I was familiar with Kirk but had never seen this collection, so even though I had a million other books to read for my classes and not much disposable income, I couldn't resist buying it. While I waited in line, a classmate approached me to say hello, saw the title, and asked, "A conservative reader? What's in *that*?" You didn't have to be a grad student to understand the subtext: he was skeptical that there was enough conservative thought to fill a 700-page anthology.[1] To answer his question, though: the anthology includes selections from Edmund Burke, *The Federalist Papers*, William F. Buckley Jr., and Michael Oakeshott—not to mention William Wordsworth, Nathaniel Hawthorne, Joseph Conrad, Rudyard Kipling, and other literary giants.

That encounter has stayed with me not only because it's the perfect illustration of how many people on the Left think "conservative thought" is an oxymoron, but also because the book helped shape how I understand that intellectual tradition. As a cradle conservative, it was easy for me to take some conservative principles for granted. A resource that gathered some of the most profound expressions of these ideas was invaluable in helping me better understand certain foundational ideas and precepts—and to recognize that they were part of a long and impressive conversation between great writers over the centuries, including in poems and stories. I hope this book does something similar for you. In the process, I also hope it refreshes how conservatives talk about fiction—that it restocks the conservative bookshelf.

When conservatives discuss novels that best reflect our views of the world, we tend to mention the same handful of works. We cherish a reliable and sturdy stock that hasn't been replenished in a generation or two. This stock includes J.R.R. Tolkien's fantasy trilogy *The Lord of the Rings* and its prequel, *The Hobbit*, which allegorize Christian belief; George Orwell's *1984*, which shows how a totalitarian government uses force and violence to control its subjects; and Aldous Huxley's *A Brave New World*, which demonstrates how a totalitarian government may also use ease and comfort to do the same thing.

That rad trad friend of yours, the one with the floppy hair and tweed blazer, gives his friends copies of Evelyn Waugh's *Brideshead Revisited*. Your uncle's been telling you for years about *The Bonfire of the Vanities*, Tom Wolfe's send-up of 1980s New York City politics, Wall Street, journalism, and race relations. And your libertarian buddy from college recommends Ayn Rand's *Atlas Shrugged* for its vision of individual defiance against the regulatory state. I don't mean to shame anyone for enjoying these novels—I love a lot of them myself. Yet the frequency of these recommendations reminds me of the advice provided from an internet meme from a few years ago: READ ANOTHER BOOK.

That admonition sprung up shortly after the first election of Donald Trump in 2016, when supporters of Hillary Clinton on Facebook and what was then called Twitter compared the president-elect and his supporters to some nefarious character or idea from the Harry Potter series, or to compare what was calling itself "the Resistance" to the noble young wizard and his allies. These political applications of the Wizarding World were not new: during the George W. Bush administration, bumper stickers that declared *Republicans for Voldemort* were a common appearance in the university town where I lived.

It's not surprising that so many people referred to Harry Potter. The novels and movies are a cultural touchstone for many Millennials, who spent their childhood immersed in the elaborate world concocted by J.K. Rowling. (It's one of the great ironies of the past several years that Rowling has become *persona non grata* for many on the Left because she rejects basic tenets of the transgender movement.) It's natural for people to relate a shared point of reference to contemporary events. Such analogies can be surprising, funny, and sometimes even instructive. On the other hand, this perpetual prattle about Potter descends into a weird obsession that reduces all experiences to the characters and events from a story written for nine-to-twelve-year-olds. The people who resort to the comparisons seem like they're in a state of arrested development and could benefit from expanding their cultural references. Isn't it time they moved on? Shouldn't they . . . READ ANOTHER BOOK?[2]

The publisher of the book in your hands wisely decided that, for sales purposes, *Read Another Book* is not a good title—readers are likely to take the title's advice without actually buying the thing. But those three words offer a helpful way of understanding why I wrote it. In some regards, what I'm suggesting is comparable to an argument that became common on campuses in the 1980s and 1990s, when many academics and students argued that programs needed to expand the curriculum beyond classic texts of the Western canon. They argued, to put it simply, that there were too many dead white men and not enough women and people of color (dead or alive) on college syllabuses. The current manifestation of this movement has the catchphrase *decolonize the canon*.

Now, I do not think Tolkien or Rand are too white or Western to be worthwhile. The problem is that our reliance on them obscures the significance and abundance of conservative ideals and principles in literature more broadly. The result is a sort of self-inflicted myopia to many cultural contributions of our ideological predecessors, and even of the exemplary literary expressions of our shared beliefs from writers who probably would not call themselves conservative. We stand on the shoulders of giants—but there are more giants than we realize.

A Nation of Non-Readers

Unfortunately, the most basic obstacle to recognizing our novelistic patrimony is that few of us are actually reading any fiction. In 2002, the National Endowment for the Arts (NEA) found that 46.7 percent of American adults read literature, a 10 percent drop from the early 1980s. That decline spanned across education levels, race, age, and gender, but was especially dramatic among eighteen-to-twenty-four-year-olds: in the early 1980s, that age group had the second-highest percentage of readers (59.8 percent). By the early 2000s, only the seventy-five and older demographic had a lower percentage (42.8 percent).[3]

A 2009 NEA report—with the hopeful title of "Reading on the Rise: A New Chapter on American Literacy"—gave cause for optimism when it found a growth in the literature-reading public for the first time since the early 1980s, and even a 4 percent bump in the reading of fiction in particular since 2002.[4] But that study's upward trend has steadily evaporated. In 2018, the NEA reported that fewer American adults were reading fiction than ever in the twenty-first century—only 41.8 percent, nearly a 3.4 percent drop in five years.[5] That decline intensified in the Endowment's 2023 report, which found just 37.6 percent of adults had read novels and short stories the preceding year, "the lowest share on record with the survey" and a 4.2 percent decrease from the previous, already dire, findings.[6]

Other surveys are no more heartening. In 2021, the Pew Research Center found that "roughly a quarter of American adults (23%) say they haven't read a book in whole or in part in the past year."[7] It is safe to assume that the percentage of adults whose shadow darkened the pages of a novel specifically is even smaller. Similarly, Gallup found that in 2021, Americans read many fewer books than just a few years before: the average American reported reading 15.6 books in 2016—and 18.5 in 1999!—but only 12.6 in 2021. In 2016, 35 percent of Americans reported reading at least 11 books over the year; that number dipped to 27 percent in 2021. The only positive way to spin these numbers is to assume that poll respondents have become more honest or modest. A remarkable element of the Gallup poll is its loose definition of "reading," which encompasses not only books and e-books, but audiobooks as well, as if listening and reading are the same acts.[8] Even with that expanded definition, engagement with books is dropping.

Any free marketeer will have an easy time identifying the reason for this decline: there's a lot more competition for our time. Dana Gioia, a poet and critic who chaired the NEA between 2003–2009, pointed this out in the Endowment's 2004 report, observing that "reading a book requires a degree of active attention and engagement . . . . [It] is a progressive skill that depends on years of education and practice. By contrast, most electronic media such as television, recordings, and radio make fewer demands on their audiences, and indeed often require no more than passive participation."[9] Keep in mind Gioia wrote that before the advent of YouTube, Google, Facebook, Instagram, X, TikTok, Netflix and other streaming services, remarkable developments in video gaming, and the countless other services and technologies that now consume our free time (and, if the shocking rumors I've heard are true, even some peoples' work time). These are all easier than reading even the breeziest genres of fiction, pot-boilers, and romance novels.

An anecdote in a recent *New Yorker* story captures this trend. Discussing the decline in the number of students studying English, James Shapiro, a Shakespeare scholar at Columbia University, explained that he once believed the trend could be reversed. He doesn't anymore:

> Technology in the last twenty years has changed all of us. How has it changed me? I probably read five novels a month until the two-thousands. If I read one a month now, it's a lot. That's not because I've lost interest in fiction. It's because I'm reading a hundred Web sites. I'm listening to podcasts.[10]

It's not just Millennials and younger people who have never known life without the internet and social media—their Boomer professors are trading in novels for the internet, too. And the more time we spend online instead of between pages, the harder it is to get back into the habit when—or if—we try.

In *The Decline of the Novel*, critic Joseph Bottum observes that the novel is the cultural form through which Western Europeans explored the problems of the modern self most fully. As the title of his book implies, however, the artform no longer enjoys a privileged place. Setting aside Bottum's reasons for this decline (which are provocative but beyond the scope of my project), it's hard to argue with his premise. As he puts it:

> serious novels have largely disappeared from public intellectual life. You can read them if you want, but you

don't have to read them to participate in the serious public discourse of America. Over lunch one day, the wonderful magazine-essayist Andrew Ferguson gave me what he called the Cocktail Party Test for new books: Would you be embarrassed to show up at a get-together of writers and public-intellectual types without having read it? And the last novel he could remember for which that seemed true was Tom Wolfe's *Bonfire of the Vanities* in 1987. . . . A fundamental art of Western civilization for hundreds of years just doesn't seem to count for much anymore.[11]

I suspect that some readers might object and suggest one or two more recent titles. One that comes to my mind is Jonathan Franzen's 2010 work *Freedom*, but I may be overestimating its cultural relevance because Leslie Knope mentioned it on an episode of *Parks and Recreation*. Still, Bottum's overall point is unassailable: the novel simply does not have the cultural significance it did a generation ago.

Why Read Fiction?

A skeptic may be asking, "So what? If I want to learn about conservatism, why don't I just re-read my favorite biography of Winston Churchill, a memoir by a prominent conservative politician, or the latest edition of a thoughtful periodical? What can I get out of fiction that I can't get out of a book about things that really happened or are really happening?"

Simple: great fiction is a source of beauty, and beauty is good. Great fiction is also a source of truth, but (per Emily Dickinson's advice) truth told slant. Perhaps this is why some of America's most influential modern conservative thinkers have recognized the power of fiction enough to try their hand at it. William F. Buckley Jr.,

xvi   13 Novels Conservatives Will Love

founder of *National Review*, wrote many novels. Russell Kirk wrote three novels and nearly two dozen short stories. Irving Kristol dabbled in fiction on his way to godfathering neoconservatism. Even Leo Strauss quoted Sherlock Holmes.

As Horace declared in *Ars Poetica*, great literature instructs and delights. And much of the best literature shows us how to live. Kirk argued that "the end of great books is ethical—to teach us what it means to be genuinely human."[12] Or as John Agresto has recently argued about the liberal arts more generally, "While our books might not make us 'more humane,' they can surely show us and lead us to think about all the aspects, high and low, of our humanity."[13] Kirk takes that premise a step further to suggest that "every major form of literary art has taken for its deeper themes the norms of human nature. . . . [Authors] assumed that the writer is under a moral obligation to normality—that is, explicitly or implicitly, to certain enduring standards of private and public conduct."[14] Kirk's reference to "normality" may raise some eyebrows, but his general point may be less controversial: great literature can show us how to lead a better life.

Given this broad purpose, it's not difficult to see potential political applications, or to understand what someone interested in being a better citizen could glean from fiction. The novelist Ralph Ellison offers one connection between politics and narrative art, as both "thrust toward a human ideal," and helps us understand how we might achieve that ideal:

> [If] the ideal of achieving a true political equality eludes us in reality—as it continues to do—there is still available that fictional *vision* of an ideal democracy in which the actual combines with the ideal and gives us representations of a state of things in which the highly placed and the

lowly, the black and the white, the northerner and the southerner, the native-born and the immigrant are combined to tell us of transcendent truths and possibilities such as those discovered when Mark Twain set Huck and Jim afloat on the raft.[15]

Fiction can show us, as the title of an Anthony Trollope novel puts it, *The Way We Live Now*; it can also gesture toward things as they should be and to what democratic citizens can aspire. In their introduction to *What So Proudly We Hail: The American Soul in Story, Speech, and Song*, Leon Kass, Amy Kass, and Diana Schaub explain the value of story-telling for national character:

> [To] hear—or read—and discuss the best stories told by the best storytellers is more than a way of passing time. It is a way of deepening time, by taking us to the profoundly humanizing truths contained in the ordinary surfaces of our experience. With the help of a great storyteller, we can see in the commonplace the things that really matter. Yes, stories are entertaining, but at their best they inform and reform us by dramatizing belief and rendering feeling thoughtful.[16]

Inform, reform, humanize—these are powerful capabilities. And part of that humanizing experience, part of how we're reformed, and what we're informed of, relates to how we see other people.

At the risk of alienating readers by quoting a conservative *bête noire* approvingly, I think former president Barack Obama's testimonial for fiction's ability to shape democratic engagement is very powerful. In an interview with the novelist Marilynne Robinson for *The New York Review of Books*, Obama attributed an important component of his political education to the fiction he read: "the most important set of understandings that I bring to that position of citizen, the most important stuff I've learned I think I've learned from novels." What exactly was that most important component? This brings us to a facet of fiction that, while possibly overstated, is important nonetheless. Here's how President Obama described it:

> It has to do with empathy. It has to do with being comfort-able with the notion that the world is complicated and full of grays, but there's still truth there to be found, and that you have to strive for that and work for that. And the notion that it's possible to connect with some[one] else even though they're very different from you.[17]

This belief in the empathetic powers of fiction has been reinforced by a number of scientific studies. The *Harvard Business Review* reports that "reading literary fiction is an effective way to enhance the brain's ability to keep an open mind while processing informa-tion, a necessary skill for effective decision-making."[18] Keith Oatley, a professor emeritus of cognitive psychology, claims that "reading novels enables us to become better at actually understanding other people and what they're up to."[19] These claims strike me as entirely plausible, and I suspect it's no coincidence that the novel developed in Britain at a time when thinkers like David Hume and Adam Smith were immersed in theories of sympathy. Indeed, one of the earliest sub-genres of fiction in eighteenth-century Britain was the novel of sensibility, in which characters demonstrated their virtue and goodness by expressing sympathy for those around them, as well as being sensitive about their own troubles.[20]

Empathetic abilities are obviously important to citizens in a pluralistic democracy like our own, which relies on compromise and no small amount of tolerance for difference. Still, it's also true that many great novels, including at least one I explore here, are more interested in ridiculing than empathizing. In 1960, the great American short-story writer Flannery O'Connor complained, "It's considered an absolute necessity these days for writers to have compassion. . . . Usually I think what is meant by it is that the writer excuses all human weakness because human weakness is human. The kind of hazy compassion demanded of the writer now makes it difficult for him to be anti-anything."[21] There's a lot to be said for the literature of antipathy, writing—especially satirical work—that condemns characters who commit evil, and ridicules the foolish, even as it recognizes the complexities and ambiguities of our world.

One way fiction immerses us in the minds of others by immersing us in language. Television and cinema are rich and rewarding media; yet while they do many things a novel could never hope to do, there are many techniques closed off to them and many ways they cannot appeal to us. Appealing directly to the eye, they rely much less on language. Fiction conjures images through words. That's an obvious statement, but the difference is profound. For all of our technological advances, language is still our primary form of communication. Like all great literature, great fiction reminds us of the power of language, renews our wonder in the possibilities of that astonishing mode of human expression. To read a great sentence written by any of the novelists in this book is to be awestruck by a combination of music and precision, imagination and wisdom.

Finally, conservatives should embrace the novel because it is one of the great achievements of Western culture. It is the form through which many of the most talented creative minds of the past three centuries have expressed their ideas, explored their times and places, and both reflected and formed the minds and characters of their audiences. To understand the heights our language and culture are capable of, we must be familiar with the heritage of the novel.

Why These *Novels?*

Lists will inevitably raise objections, and I am certain that anyone looking through this book's table of contents will protest an inclusion or, more likely, an omission. Before you take the time to write me a terse email to vindicate the works of your favorite author, let me explain my basic approach.

As I hope is already clear, I have avoided including works that, in my experience, conservatives already frequently recommend to each other. Secondly, I tried to cover a broad timeframe—not quite from the earliest days of the novel (I would have chosen Daniel Defoe's *Robinson Crusoe* or Henry Fielding's *The History of Tom Jones, a Foundling*), but from the mid-eighteenth century, when it was still a relatively new and indeed novel form, and spreading out selections across decades, centuries, and continents. I chose from this broad range not to make any point about the development of the novel, but to illustrate the long shelf-life of conservative ideas, the echo across ages of certain values and principles.

It's unlikely that many conservatives need to be told that it's valuable to read old works, but just in case, I appeal to the wisdom of C. S. Lewis, who wrote that each age has its own "characteristic blindness" that "none of us can fully escape." But we risk increasing the errors of our age "if we read only modern books." He continues:

> Where they are true they will give us truths which we half knew already. Where they are false they will aggravate the error with which we are already dangerously ill. The only palliative is to keep the clean sea breeze of the centuries

blowing through our minds, and this can be done only by reading old books.[22]

"The clean sea breeze of the centuries"—what a beautiful image for the purifying wisdom of the past. At the same time, it's worthwhile for conservatives to recognize that writers still convey enduring wisdom to modern audiences in modern language and modern idioms. Conservatives must not believe that their vision is impossible to convey in the present, which is why I wanted to include novels of more recent vintage.

Additionally, my focus here is on literary fiction.[23] With this decision to generally exclude science fiction, fantasy, mystery, and romance, I may be playing into the worst stereotypes of conservatism—though all of those genres draw many conservative fans. But I acknowledge that plenty of genre fiction (particularly science fiction, detective fiction, and the western) reflects conservative attitudes toward, for example, progress, technology, crime, and some of the problems created by a culture preoccupied with leveling all distinctions. (See, for example, Kurt Vonnegut's short story "Harrison Bergeron.") But I believe that literary fiction's greater emphasis on characterization and psychology rather than plot and action makes it a more rewarding and enriching form of fiction. I also decided to focus on literary fiction because, to put it bluntly, it is the kind of book I like to read.

That brings me to another important criterion for inclusion: these are all books I enjoy, which means my choices may strike some readers as idiosyncratic or just plain weird. For example, during many conversations with friends and colleagues about this project, a number of people have asked whether I'd be including anything by the novelist, philosopher, and National Book Award winner Walker Percy (and especially his debut novel, *The Moviegoer*). The answer to

xxii   13 NOVELS CONSERVATIVES WILL LOVE

that question is no, for the simple reason that I do not enjoy his novels as much as many people whose tastes I otherwise share. The same can be said of Cormac McCarthy, whose many admirers see his clear vision of good and evil, and his understanding of the brokenness of human nature, as amenable to their principles; but I confess that his style has always left me a bit cold. (I discuss this a bit more in my chapter about Leif Enger's *Peace Like a River*.)

As long as I'm discussing my rationale for excluding specific authors, I should explain why I have not included any Jane Austen. It's not because she's not excellent (she is), but because the choir that is perpetually singing her praises does not need me to join the chorus. Instead, I've focused on great novels that have not yet been adapted into roughly one thousand movies and mini-series, self-help books, memoirs, travelogues, and fan fiction featuring zombies. That said, I confess that I have long suffered from a severe case of Anglophilia, and my research and teaching focus during my former life as an English professor was eighteenth- and nineteenth-century British literature, which is why much of this book has an English accent. Just not Emma Woodhouse's or Elizabeth Bennet's.

I've tried to include books by well-known authors and perhaps titles that you've heard of, but my hunch is that few casual readers have read more than a couple of the works on this list. It's also likely that if they have read, say, *Their Eyes Were Watching God*, it was a very long time ago, and they did not approach it from a specifically conservative point of view, so the interpretations and analysis I offer may be new. I also made the difficult decision of only including novels in the Anglophone tradition. Everything on this list was originally written in English. This is not because I'm so outraged by Vladimir Putin's invasion of Ukraine that I can't bring myself to include *The Brothers Karamazov*. The decision is practical, not political: I needed to refine my search filter and couldn't imagine including Fyodor Dostoevsky without also inviting Alessandro Manzoni's nineteenth-century Italian masterpiece *The Betrothed*, or a contribution by Peruvian Nobel Laureate Mario Vargas Llosa, or one of French novelist Michel Houellebecq's controversial works. I was especially tempted to include *Darkness at Noon*, Arthur Koestler's novel of Soviet injustice, using the thin rationale of bad precedent: when the Modern Library compiled a list of the twentieth-century's best novels in the English language, it placed Koestler in eighth place, even though he wrote his classic in German.[24] I ultimately decided that the project was imposing and, I hope, fruitful enough when only looking at literature in English, so you'll have to wait for *Thirteen More Novels Conservatives Will Love* for any foreign-language recommendations.

Another major question looming over this project is how to define conservatism. Over the past decade or so in America, the meaning of this word has been subject to debate; many members of the GOP, the political party most associated with conservatism in the United States, are challenging some priorities that had been central to its platform for decades. I do not purport to offer a concise definition here; nor did I select these novels because they, even collectively, explore or represent every principle that is central to conservative thought. They certainly do not constitute a list of policy prescriptions for a conservative political party in the twenty-first century. There isn't a novel here that presents a coherent corporate tax policy, a winning strategy toward China, or a blueprint to reform public education.

Instead, I work from some basic tenets that have been central to Anglo-American conservative thought for generations. They include the preference for gradual social and political change over sudden innovation and revolution; the recognition of the imperfectability of mankind and the consequent dangers—and inevitable doom—of utopian projects; an inclination toward time-tested traditions over abstract theory and untested innovation; a respect for religious belief, particularly in the Judeo-Christian tradition; and an emphasis on the institutions of civil society, especially the family. These works also include plotlines relevant to education, national identity, immigration, the American Dream, postcolonial ideology, demographic decline, the relationship between the sexes, cancel culture, social propriety, racial identity, and competing ways of understanding the world around us.

Just as not every conservative cherishes all of the above principles equally, so not every novel I discuss in this book expresses all of them. Some works here, like *Waverley* and *The Blithedale Romance*, have explicitly political subjects and applications. Others, like *My Ántonia* and *Peace Like a River*, are more focused on interior and domestic life. What's more, it would be a mistake to categorize all of these authors as unambiguously conservative. But that an American novelist whose Subaru is adorned with a *Republicans for Voldemort* bumper sticker might recognize, for example, the importance of what we the Burke-besotted call *little platoons* does not make that value any less conservative. Too often we confuse mere contrarianism with conservatism. That's a mistake. Conservatives should recognize the broad appeal of certain beliefs as both an opportunity to engage with individuals who don't seem to think like us, as well as a sign that certain cherished principles are more widely shared than we sometimes realize.

Two more qualifications before I send you on your way. I do not want to give the impression that anyone should only read fiction that corresponds to or confirms one's political point of view. That would be boring, and it would deprive you of one of the great joys of literature, which is to encounter lives and ideas unlike your own. So no, the point isn't that these are the only novels you'll ever need to read. Instead, I'm working under the premise that many conservatives—and liberals, too—want to both know more about conservatism and to read more great literature. These books kill both those birds.

Finally, it's crucial to understand that no art can achieve greatness by virtue of its message alone. Any artist who elevates his political point above the techniques and elements of his craft is creating propaganda, not art. The late English philosopher Sir Roger Scruton expressed the dangers of political art well:

> It is certainly a failing in a work of art that it should be more concerned to convey a message than to delight its audience. Works of propaganda . . . sacrifice aesthetic integrity to political correctness, character to caricature, and drama to sermonizing. On the other hand, part of what we object to in such works is their *untruthful* quality. The lessons urged upon us are neither compelled by the story nor illustrated in the exaggerated figures and characters; the propaganda message is not part of the aesthetic meaning but extraneous to it—an intrusion from the everyday world which only loses conviction when thrust on us in the midst of aesthetic contemplation.[25]

The point is not that great art must be morally ambivalent or politically neutral, but that the artists demonstrate exceptional technical skill and aesthetic judgment as they convey what Kirk called "standards of private and public conduct." Similarly, what the critic Micah Mattix writes about poetry is also applicable to fiction: "To value it primarily for *what* it says rather than *how* it says it is to undermine its integrity. The form of poetry is valuable in its own right. It is inherently pleasing. If poetry is to regain its integrity in

American intellectual life, we must take seriously not only *what* it says but *how* it says it."[26]

This general belief in the integrity of the novel as an artform has guided my selections: none of these novelists sacrifices their art to convey political insights. I think anyone who enjoys fiction will love almost all of these novels, even if he or she disagrees with the ideas they intimate or (God forbid!) my readings of them. To underscore the significance of these aesthetic elements, I'll occasionally linger on remarkable passages and shed light on what makes them so effective, funny, or otherwise fantastic. Because my audience is the general reader rather than the academic, I generally refrain from incorporating contemporary literary theory (you can thank me later) and only sometimes refer to recent scholarly conversations about specific works. And while each chapter focuses on one novel, I also say a word or two about the lives and careers of the authors, situate the work within its cultural context, discuss other works by the author—or works by other authors—that help develop our understanding of the novel. The chapters necessarily include summaries of the plots, but those summaries are by no means exhaustive, and I try to avoid spoilers so that you'll still want to read the books for yourself. If you've already read any of the novels, I hope my analysis will ring true or get you thinking about the work in a fresh light.

I can't guarantee all readers will love all of these works, but I'm confident that everyone—no matter one's political beliefs or previous reading—will come away with a better understanding of many principles and beliefs shared by conservatives. With any luck, this will inspire you to explore more works by these authors, and perhaps even inspire more writers to imitate the skills and techniques they see in here to craft their own great novel.

Chapter One

Human Nature and the "Choice of Life"— Samuel Johnson, *Rasselas* (1759)

In 1750, as the novel was becoming a popular literary genre in Britain, the English essayist, poet, and lexicographer Samuel Johnson observed how different it was from older kinds of narrative fiction. As he wrote in an installment of his essay series called *The Rambler*, previous generations of readers devoured tales of knightly adventures in faraway places, whereas "the present generation seems more particularly delighted" in works of fiction that "exhibit life in its true state, diversified only by accidents that daily happen in the real world, and influenced by passions and qualities which are really to be found in conversing with mankind."[1] This created a great challenge for writers. In the past, when realism mattered little, a writer could simply "let loose his invention, and heat his mind with incredibilities" without worrying about accurately depicting nature or life.[2] The new breed of fiction writers had higher standards to meet because their readers expected, and would recognize, realistic depictions of the everyday.

More significantly, though, Johnson was anxious about what this realism meant for the readers of this new fiction:

> These books are written chiefly to the young, the ignorant, and the idle, to whom they serve as lectures of conduct and

introductions into life. They are the entertainment of minds unfurnished with ideas, and therefore easily susceptible of impressions; not fixed by principles, and therefore easily following the current of fancy; not informed by experience, and consequently open to every false suggestion and partial account.[3]

Because of that impressionable audience, novelists had to take care to not corrupt their readership by representing people and actions about which ignorance was bliss, or at least a virtue. Johnson argued that because "the power of example is so great as to take possession of the memory by a kind of violence, and produce effects almost without the intervention of the will, care ought to be taken that, when the choice is unrestrained, the best examples only should be exhibited; and that which is likely to operate so strongly should not be mischievous or uncertain in its effects." Artists should "imitate nature"—but only "those parts of nature which are most proper for imitation."[4] Johnson saw moral formation as a crucial component of literature, including fiction. He warned that no matter how realistically rendered, "many characters ought never to be drawn," and certain knowledge about the world is more likely "to make men cunning than good." Johnson presented a clear moral vision for the new fiction:

> The purpose of these writings is surely not only to show mankind, but to provide that they may be seen hereafter with less hazard; to teach the means of avoiding the snares which are laid by Treachery for Innocence, without infusing any wish for that superiority with which the betrayer flatters his vanity; to give the power of counteracting fraud, without the temptation to practise it; to initiate the youth

by mock encounters in the art of necessary defense, and to increase prudence without impairing virtue.[5]

Johnson's vision of fiction was to help form its young readers into better people—to show the dark side of human life without making it seem attractive and to prepare them to become virtuous adults. Given these particular standards, it's not surprising that when Johnson tried his hand at fiction at the end of the decade—albeit in a form unlike the realistic, domestic novels he was describing in *The Rambler*—he focused on educating younger readers about proper moral conduct and certain principles of human nature. But that strange and wonderful little story, titled *The History of Rasselas, Prince of Abissinia* (though usually referred to simply as *Rasselas*), is rewarding not only for young people, but for anyone seeking guidance on the purpose of life or in making major decisions.[6]

The Age of Johnson

Literary scholars once divided the period of English literature spanning the late-seventeenth century into the late-eighteenth into three epochs, each named after a specific writer who outshone all peers. There was first the Age of Dryden, after the critic, essayist, playwright, and poet John Dryden; this was followed by the Age of Pope, after the poet Alexander Pope; and finally, the Age of Johnson. Dividing the periods that way has fallen out of fashion, but it gives you a sense of the esteem with which Johnson was once held.

Born in Lichfield, England—just north of Birmingham— Johnson briefly attended Oxford before dropping out because his family could not afford the tuition. (This was before there were executive orders canceling student loans.) After getting married and trying (and failing) to open a school, he moved to London in 1737 to start his literary career. The variety of his output apart from *Rasselas* was remarkable. As a journalist, he wrote summaries of parliamentary debates; he wrote two great poems, exceptional literary biographies, dozens of essays, and drama. He also wrote political tracts, edited an edition of William Shakespeare's works, and published an account of his travels into Scotland. Johnson's most impressive accomplishment was his *Dictionary of the English Language*, which he began in 1746 and first published in 1755. Johnson's dictionary wasn't the first of the language, but it was the best of its time and remains a helpful and entertaining guide for understanding the history of our language.

As varied as Johnson's output was, his works are bound together by recurring themes, an abiding interest in and knowledge of human nature, an authoritative moralistic tone, and a remarkable quotability. To give you some sense of his fame: in the years immediately following his death in 1784, four biographies about him were published—including one of the greatest biographies in English, *The Life of Samuel Johnson* by his friend James Boswell.

Johnson wrote *Rasselas* over the course of a week in 1759 quite simply because he needed the money: his mother was dying and her funeral had to be paid for. It was Johnson, remember, who said "no man but a blockhead ever wrote except for money."[7] In this case, at least, you can understand why. Those circumstances help explain the work's tone: it is dark and somber. It was published anonymously, but the voice was so like that which he used in his essays that his identity as the author was not a long-held secret. The work's conceit was in keeping with the era's vogue for travel writing. In fact, Johnson's first published work was a translation of a French priest's travels, titled *A Voyage to Abyssinia* (1735). (Abyssinia refers to what we now know as Ethiopia.) You may already be familiar with other works that were part of this trend, such as Daniel Defoe's *Robinson Crusoe* (1719) or

Jonathan Swift's *Gulliver's Travels* (1726). Toward the end of his life, Johnson would publish a non-fiction travel work, titled *A Journey to the Western Islands of Scotland*.

This story concerns a young man—which the title helpfully identifies as *Rasselas, Prince of Abissinia*—who, as a member of the royal family, lives in a palace sealed off from the troubles and concerns of the real world.[8] The name of this home is Happy Valley, and it sounds it: "All the diversities of the world were brought together, the blessings of nature were collected, and its evils extracted and excluded."[9] In this remarkable refuge, "the sons and daughters of Abissinia lived only to know the soft vicissitudes of pleasure and repose, attended by all that were skilful to delight, and gratified with whatever the senses can enjoy."[10]

As enticing as this sounds, Rasselas is unhappy, and he longs to see more of the world outside of his secluded valley. With the guidance of a wise man named Imlac, Rasselas, his sister Nekayah, and her servant Pekuah escape the valley and travel as far as Cairo, experiencing and reflecting on different ways of life. What does Rasselas hope to gain from this experience? He's convinced that, "if I had the choice of life, I should be able to fill every day with pleasure."[11] And even after the wise Imlac warns him that life is full of disappointment, Rasselas is more convinced than ever that he needs to make his escape and see the world for himself: "I am resolved to judge with my own eyes of the various conditions of men, and then to make deliberately my *choice of life*."[12]

Choice of life—the phrase is central to *Rasselas*. Although it doesn't first appear until chapter twelve (admittedly, these are concise chapters), it or some variation of it occurs eleven times, often in italics, the typographical equivalent of alarm bells. So important is this phrase to the purpose of the work, it was also Johnson's working title. That emphasis on choosing a life's path makes this work particularly appropriate for readers on the verge of adulthood (though Rasselas himself is twenty-five when the book begins, and closer to thirty when he finally sets out on his travels. Slacker!). Again and again, *Rasselas* raises important questions about what to choose—and expect—from life. And because it offers so many examples of people trying to make up their own mind, or explaining their own decisions, it does what so much great fiction does: help us live vicariously through the characters and learn from their experiences, mistakes, and insights.

Tell 'em That It's Human Nature

That potential in fiction relates to one of the most important themes in *Rasselas*: that we are able to learn from the lives and ideas of other people, including people of distant times and places. And that rests on an important assumption about human nature, an assumption that was central to Johnson's work—and to the work of other Enlightenment thinkers with whom you're probably more familiar. This is a belief in a universal, consistent human nature, a set of desires and behaviors that are constant over time and cultures. It's not the same as the belief that everyone is identical and there is no variation in human thought, belief, or outcome—but that everyone is capable of reason, and also vulnerable to the same set of passions and vices, albeit to varying degrees.

As Imlac tells Rasselas, "Every man . . . may by examining his own mind guess what passes in the minds of others."[13] This guess isn't necessarily correct, of course, but the possibility of being able to understand others by imagining ourselves in their situations is a sympathetic act that rests on the premise that people share fundamental passions, desires, emotions, and rational abilities. In fact, that is crucial to the broader concept of sympathy that was central to eighteenth-century philosophy and fiction. It's no coincidence that the century that saw the rise of the novel also saw the advent of such works as Adam Smith's *The Theory of Moral Sentiments* (published, like *Rasselas*, in 1759) that explored why people feel sympathy for others. The eighteenth century's cult of sensibility celebrated one's ability to show emotion over the sufferings and joys of others, a capacity that could be refined through works of art, including fiction.

Johnson expresses his belief in a universal human nature throughout his essays, including in *Idler* 51—published the same month as *Rasselas*:

> Men, however distinguished by external accidents or intrinsick [sic] qualities, have all the same wants, the same pains, and, as far as the senses are consulted, the same pleasures. The petty cares and petty duties are the same in every station to every understanding, and every hour brings some occasion on which we all sink to the common level. We are all naked till we are dressed, and hungry till we are fed; and the general's triumph, and sage's disputation, end, like the humble labours of the smith or ploughman, in a dinner or in sleep.[14]

Johnson was no leveler; he believed in the importance of social hierarchies for maintaining order. Yet this passage expresses his belief in a "common level," according to which people of all ranks and, presumably, races share important traits. Similarly, see the opening lines of his greatest poem, "The Vanity of Human Wishes," published ten years earlier:

> Let observation with extensive view,
>   Survey mankind, from China to Peru;

Remark each anxious toil, each eager strife,
And watch the busy scenes of crowded life;…
How rarely reason guides the stubborn choice,
Rules the bold hand, or prompts the suppliant voice,
How nations sink, by darling schemes oppress'd,
When vengeance listens to the fool's request.[15]

Much in this passage—the battle between reason and the passions, the futility of wishes expressed by the title—anticipate central themes of *Rasselas*. There, Johnson half-jokes that the master observer of these general traits is the poet, as Imlac explains:

This business of a poet … is to examine, not the individual, but the species; to remark general properties and large appearances. He does not number the streaks of the tulip, or describe the different shades of the verdure of the forest. He is to exhibit in his portraits of nature such prominent and striking features as recall the original to every mind, and must neglect the minuter discriminations, which one may have remarked and another have neglected, for those characteristics which are alike obvious to vigilance and carelessness.[16]

In this analogy, Johnson paraphrases the theories of his friend, the painter Sir Joshua Reynolds, to explain how poets should represent their subject matter. It's advice that Johnson follows when he represents his characters in *Rasselas*. They are very broadly sketched: we don't know much about their appearances, for example, or their distinctive personalities. Instead, Johnson gives us a relatively general picture of their beliefs and their desires. Even the earliest British novels, like Daniel Defoe's *Moll Flanders* (1722) and Samuel

Richardson's *Pamela* (1740), offer much more individualized characters (and many more pages).[17] Nonetheless, the conversations between the characters in *Rasselas* and the ideas they express are memorable.

One reason Johnson's belief in general human nature is remarkable is he assumes that when he writes about African characters, his British readers will accept the applicability and validity of their ideas, observations, feelings, and desires. There aren't many eighteenth-century works of fiction in which that is the case. (Though, again, Johnson does not try to make the characters distinctively Abyssinian.) In fact, Johnson underscores the differences between his characters and his readers only once, when Imlac tells Rasselas about his encounters with Europeans. This passage clearly endorses the idea of Western supremacy, for which reason it's likely to rub modern readers the wrong way, as Imlac observes that Europeans "appeared almost another order of beings" compared to "the natives of our own kingdoms."[18] Imlac explains why:

> "They are more powerful, sir, than we," answered Imlac, "because they are wiser; knowledge will always predominate over ignorance, as man governs the other animals. But why their knowledge is more than ours I know not what reason can be given but the unsearchable will of the Supreme Being."[19]

This passage is unlikely to satisfy the modern reader, but it's worth noting that nothing in the work suggests the inferior wisdom of the central characters. Johnson focuses on what he believes all peoples have in common, as when Imlac reminds his young friend that "Europeans . . . are less unhappy than we, but they are not happy.

Human life is every where a state in which much is to be endured, and little to be enjoyed."[20]

If Johnson's belief in a universal human nature strikes you as a little odd or naïve, it shouldn't—in fact, it should feel familiar to you. Johnson shared this principle with America's Founding Fathers. As products of—or participants in—the Enlightenment, they all believed in a cross-cultural shared human nature. As the diplomat Howard Trivers wrote in an essay commemorating our bicentennial, "The Enlightenment was characterized by its universalism, the affirmation of universal principles in human affairs, and a cosmopolitan vision of mankind."[21] This is clear from the very first utterances of our nation as such, which are a series of universalist claims: "We hold these truths to be self-evident, that all men are created equal, that they are endowed by their Creator with certain unalienable Rights, that among these are Life, Liberty and the pursuit of Happiness." The Declaration proceeds to make general statements about the purpose of government and the rights of citizens, before moving into the specific political situation of the colonies. It is essentially an exercise in deductive reasoning based on universalist principles.

Not that this means Johnson supported the American Revolution. His 1775 pamphlet *Taxation No Tyranny* features the caustic question, "how is it that we hear the loudest yelps for liberty among the drivers of negroes?"[22] Despite this difference about the status of the colonies, though, Johnson and his American cousins held a shared faith in universal human nature. To some degree, this attitude endures in the United States. The most famous—or depending on your perspective, the most notorious—modern example could be what President George W. Bush said before the United Nations in 2004: "The desire for freedom resides in every human heart."[23] It's a bipartisan belief: in 2022, President Joe Biden referred to "humankind's unending search for freedom."[24]

Universalist principles of the Enlightenment are in many ways, to use a favorite word of the "Great Awokening," *problematic*, at least in the twenty-first century. Our age prefers illiberal identity politics and tribalism, ways of thinking and perceiving which cut against the best of our liberal traditions by focusing on racial differences. The Enlightenment mindset assumes commonality and similarity; the current intellectual trend emphasizes differences and steers us toward fracture. At the same time, it would be a mistake for a belief in human nature to mean that there are no emotional, intellectual, or other major variations between people—we'll see how important these differences are when we discuss George Eliot's *Daniel Deronda*, in particular. To use the example from the preceding paragraph, a common belief in freedom does not mean that we all want the same kind or amount of freedom. This is the case made in the famous Grand Inquisitor passage from Dostoevsky's *The Brothers Karamazov*; we will see it for ourselves when we come to P. D. James's *The Children of Men*.

Nonetheless, the rejection of some baseline of human nature and the embrace of what Steven Pinker calls "a pliant human nature" opens the door for efforts to control environments and behavior. As Pinker puts it, "the issue is not whether we can change human behavior, but at what cost. . . . Inborn human desires are a nuisance to those with utopian and totalitarian visions, which often amount to the same thing."[25] Similarly, George F. Will has pointed out that "if human nature is a fiction, a pre-modern superstition . . . then controlling the culture becomes imperative. And politics must saturate every nook and cranny of life."[26] As paradoxical as it may sound, a belief in general human nature helps protect individual liberty.

If you'll indulge me for one moment before moving on to specific elements of human nature that Johnson explores in depth, I can't help but think of the Founders when I read this passage from *Rasselas*, in which Imlac delineates some limits of political power:

> [N]o form of government has been yet discovered by which cruelty can be wholly prevented. Subordination supposes power on one part and subjection on the other; and if power be in the hands of men it will sometimes be abused. The vigilance of the supreme magistrate may do much, but much will still remain undone. He can never know all the crimes that are committed, and can seldom punish all that he knows.[27]

This vision of human imperfection—and therefore the imperfection of human institutions—calls to mind James Madison's famous passage from *Federalist*, no. 51, published about thirty years later, in which he explains the need for the separation of powers:

> But what is government itself, but the greatest of all reflections on human nature? If men were angels, no government would be necessary. If angels were to govern men, neither external nor internal controls on government would be necessary. In framing a government which is to be administered by men over men, the great difficulty lies in this: you must first enable the government to control the governed; and in the next place oblige it to control itself.[28]

Despite the very different contexts of these passages, they both offer keen insights into human frailty and the limits of governmental power. What separates Madison from Johnson is that the American Founder believes the structure of government can "control"—not stop—the un-angelic behavior of both those who are governed and those who govern.

Rasselas the Restless

From Johnson's general belief in a universal human nature, let's turn to some of the specific elements of that nature that he explores in *Rasselas*. One of the most important qualities is hinted at in the character's very name: Rasselas is restless. Or, as Johnson himself defined restless in his dictionary, Rasselas feels "unquiet, without peace."[29] Although he has every material comfort and entertainment at his disposal, he is bored. "Man has surely some latent sense for which this place affords no gratification," he observes, "or he has some desires distinct from sense which must be satisfied before he can be happy."[30] Rasselas understands that healthy human nature craves a purpose: "That I want nothing . . . or that I know not what I want, is the cause of my complaint; if I had known any want, I should have a certain wish; that wish would excite endeavor" and with that ambition, he would no longer languish.[31] Ironically, Imlac finally provides Rasselas that "want" when he tries to convince him just how good he has it, how difficult life is for most people outside of Happy Valley: Rasselas explains, "you have given me something to desire; I shall long to see the miseries of the world, since the sight of them is necessary to happiness."[32] This longing, in turn, gives Rasselas some respite from his misery through what the narrator calls "a subject of thought."[33] What we see through Rasselas is that enduring (which is not to say constant) happiness requires well-ordered desire—we need to pursue something of value, and we need to have some goal beyond ourselves to feel satisfied.

Closely related to this quality of human nature is that a full life requires motion and activity—as Imlac tells his young followers, "some desire is necessary to keep life in motion; and he whose real wants are supplied must admit those of fancy."[34] This point is underscored by the constant references to water throughout the work, represented most vividly by the Nile, along which they travel. Again, Imlac: "Do not suffer life to stagnate: it will grow muddy for want of motion; commit yourself again to the current of the world."[35] But Imlac never says that this motion will always be smooth. In fact, he's quite clear about the opposite being true when he warns Rasselas at the outset of their journey:

> The world, which you figure to yourself smooth and quiet as the lake in the valley, you will find a sea foaming with tempests, and boiling with whirlpools: you will be sometimes overwhelmed by the waves of violence, and sometimes dashed against the rocks of treachery. Amidst wrongs and frauds, competitions and anxieties, you will wish a thousand times for these seats of quiet, and willingly quit hope to be free from fear.[36]

Part of that motion is the never-ending need to need. That is the paradox driving the work: desire is necessary. We need a purpose ahead of us to be happy, but the happiness we feel in realizing that purpose is temporary—either it won't be exactly as we hoped, or we'll grow restless for another desire or purpose. As Rasselas's sister Nekayah observes, "Such . . . is the state of life, that none are happy but by the anticipation of change; the change itself is nothing; when we have made it, the next wish is to change again. The world is not yet exhausted; let me see something to-morrow which I never saw before."[37] And there are also cases in which our focus on the purpose itself deludes us, warps our minds and disconnects us from our community and the world around us. That is the case of an astronomer they meet, who becomes so convinced that he can control the weather that he believes the fate of the world rests in his hands. Despite all of his knowledge, the astronomer lets himself become the victim of his fancy, and so a warning to us all. As Imlac explains, "Of the uncertainties of our present state, the most dreadful and alarming is the uncertain continuance of reason."[38]

Rasselas is certainly instructive and entertaining, but it's nobody's idea of a fairy tale. The policy wonk equivalent of the book's moral is the economist Thomas Sowell's insight that "there are no solutions; there are only trade-offs."[39] No choice in life will bring constant pleasure, as Rasselas had hoped. Every choice of life brings disappointment, frustration, and a desire for change. That's why it's so remarkable that at the end of the story, Johnson's characters finally address religious belief. Rasselas admires monks, who "support, without complaint, a life, not of uniform delight, but uniform hardship." They are happier in their poverty than Rasselas had been in his luxury because they work and pray with an eye toward an eternal reward. Imlac envisions that "state of future perfection, to which we all aspire," as one of "pleasure without danger, and security without restraint."[40] And as they visit catacombs, Nekayah utters perhaps the most profound lines of the work: "To me . . . the choice of life is become less important; I hope hereafter to think only on the choice of eternity."[41] Of course, implicit there is another question: which choice of life leads one to one's choice of eternity? Johnson raises these questions at the end of the book to underscore the ultimate purpose of any choice of life.

A remarkable element about the conclusion of *Rasselas* is that nothing seems to be resolved. The narrator walks us through the young characters' final choices of life: Pekuah wants to be "fixed in some unvariable state." Nekayah wishes to "learn all the sciences" and found a woman's college. Rasselas hopes to become a monarch "and see all the parts of government with his own eyes." But they all realize that "of these wishes that they had formed . . . none could be obtained. They deliberated a while what was to be done, and resolved, when the inundation should cease, to return to Abissinia."[42] That's a fascinatingly ambiguous last paragraph. Why do they know they can't realize their choice in life? And by returning to Abissinia, are they just giving up on even pursuing their choices of life because they know they will never achieve them?

A reasonable interpretation of the work lands at a *yes* to those questions. But an even better reading answers, *not so fast*. This optimistic reading would note that the text is unclear about where they intend to go—the narrator only says Abissinia, not Happy Valley, so it's possible they return to their kingdom and pursue their lives away from the palace. (Besides, how would they get back in?) And the reason they know they won't realize their choices is simply because their choices are extreme: nobody can know all the sciences. Nobody can live an unvaried life. No ruler can see all the parts of government. But they have clear pursuits now, and that clarity will bring them purpose and more happiness than anything they could have in Happy Valley. Similarly, their awareness of inevitable frustrations and disappointments will make those frustrations and disappointments more bearable.

In their valuable book *Why We Are Restless: On the Modern Quest for Contentment*, Benjamin Storey and Jenna Silber Storey touch on what Johnson is conveying here when they describe the situation in which exceptional college students and recent graduates often find themselves. Well-educated and ambitious, these young men and women are uncertain about how to approach their next steps, so they approach the problem as they've been taught to solve others:

> looking up countless opportunities, tabulating pluses and minuses, making spreadsheets to keep track of it all. But

the question of how to live cannot be answered by aggregating qualities. We must rather think about it by attending to the strange and contradictory qualities that make us human—that we are free, rational, and open to the divine but also frail, fallible, and subject to death. How can such a patchwork being pull itself together to make a meaningful life?[43]

This situation can seem paralyzing, making young people hold off on making a final decision for as long as possible. What the Storeys call this "love of indeterminacy" even bleeds into adult life, as professionals seek to be everything at once.[44] The Storeys contend that a proper liberal education can teach students what they call "the art of choosing." In the poignant last sentence of their book, they write: "The art of choosing cannot bring our restless hearts to a standstill. But it may help us turn our pointless busyness into a pointed quest."[45]

That, I think, is very close to the moral of *Rasselas*. Restlessness is inevitable. It is part of human nature. The problem arises when restlessness has no purpose. We can find that purpose, the Storeys suggest, because "the true adventure of the human soul begins not on study abroad but right here—alone in our rooms."[46] Engaging with books like *Rasselas*, or any of the other novels covered in the following chapters, helps us start our voyage to understanding human nature and individual people. That is only the beginning, though, and at some point we have to venture abroad like Rasselas and his companions. (And, as we'll discover in our discussion of *Waverley*, reading carelessly can have disastrous consequences.)

Like the bridegroom after hearing the ancient mariner's tale, you are likely to leave *Rasselas* "sadder but wiser." If the book's ending is too ambiguous or even dark for you, let me brighten it with the ending of an essay Johnson wrote about a decade before *Rasselas*. That piece begins with ideas much like ones Imlac expressed:

> Every man is sufficiently discontented with some circumstances of his present state, to suffer his imagination to range more or less in quest of future happiness, and to fix upon some point of time, in which, by the removal of the inconvenience which now perplexes him, or acquisition of the advantage which he at present wants, he shall find the condition of his life very much improved.
>
> When this time, which is too often expected with great impatience, at last arrives, it generally comes without the blessing for which it was desired; but we solace ourselves with some new prospect, and press forward again with equal eagerness.[47]

Here again is the cycle of dissatisfaction, desire, and disappointment that we see in *Rasselas*, as well as the comfort we find in setting our sights on pursuing a new desire. Yet Johnson concludes the essay on a more positive note than he did the fiction, and with words directed specifically at young readers, though they will also resonate with the old. Johnson advises, "He that enlarges his curiosity after the works of nature, demonstrably multiplies the inlets to happiness" and encourages "the younger part of my readers, to whom I dedicate this vernal speculation . . . to make use at once of the spring of the year, and the spring of life." What does making use of the literal and figurative springs entail? Johnson explains that young people should form "a love of innocent pleasures, and an ardour for useful knowledge," while also remembering "that a blighted spring makes a barren year, and that the vernal flowers, however beautiful and gay, are only intended by nature as preparatives to autumnal fruits."[48]

This passage differs from *Rasselas* insofar as it does not explore a particular choice in life, but its overall point coincides with the fiction's: Johnson's young readers should study that knowledge which is useful to their flourishing, in preparation for what the great moral philosopher Francis Albert Sinatra called the September of their years—as well as their choice of eternities. *Rasselas* itself is an evergreen source for the "useful knowledge" that can prepare young readers. And for older readers, those who are already in their autumnal years, there is a certain pleasure in having one's experiences confirmed (or challenged) in a classic work you somehow overlooked, or failed to appreciate at the time—or took to heart decades ago and whose wisdom you've cherished since. When I was discussing this book project with a prominent political philosopher, his eyes lit up when I told him that I'd be writing about *Rasselas*. He then recited a line and told me how much he enjoyed the book when he first read it, nearly fifty years before. It had provided worthwhile subjects of thought for his voyage along the river of his life.

Chapter Two

Minding Our Manners—Frances Burney,
Evelina (1778)

uring his famous travels across America in the nineteenth
century, the French political theorist and keen cultural
observer Alexis de Tocqueville noted that a democratic
form of government inspired very different manners than an aristocracy. "In aristocratic societies, where a few individuals direct all
things," he speculated, "external relations among men are subject to
nearly fixed connections. Each then believes he knows in a precise
manner by what sign it is fitting to show respect or to signal good
will, and etiquette is a science of which one does not assume ignorance." That is, the clear class and social distinctions of an aristocracy
breed strict, tightly observed manners of conduct, the breaking of
which could send unintended messages to one's peers and social
circle. The blurred social distinctions of a democracy bring with
them looser norms of decorum: "as men diverse in their education
and birth are mixed and confused in the same places, it is almost
impossible to agree on the rules of social graces. . . . one becomes
attached, therefore, to the substance of the actions rather than to the
form, and one is at once less civil and less quarrelsome." In the
process, a man's "manners become less courteous and his mores
simpler and more manly."[1] It's a reasonable observation—Americans

in particular are proud of our informality and relative lack of stuffiness. We expect even our presidential candidates to be able to roll up their shirt sleeves and eat hot dogs at a state fair or spend an hour serving french fries at a drive-thru.

Nonetheless, there is abundant evidence to suggest that Americans still take certain manners seriously. In the fall of 2023, Senate Majority Leader Chuck Schumer, a Democrat from New York, announced that he was waiving the long-standing rule of the Senate that required all members of the upper house to wear business attire on the floor. The move was widely recognized as an accommodation to the junior senator from Pennsylvania, John Fetterman, a Democrat from Pennsylvania who had built a reputation as a man of the people by dressing like fellow Pennsylvanian Rocky Balboa during a training montage. The response was swift. Republicans, as media outlets like to say, pounced. Forty-six GOP senators signed a letter, declaring that "casual clothing on the Senate floor disrespects the institution we serve and the American families we represent."[2] Peggy Noonan, a *Wall Street Journal* columnist and former speechwriter for President Ronald Reagan, lamented the decision because dressing well in the Senate sends an important message to Americans: "It shows . . . that you understand that as a high elected official of the United States you owe the country, and the world, the outward signs of maturity, judgment and earnestness."[3] Even the *Washington Post*'s editorial board agreed with the Republicans: "Putting on a suit creates an occasion for lawmakers to reflect, just for a moment, on the special responsibilities with which the people have entrusted them and on a deliberative process that at least aspires to solemnity."[4] Before long, a bipartisan resolution to institute a formal dress code passed by unanimous consent.

This admittedly minor episode in the annals of American politics was nonetheless instructive for what it demonstrated about

Americans and manners and decorum.[5] For as much as Americans embrace an egalitarian ethic, we—and conservatives, in particular—also recognize that certain occasions and institutions require particular respect, and that respect is demonstrated by behaving according to certain customs and expectations. A degradation in manners implies the threat of lower standards more generally.

Frances Burney's debut novel, *Evelina, or the History of a Young Lady's Entrance into the World*, offers insights into the significance of the unwritten rules of behavior. In this story of a young woman's introduction to English society, the character (along with readers) learns important lessons about how to treat people in specific social situations, how to demonstrate care and sympathy toward others, and how to defend those in danger. Ultimately, and with a good deal of very funny social satire, the novel suggests that corrupt manners can have violent, degrading consequences, while respect for civil behavior signals broader sympathy and concern for others.

The Kernel of Life

Writing in her journal several months after the publication of *Evelina*, the twenty-five-year-old Burney proclaimed, "This year was ushered in by a grand and most important Event,—for, at the latter end of January, the Literary World was favoured with the first publication of the ingenious, learned, and most profound Fanny Burney!—I doubt not but this memorable affair will, in future Times, mark the period whence chronologers will date the Zenith of the polite arts in this Island!" This celebration, albeit tongue-in-cheek, belies the nervousness with which Burney approached publication. Like many eighteenth-century fictional works (including *Rasselas*), Burney's first novel was published anonymously. Burney even went a step further and kept it a secret from her father, the musician Dr. Charles Burney, with whom she enjoyed an otherwise close relationship. Burney explained that she wrote "my little Book simply for my amusement; I printed it . . . merely for a frolic, to see how a production of my own would figure in that Author like form: but as I had never read any thing I had written to any human being but my sisters, I had taken it for granted that They, only, could be partial enough to endure my compositions."[6] The novel met with great success, however, and opened doors for her. One of its biggest fans was none other than Samuel Johnson. He and his friend Hester Thrale compared their young friend's new work favorably to the towering achievements of foundational British novelists Samuel Richardson and Henry Fielding: "'Harry Fielding,' [declared] Dr Johnson, 'knew nothing but the shell of Life.' 'So *You*, Ma'am,' added the flattering Mrs. Thrale, 'have found the *kernel!*'"[7]

Burney conveyed the kernel of life through the story of a seventeen-year-old orphan named Evelina Anville, who lived a secluded life while being raised by an acquaintance of her deceased grandfather named Arthur Villars. Villars had a long history with Evelina's family, and he knew that her mother had entered into a rash marriage with "a very profligate young man" named John Belmont. Belmont, disappointed that his wife did not inherit a fortune he had expected her to, abandoned her and their newborn daughter, Evelina.[8] Evelina's mother died soon thereafter, and the girl was cared for by Villars. The majority of the book recounts Evelina's entrance into society and, to a lesser degree, the efforts to claim her rightful estate.

This is an epistolary novel, meaning Burney presents the narrative through a series of letters, in this case primarily from Evelina and Villars. The first letter, though, is addressed to Villars from an old acquaintance named Lady Howard, informing him that Evelina's despicable grandmother wants Evelina to live with her in Paris. Villars is reluctant, but he realizes that Evelina must acquire new experiences and meet new people—"the time draws on for experience and observation to take place of instruction," as he puts it—so he agrees to send her to stay with a family friend.[9] He warns his friend, "You must not . . . expect too much from my pupil. She is quite a little rustic, and knows nothing of the world."[10] Evelina also receives guidance, much of it unwanted, from her tacky grandmother, Madame Duval.

Evelina, then, is the story of how its naïve title character comes to know something of the world through a series of travels and excursions—and not just to know, but to judge and act for herself. As Evelina writes to Villars, "Unable as I am to act for myself, or to judge what conduct I ought to pursue, how grateful do I feel myself, that I have such a guide and director to counsel and instruct me as yourself!"[11] Burney explains in the novel's preface that her intention was "to draw characters from nature, though not from life, and to mark the manners of the times." Evelina is the vehicle for these observations about contemporary manners, as "her ignorance of the forms, and inexperience in the manners of the world, occasion all the little incidents which these volumes record."[12]

To that end, the innocent, beautiful, and virtuous Evelina gains experience and wisdom during stays with various friends and relatives, attending an array of social events, and visiting a sundry of attractions, especially in London and Bristol. In this regard the novel is comparable to *Rasselas*, but with an attention to character and particular detail absent from that work. Indeed, this specificity is crucial to its purpose as what is known as a novel of manners. As the literary critic M.H. Abrams explained, this type of "realistic novel focuses on the customs, conversation, and ways of thinking and valuing of the upper social class."[13]

Burney engages the readers' attention with several recurring themes and plotlines. Like so many characters from eighteenth- and nineteenth-century fiction, Evelina is in search of her parentage and rightful inheritance. In this case, she knows who her father is, but he refuses to recognize her, and his reasons for this are unclear until the end. The novel also includes a romantic subplot involving Evelina's relationship with Lord Orville, a refined gentleman who is initially unimpressed by her but gradually falls in love. (Much about their relationship, and particularly the negative first impressions, may remind readers of Elizabeth Bennet and Mr. Darcy's romance in Jane Austen's *Pride and Prejudice*.) There are several other men in pursuit of the naïve Evelina, most notably a scheming cad named Sir Clement Willoughby. Evelina must determine for herself which of these suitors best suits her—though, in fact, the bigger challenge, Evelina finds, is the most appropriate way to reject men. That challenge is very much in keeping with the novel's general preoccupation with good—and bad—manners. Much of the novel's pleasure derives from the assortment of boorish characters who move in and out of the plot. Burney excels at depicting social incompetence in various ways, and showing how Evelina learns how to behave herself.

Impertinent People

When you encounter an uncommon word many times in a literary work, chances are the author wants to draw your attention to an important concept or theme. Shakespeare, for example, will have various characters in different scenes discuss the same concept—such as honor, virtue, or love—to reveal the characters' differing perspectives and values. In the case of *Evelina*, Burney draws our attention to the importance of manners—and the frequency with which people violate good manners—through the ubiquity of the word *impertinence*. This isn't a word we use every day. What it means in the context of *Evelina* is, as the *Oxford English Dictionary* puts it, "not appropriate to the time or circumstances; incongruous, unsuitable, untimely." (The *OED* lists this definition as "obsolete," and puts its year of death at 1849. So if you haven't heard it used in this way often, don't feel bad—that just means you hang out with people who don't speak in archaisms.) According to my calculations (that is, through a Ctrl+F search), *impertinent* and *impertinence* appear a total of fifty-eight times in *Evelina*. If you were bored enough to make a drinking game out of the word, you'd throw your first shot back during the preface, when Burney avers, "the candour of my readers, I have not the impertinence to doubt."[14] The related words *propriety* and *impropriety* appear another twenty-four times, and *improper* another ten. Burney leans heavily on the vocabulary of decorum.

To a great extent, the novel's action is a series of gaffes, faux pas, and generally rude behavior. Part of the fun is the variety of rudeness it catalogues—sometimes violent, sometimes intentional, often clueless. Nearly everyone commits some social misstep, including Evelina. Being a virtuous naïf, her errors arise out of ignorance rather than malice. For example, at a dance early in her time away from Villars, an affected and foolish fop named Lovel asks her to dance; she declines by telling him she had no interest in dancing with anyone that night. When he finds her dancing with the gallant Orville later, however, he expresses surprise at her "ill manners" for her earlier rejection of him. At that moment, she writes to Villars, "a confused idea . . . entered my head, of something I had heard of the rules of assemblies; but I was never at one before,—I have only danced at school,—and so giddy and heedless I was, that I had not once considered the impropriety of refusing one partner, and afterwards accepting another." She confesses that she "was thunderstruck at the recollection" and "was ready to die with shame."[15] She's a quick study, though, and behaves differently in subsequent comparable situations. Many other characters never learn—and don't seem to care. Their social mistakes are unfailingly entertaining, as well as bright red flags.

At the same time, several of Burney's rude characters are also voices of important insights. They express valuable ideas—they just do so without tact, so their ideas are taken less seriously than they should be. One such character is Mrs. Selwyn, an old family acquaintance who joins Evelina late in the novel. Although she has good instincts in many matters, Selwyn possesses an "unmerciful propensity to satire" that discomfits those around her. [16] She generally uses her satirical superpowers for good, often mocking the fops and cads around Evelina. That approach corresponds to Burney's own delight in satirizing ridiculous characters. But personal interactions demand more delicacy, and Selwyn has a bluntness Evelina finds mannish: "She is extremely clever: her understanding, indeed, may be called masculine: but, unfortunately, her manners deserve the same epithet; for, in studying to acquire the knowledge of the other sex, she has lost all the softness of her own." In short, Selwyn lacks "gentleness; a virtue which, nevertheless, seems so essential a part of the female character, that I find myself more awkward, and less at ease, with a woman who wants it, than I do with a man." [17]

Selwyn's harsh lack of tact is most evident in the final letters. Here we discover that for years, another girl—the daughter of Evelina's first wet-nurse—has been living in Evelina's rightful place as John Belmont's daughter while Evelina had been shunned. In large part through Selwyn's machinations, Belmont finally recognizes Evelina as his own—great news for our heroine; awful news for the Girl Previously Known as Belmont. Yet Selwyn has no concern for the other girl's feelings. As far as she's concerned, there's nothing that can "prevent her being eternally stigmatized" as an imposter. She explains to Evelina that "though compassion may make us wish to save the poor girl the confusion of an immediate and public fall, yet justice demands" a less merciful resolution. [18] Selwyn's desire to address the wrongs committed against Evelina is understandable, but her lack of compassion for the other young woman is startling, especially considering the imposter did nothing sinister herself; the deception by which she was presented as Belmont's daughter was the work of her mother. Fortunately, the more compassionate Orville devises a way to spare the unwitting imposter public humiliation while still ensuring Evelina's new status. Evelina's explanation of the arrangement to Villars emphasizes Orville's tact: "this noblest of men had insisted the so-long-supposed Miss Belmont should be considered, *indeed*, as my sister, and as the co-heiress of my father! though not in law, in justice, he says, she ought ever to be treated as the daughter of Sir John Belmont."[19] The distinction she identifies here between law and justice runs contrary to Selwyn's more hard-headed belief that justice and compassion were at odds in this circumstance. Orville demonstrates his suitability for Evelina by finding a way to unite the two virtues.

What Burney demonstrates through Selwyn's uncaring conduct is the connection between good manners and care for others. Frequently, the rudest people in this novel are also just plain mean; propriety implies sympathy. The connection between good manners and sympathy is most apparent when Evelina encounters the Branghtons, relatives of Madame Duval who live in London. Mr. Branghton, a silversmith, has three children; Evelina describes one daughter as "very foolish, very ignorant, very giddy" and the other as "proud, ill-tempered, and conceited"; the son's "gaiety is that of a foolish, overgrown schoolboy, whose mirth consists in noise and disturbance. . . . he seems himself to have no talents, spirit, or generosity."[20] They show no discretion or sympathy when they learn of Evelina's personal misfortunes and treat their new acquaintance not with friendliness but "with great familiarity."[21] Their impertinence hits its nadir when, without Evelina's permission, they use her name to gain access to Lord Orville's chariot, a presumption that mortifies her.

The line between bad manners and meanness blurs the most in relation to their treatment of a young man lodging in their house, an impoverished Scottish poet named Mr. Macartney. One morning, Evelina sees him preparing to commit suicide. She intervenes by physically restraining him and urging him to "have mercy on yourself!"[22] This melodramatic demonstration of Evelina's compassion and sympathy contrasts the Branghton family's callousness toward their suicidal lodger. Evelina explains:

> Mr. Branghton said, that his first thought was instantly to turn his lodger out of doors, "Lest," continued he, "his kill-ing himself in my house, should bring me into any trouble; but then, I was afraid I should never get the money that he owes me, whereas, if he dies in my house, I have a right to all he leaves behind him, if he goes off in my debt. Indeed, I would put him in prison,—but what should I get by that? he could not earn anything there to pay me[.]"[23]

Mr. Branghton eventually resolved "to ask him, point-blank, for my money out of hand." When Macartney is unable to provide that at the moment, Mr. Branghton accepts a ring as collateral. Evelina concludes, "What principles! I could hardly stay in the room."[24] She may be naïve, but the young heroine recognizes selfishness and cruelty when she sees it.

Manners and Masculinity, Cruelty and Chivalry

As gruesome as the Branghtons are, they can't out-do Captain Mirvan, the boorish father of Evelina's friend Maria. The captain is at the center of some of the novel's most entertaining but discomfiting set pieces, chaotic scenes that combine wild humor with a hint of danger and violence. Captain Mirvan derives particular pleasure from making Madame Duval miserable and, egged on by the creepy Sir Clement Willoughby, he always takes his jokes too far. At the start of the second volume, he organizes an elaborate prank to convince Duval that her love interest (a Frenchman named Du Bois) was imprisoned for spying. This scheme initially seems like harmless fun, especially because Duval is such an unlikeable character, but it gradually becomes darker and more disturbing. Duval rushes out to visit her imprisoned friend, but the Captain has arranged for fake highwaymen to stage a robbery of her coach. It's not just the captain's outrageous behavior that makes this scene so remarkable; it's also that nobody else seems willing to stop it. Sir Clement is in the best position to impede the nonsense, but the elaborate plot gives him the opportunity to flirt with Evelina. By the end of the episode, Duval is left in a ditch, tied up and alone, with only Evelina to feel pity for her. Evelina's description of what she sees when she rescues her grandmother is remarkable:

> She was sobbing, nay, almost roaring, and in the utmost agony of rage and terror. As soon as she saw me she redoubled her cries, but her voice was so broken, I could not understand a word she said. I was so much shocked, that it was with difficulty I forebore exclaiming against the cruelty of the Captain, for thus wantonly ill-treating her; and I could not forgive myself for having passively suffered the deception. I used my utmost endeavours to comfort her, assuring her of our present safety, and begging her to rise and return to the chariot.
>
> Almost bursting with passion, she pointed to her feet, and with frightful violence she actually tore the ground with her hands.[25]

To underscore the plight of Madame Duval, and the dehumanizing treatment she receives at the hands of the captain and his henchman, Evelina concludes that "covered with dirt, weeds, and filth" and the combination of dust from the road and her smeared makeup, "she hardly looked human."[26] The elaborate prank's descent into terror underscores the wanton cruelty of Captain Mirvan. This is no way to treat a lady—even if she *is* French. And although Evelina does help, it's only after the damage has been done. As Margaret Anne Doody points out, "Madame Duval enraged in a ditch is a wild illustration of feminine helplessness."[27]

A similarly disturbing scene, this time without the captain, demonstrates the cruel behavior of which Burney's high-class but low-mannered characters are capable. Two dissolute aristocrats, Lord Merton and Mr. Coverley, seek to have fun by making a friendly wager. Their initial idea is to have a carriage race, but Orville—out of concern for the women who are nervous about this idea—steers them away from that dangerous wager and proposes a more virtuous alternative: "the money should be his due, who, according to the opinion of the two judges, should bring the worthiest object with whom to share it!"[28] The others respond to this suggestion with silent stares, Evelina assumes out of shame for their selfishness; for her part, she "felt [her] eyes filled with tears" over Orville's worthy idea.[29] In contrast, Mrs. Selwyn encourages them to bet on whoever can recite the longest Horatian ode, knowing very well that none of them are smart or educated enough to accept that challenge.

The bet on which they eventually settle is grotesque: a race between two elderly poor women. As with the scene of Captain Mirvan's prank, the scene moves from humorous to disturbing. Evelina explains that the "two poor old women . . . looked so weak, so infirm, so feeble, that I could feel no sensation but that of pity at the sight." Again, though, she's outnumbered, and the other onlookers laugh at the ladies—with the exception of Orville, "who looked very grave during the whole transaction."[30] Once the race begins, the scene moves from the ridiculous to the dangerous when one of the women takes a hard fall. Evelina rushes to the old woman's aid, as she did with Duval in the ditch—only to be stopped by one of the bettors, who insists that the old woman must get up on her own. But when the competitor explains that she is too hurt to finish, the man who had bet on her "swore at her with unmanly rage, and seemed scarce able to refrain from striking her."[31] Evelina does not tell us of anyone who scolds or remonstrates this man's reaction.

Orville recognizes one of the remarkable elements of this sequence when he explains to Evelina, "the prevalence of fashion makes the greatest absurdities pass uncensured, and the mind naturally accommodates itself even to the most ridiculous improprieties, if they occur frequently."[32] That is, fashion can be dangerous—it's a kind of mob rule that blinds its participants to their own ridiculousness and, in the case of the race itself, cruelty. It takes well-formed independent minds to direct others or stand apart from them. But it's also remarkable that Orville and Evelina do not attempt to stop the race itself and the physical harm that consequently befalls one of the elderly women. Feminist critics sometimes interpret these scenes as illustrative of the vulnerability of women—particularly women beyond the age of marriage, women who have lost their sexual attraction and are therefore no longer of value to young men. This strikes me as a reasonable interpretation, though I would emphasize the absence of a proper masculine intervention. In this regard, the scenes anticipate the famous (or notorious, depending on your response to Burke's purple prose) passage in *Reflections on the Revolution in France*, in which Burke mourns the revolutionary capture of Marie Antoinette: "I thought ten thousand swords must have leaped from their scabbards to avenge even a look that threatened her with insult. —But the age of chivalry is gone. —That of sophisters, economists, and calculators, has succeeded; and the glory of Europe is extinguished for ever."[33] Rather than sophisters and the like, Evelina shows chivalry displaced by gamblers, pranksters, and drunkards.[34]

Too Much Monkey Business

There is redemption, though. In the novel's final set piece, the captain returns for another prank. This time his target is Lovel, a fop we meet early in the novel and who, like Madame Duval, does not earn any of our sympathy until Captain Mirvan takes his joke too far. In this case, the joke is that the captain says he's seen a relative of Lovel's, which turns out to be a monkey. The monkey charges into the room and causes mayhem, eventually jumping onto Lovel's face and scratching it, making the poor fop bleed. This moment, like the others, forces readers to elevate their senses of sympathy: we agree with Evelina: "I was really sorry for the poor man, who, though an egregious fop, had committed no offence that merited such chastisement."[35] But whereas Madame Duval had been left to cry in the ditch and the old ladies to fall down on the race track, Orville—after first protecting Evelina and making sure she is safe from the unleashed primate—emerges.

Before we see how he does that, it's worth taking a step back and noting that elsewhere in *Evelina*, there's the suggestion that although Orville is a charming and good person, there's something unmasculine about him. We saw before how he failed to intervene adequately during the race between the elderly women. During that same sequence, when he advises against the carriage race, Mr. Coverley jokes that "my Lord Orville is as careful,—egad, as careful as an old woman!"[36] In a more positive context, Evelina praises Orville for his "feminine . . . delicacy!"[37] He's not nearly as effeminate as Lovel, whom we first encounter approaching Evelina "on tiptoe" and in attire that "was so foppish, that I really believed he even wished to be stared at; and yet he was very ugly." (For his part, when we first see Orville, he manages to be "gayly, but not foppishly, dressed.")[38] Yet there nonetheless seems the possibility that he lacks the masculine roughness that, ironically, Selwyn has in abundance. Will he be ready to act decisively and with force when good manners aren't enough?

This final set-piece answers that question with an unequivocal yes—but he does not shed the qualities that Evelina so admires about him. As she explains, "ever humane, generous, and benevolent, he quitted his charge [Evelina herself], whom he saw was wholly out of danger, and seizing the monkey by the collar, made him loosen the ear; and then, with a sudden swing, flung him out of the room, and shut the door."[39] Lovel is bloodied and crying, so it would be an overstatement to say that Orville has saved him, but his intervention ends the violence and demonstrates his own development as a character because he acts with vigorous masculinity to protect the terrified women around him. There's hope for chivalry, that well-mannered mode of masculinity, after all!

Of course, Orville is not the only character who has changed; by the novel's conclusion it is clear that Evelina has matured into someone who is not only more polite than she was at the start of her voyage away from Villars, but also more independent. Although she has guides in Selwyn and Villars, she eventually realizes that she cannot always rely on them. Selywn in particular was never an especially appropriate guide for her young charge—Evelina notes that she is "too much engrossed in perpetual conversation to attend much to me"—and even gives her bad advice on affairs of the heart by encouraging her to pursue a relationship with the conniving cad Sir Clement.[40] As for Villars, at one point she writes to her mentor, "I know not what to *wish*;

think for me, therefore, my dearest Sir, and suffer my doubting mind, that knows not which way to direct its hopes, to be guided by your wisdom and unerring counsel."[41] Late in the novel, however, Villars provides questionable advice regarding Orville; and by the end, rather than asking for his permission to act, Evelina makes her own judgments and asks not for his advice, but for his "congratulations upon the events of this day."[42] In her short time in the world, Evelina has proven her social maturity and good judgment.

Most modern readers would not want to live in a society with manners as rigid as the one Evelina enters, but there is something impressive or beautiful about this social environment, which is one reason we still enjoy reading novels of manners. "The manners of aristocracy placed beautiful illusions over human nature," wrote Tocqueville, "and although the picture was often deceptive, one felt a noble pleasure in regarding it."[43] And even if our manners are more lax, we are still able to recognize parallels between Evelina's day and our own. When I taught this novel to college students, I put it in the context of entertainment that was more familiar to them. It's a type of comedy we still enjoy, at least on television. The legendary sitcom *Seinfeld* is often referred to as "a show about nothing," but its fans know that's not an accurate description. A typical *Seinfeld* episode is about a lot of things, and one of the things it's most often about is manners. Its immature and emotionally detached characters are confronted with questions about how to behave in situations that range from the absurd to the everyday. What do you do when someone offers you a gift you don't really want? How should you react if someone else gets credit for a meal you purchased for a friend? Is it rude to use a cell phone to call about someone's health, or is Jerry right when he warns, "It's like saying I don't want to take up any of my important time in my home, so I'll just get it out of way on the street"?[44] (This was back when people still had landlines. Manners change.) *Seinfeld*'s co-writer and co-producer Larry David continued this theme when he went solo with *Curb Your Enthusiasm*. In one episode, David's character lectures the person in front of him in line at an ice cream shop for testing too many flavors. "This is so rude!" he complains. "You're like a sample abuser, that's what you are! You're abusing your sampling privileges. One sample. Two samples the most. You can't just go on sample after sample!"[45] Larry David is more quarrelsome (to return to Tocqueville's phrasing) than the average American, who is unlikely to scold anyone over ice cream. Yet the success of David's comedy—not to mention the enduring popularity, and adaptations, of Jane Austen's fiction—points to the enduring interest in, and significance of, rules of behavior.

"Manners, properly understood," wrote Roger Scruton, "are the instruments whereby we negotiate our passage through the world, earn the respect and support of others, and form communities, which are something more than the sum of their members." They are also fragile, and "in a world where people hasten from goal to goal, with scant regard for the forms that secure the respect and endorsement of their fellows, these truths are increasingly obscured."[46] In *Evelina*, Burney gives us frequently funny but always thought-provoking examples of why manners matter and what they reveal about our sympathy and respect for those around us. Even in a democracy where, as Tocqueville observed, codes of conduct are looser and less rigorous than the aristocratic world of Burney's naïve heroine, they still speak volumes about our respect for our institutions, peers, and countrymen.

Manners, in the more general sense of customs and habits, also play an important role in our next novel, as its main character learns about the different ways of life of his countrymen—and its author attempts to preserve some of them in the mind of the reader.

Chapter Three

Rudderless Reading, Rash Rebels, and the Honorable Past—Walter Scott, *Waverley* (1814)

W hen Sir Walter Scott published his first novel, *Waverley; or, 'Tis Sixty Years Since*, in 1814, he did so anonymously, in part because he was unsure whether it would succeed. Already one of Europe's most popular poets, Scott feared that a dud of a novel would hurt his reputation. He didn't have to worry. *Waverley* was an enormous success, launching a fiction-writing career that made Scott the most widely read novelist of his time.[1] Scott is largely responsible for establishing one of the novel's most popular genres, the historical novel. In the process, he revived the critical status of the novel while also attracting ordinary readers. His works were the equivalent of a blockbuster film that also garnered prestigious awards.

A remarkable measure of his popularity is that places around the world are named after his characters and works. In North America alone, there are, by my count, seven towns named after his 1819 novel *Ivanhoe*; there's another in Australia. The sun never sets on Scott's literary empire. And while his works have been embraced by readers across the political spectrum (the Marxist literary theorist Georg Lukács was a particular fan), they are perhaps most amenable to those of a conservative disposition.

Among the people he influenced was the American political thinker Russell Kirk, who referred to Scott as "his literary mentor."[2] In *The Conservative Mind*, Kirk connected Scott's fiction to Edmund Burke's political thought as a mode of resistance against the encroachment of utilitarianism:

> Sir Walter succeeded in popularizing the proud and subtle doctrines of Burke. The *Reflections* sold by tens of thousands of copies, during the 1790s, but the Waverley novels carried Burke's ideas to a multitude which never could have been reached by pamphlets. . . . Scott makes the conservatism of Burke a living and a tender thing.[3]

That is a hallmark of great fiction: to adapt major ideas—including about politics and culture—into a compelling and credible narrative. John Henry Newman, the Anglican priest turned Catholic cardinal who was canonized a saint by the Catholic Church in 2019, also admired Scott. He once declared, "I have ever had such a devotion, I may call it, to Walter Scott. As a boy, in the early summer mornings, I read *Waverley* and *Guy Mannering* in bed, when they first came out, before it was time to get up; and long before that—I think when I was eight years old—I listened eagerly to *The Lay of the Last Minstrel*, which my mother and aunt were reading aloud."[4] As Newman saw it, Scott's works elevated readers:

> The general need of something deeper and more attractive than what had offered itself elsewhere, may be considered to have led to his popularity; and by means of his popularity he re-acted on his readers, stimulating their mental thirst, feeding their hopes, setting before them visions, which, when once seen, are not easily forgotten, and

silently indoctrinating them with nobler ideas, which
might afterwards be appealed to as first principles[.]

Compared to the works of other prominent novelists and poets,
Scott's works "stand almost as oracles of Truth confronting the
ministers of error and sin."[5]

Scott's influence meant that he also had his share of detractors.
The most prominent of them was Mark Twain, who absurdly blamed
Scott for starting the Civil War and named the sinking boat in
Huckleberry Finn the *Walter Scott*. Despite what Twain would have
you believe, Scott was also popular among opponents of slavery. A
statue of him was erected in New York's Central Park in 1872. And
when a slave named Frederick Bailey escaped to freedom, he looked
to a character in a Walter Scott poem for his new last name and
became Frederick Douglass.[6]

Today, it's fair to say that Scott's nickname of "The Wizard of the
North" is more likely to conjure up images of Harry Potter than
Edward Waverley—which is ironic, as J.K. Rowling began writing
her famous series in an Edinburgh café near the city's monument to
Scott, as well as the train station named after the hero of his first
novel. There isn't room here to explore why he's has fallen out of favor
(I have my theories), but whatever the cause, Scott's downfall is a
serious loss for modern readers.

The History behind the Historical Novel

In *Waverley; or, 'Tis Sixty Years Since*, Scott traces the mistakes and
maturation of Edward Waverley, a young Englishman who finds himself caught in the middle of the Jacobite Rising of 1745. The historical
backdrop, familiar to Scott's initial readers, is that the Jacobites supported the Stuart dynasty's claim to the British throne; as such, they

sought to replace the reigning Hanoverian monarchy with the exiled Stuart, James Francis Edward. (*Jacobus* is Latin for James, which is why a supporter of James's claim was called a Jacobite.) The so-called Old Pretender's father had been James II, the last Catholic king of England and Scotland, who was deposed through the Glorious Revolution in 1688 and replaced by his Anglican daughter Mary and her husband, William of Orange. The subsequent Act of Settlement of 1701 ensured the Protestant succession of the throne, and in 1702 Queen Anne, a Stuart but an Anglican, ascended. Because she died in 1714 without any surviving male heirs, the crown passed to the German George, Elector of Hanover.

The first Jacobite risings took place shortly after James II abdicated the throne and another significant one occurred the year after Anne's death, but *Game of Thr*—I mean *Waverley* centers on the most serious one, which began in 1745. Led by James II's son, Charles Edward Stuart (nicknamed Bonnie Prince Charlie), these Jacobite forces gathered in the Scottish Highlands—the Stuart dynasty began in Scotland, so that's where Jacobite risings tended to begin—and made it forty miles outside of London before beginning their retreat and eventually suffering their final defeat at Culloden in April of 1746. Afterward, to ensure that was the last such uprising, the British government doled out harsh penalties against the insurgents, increased its military presence in the Highlands, and passed legislation to break up the feudal clan system.

In Scott's novel, Edward Waverley is the scion of a landed English family that had supported the Stuart claim to the throne. His uncle, Everard, was involved in the rising of 1715 and has since lived quietly with his sister Rachael at the family estate of Waverley-Honour. But Edward's father, Richard Waverley, sees more hope for his desired future in Parliament as a whig supporting the reigning Hanoverian monarchy. While this causes tension between Richard and his older siblings, they reconcile when Edward is a young boy. Eventually, Edward—the last of the family line and set to inherit the estate—spends most of each year with his uncle and aunt at Waverley-Honour.

So much for the historical and familial context. The novel's conflict arises when Edward becomes a commissioned officer in the British military and is stationed just north of Edinburgh. After some initial training, Edward goes on leave and visits a family friend in the Highlands and then, through a series of deceptions, mistakes, and misunderstandings, finds himself traveling among Jacobite Highlanders and eventually in the presence of Bonnie Prince Charlie himself. Abandoning his commission, he takes up arms for the doomed Jacobite cause before realizing that, in the words of Gob Bluth, he'd made a huge mistake.

What makes this young and smart Englishman take up arms against the king in whose army he had been an officer?

The Miseducation of Edward Waverley

You may have noticed that when parents and teachers discuss the reading habits of their children and students, they tend to look at the bright side. If the material is never challenging—say, if a high school student reads only graphic novels—they often resort to some variation of the common refrain, "Well, at least they're reading!" In some regards, this reaction is understandable. In an age with countless distractions pulling us all away from the written word, it's a relief to find a young person looking at print of any type. I feel that sense when I see one of my children with a book instead of a video game controller or tablet in hand.

Waverley suggests a problem with this attitude: if we take reading seriously, if we believe it can shape how people think and behave, then the quality and content of what we read matters. What we read can form our behavior, our expectations, even what we think about when we're not reading. Conservatives in America have stressed this for generations. It's why we've tended to emphasize the importance of character formation in education, going back to at least William Bennett's tenure at the Department of Education during the Reagan administration. It's evident in the current interest in the classical education movement.[7]

Waverley explores the ramifications of an education that does not direct and guide students, and in particular the consequences of an undisciplined approach to reading. Scott describes his hero's learning in blunt terms: "The education of our hero, Edward Waverley, was of a nature somewhat desultory."[8] That last word isn't one we use much today, but it comes up often in *Waverley*. The *Oxford English Dictionary* defines it as "skipping about, jumping or flitting from one thing to another; irregularly shifting, devious; wavering, unsteady," as well as "pursuing a disconnected and irregular course of action; unmethodical."[9] Both of these senses clarify how Scott uses the word in *Waverley*, and the first sense's use of "wavering" is itself a red flag for its importance to the title character, whose surname hints at his "somewhat desultory" education, and the unsteady habits and poor judgment that develop as a result.

Edward's inadequate education results from an absence of parental engagement and consistent guidance. Parental guidance could have helped "prevent the dissipation of mind incidental to such a desultory [there's that word again!] course of reading."[10] But Edward's mother died when he was young, his father was too preoccupied with his own political ambitions to be concerned about his son's education, and his uncle and aunt nurture the false belief that any reading is good reading—or, as the narrator describes this misconception:

the vulgar doctrine, that idleness is incompatible with reading of any kind, and that the mere tracing the alphabetical characters with the eye, is in itself a useful and meritorious task, without scrupulously considering what ideas or doctrines they may happen to convey.[11]

Edward's part-time tutor is no help, either. An "old and indulgent" chaplain, he permitted his student to "to learn as he pleased, what he pleased, and when he pleased."[12] A better instructor, and more perceptive guardians, would have discerned that Edward's "desire of amusement" required guidance to mature into a more appropriate "thirst for knowledge." As it was, "young Waverley drove through the sea of books like a vessel without a pilot or a rudder"—or, for that matter, a compass. This "indulgence of his tutors" in allowing the young man "to seek his instruction only according to the bent of his own mind" would, the narrator warns, have "evil consequences, which long continued to influence his character, happiness, and utility."[13]

How could something as basic as his reading habits inflict so much harm on Edward? Because what and how Waverley read distorted what and how he thought. He fails to develop intellectual discipline:

> Alas! while he was thus permitted to read only for the gratification of his own amusement, he foresaw not that he was losing for ever the opportunity of acquiring habits of firm and incumbent application, of gaining the art of controuling, directing, and concentrating the powers of his own mind for earnest investigation.[14]

In other words, he would remain and unserious and flighty boy incapable of elevating his thought. Edward's education also retards his moral development because for as much as the young boy has read, he learned "little of what adds dignity to man, and qualifies him to support and adorn an elevated situation in society."[15] His reading does not improve his mind or his character, does not help him contribute to society, and serves no greater purpose apart from the moment of reading itself. If you think I'm being harsh, you should hear the narrator, who concludes that "the dainty, squeamish, and fastidious taste acquired by a surfeit of idle reading, had . . . rendered our hero unfit for serious and sober study."[16]

The scholar Alan Jacobs is certainly right to argue that "it should be normal for us to read what we want to read, to read what we truly enjoy reading"; we don't need a literary diet restricted to the canon of Great Books.[17] But a proper education means developing the ability to engage with, understand, and learn from a variety of challenging literary works. Edward lacks that, and the details of his mis-education prepare us for demonstrations of "the wild and irregular spirit of our hero."[18]

The implications of his educational malpractice first become clear when Edward joins the British army as an officer in the mounted infantry. The impetus behind this decision is sensible enough: because Edward is to inherit a substantial estate and is the sole male descendent in his noble line, his father and uncle agree that he should learn more about the outside world before getting married and taking on the responsibilities of a landed gentleman. Everard and Rachael want to send him to Europe, but Richard, fearing that Edward will be introduced to Jacobite intrigues abroad, pulls strings to get Edward a commission as a captain.

It is a position for which Edward is ill-suited, requiring careful thinking, steady focus, "and a cool and reasoning head to bring them into action"; but Edward's "vague and unsatisfactory course of reading" gave him only "that wavering and unsettled habit of mind which is most averse to study and riveted attention."[19] To his credit, Edward is perceptive enough to recognize his shortcomings and feel an appropriately "painful sense of inferiority."[20] But Edward is unable to apply himself and develop his abilities as an officer. As soon as summer comes, he requests a leave so he can see more of Scotland. He enjoys his journey into the Highlands so much that he requests an extension of his leave. These decisions will have dire consequences.[21]

Edward under the Influence

Six weeks into his visit, an event occurs that stokes the fire of Edward's romantic imagination: a group of Highland bandits steal cattle belonging to his host. Edward is amazed by the stories he hears about blackmail payments to the local clan chief, Fergus Mac-Ivor, and "could not help starting at a story which bore so much resemblance to one of his own day-dreams."[22] Following a Highlander on a hike to recover the stolen steer, he "give[s] himself up to the full romance of his situation."[23] The lack of discipline, as well as the fondness for romance that his reading and imagination fostered in him, blind Edward to the dangers presented by his new surroundings and associates, who scheme to use his status to further the Jacobite cause.

A less manipulative Jacobite he encounters is Flora Mac-Ivor, but even here Edward's education hurts him. A beautiful young Highland woman, Flora entrances Edward because she seems as if she stepped out of the pages of a romance. Scott frequently draws our attention to how Edward's experiences with her correspond to the subject matter of his reading: Waverley is compared to "a knight of romance"; a waterfall is "romantic"; he experiences "wild feelings of romantic delight"; in short, Waverley falls for Flora and her home because he is "a youth of romantic imagination."[24] Still besotted with his unguided readings, Edward drifts through the Highlands in a dream.

Waverley's inadequate education contrasts the one received by Flora's brother, Fergus. Fergus has benefited from rigorous study abroad which, combined with worldly experience, helps him hold sway over the inexperienced Englishman through "bold and prompt habits of thinking, acting, and speaking."[25] This educational advantage helps him manipulate the naïve young Englishman, who is overcome by "the bold and decisive activity of an intellect which was sharpened by the habit of acting on a preconceived and regular system"—a far cry from the rudderless, pilotless vessel of Edward's education.[26]

Meanwhile, the political scheming of Edward's father, Richard, backfires and costs him his position in government. Though he only has himself to blame, Richard (with help from his siblings) convinces Edward that his downfall is more evidence of the unworthiness of the Hanoverian government, and they encourage him to resign his military commission. Poor Edward is incapable of thinking for himself and understanding the truth of the situation:

> From the desultory style of his studies, he had not any fixed political opinion to place in opposition to the movements of indignation which he felt at his father's supposed wrongs. Of the real cause of his disgrace, Edward was totally ignorant; nor had his habits at all led him to investigate the politics of the period in which he lived, or remark the intrigues in which his father had been so actively engaged.[27]

The shoddy education provided by Edward's guardians make him susceptible to the dangerous persuasions of those same guardians. The young man's sense of injustice is further inflamed when his commanding officer informs him that he must return to camp or be reported to the War Office. Instead, he resigns his commission.

Before long, through a series of calculated efforts, Fergus capital-
izes on Edward's vulnerability and frustration by immersing him in
the romance of the Highland army and eventually introducing him
to Bonnie Prince Charlie himself. If the manners and habits of a
Highland chieftain can hypnotize Edward, what chance does he stand
against the charms of a prince? Before long, all of Edward's "prudential
motives" are overcome by "the address and manner of a polished
court" and the Young Pretender's similarities to "a hero of romance."
It helps that the prince's flattery makes Edward feel more important
and relevant to the Jacobite cause than he had been to the British
military. At the end of his first encounter with the prince, Edward
kneels before the Young Pretender and "devote[s] his heart and sword
to the vindication of his rights."[28] None of this would have happened
if Edward's educators had provided him direction and guidance to
temper his obsession with romance.

Earlier in this chapter, I mentioned John Henry Newman's admiration of Scott; perhaps some of that admiration stems from their
similar attitudes toward education. In his influential work *The Idea
of a University* (1852), Newman addresses efforts to educate the
working-class with programs that offer "interesting and instructive
reading." He asks a familiar question: "what *permanent* advantage
[does] the mind [get] by such desultory reading and hearing, as this
literary movement encourages"? Newman's use of the d-word signals
that the answer is not much, because there is an important difference
"between the mere diversion of the mind and its real education."
Newman expounds upon the distinction:

> A man may hear a thousand lectures, and read a thousand
> volumes, and be at the end of the process very much where
> he was, as regards knowledge. Something more than
> merely *admitting* it in a negative way into the mind is

necessary, if it is to remain there. It must not be passively
received, but actually and actively entered into, embraced,
mastered. The mind must go half-way to meet what comes
to it from without.[29]

To learn something, to retain the knowledge conveyed in what one
reads, requires conscious engagement, what we might now call (perhaps too often) critical thinking. This is the kind of reading that leads
to knowledge and wisdom. This is precisely what Edward lacks and
why he participates in a doomed attempt to shake the foundations
of Britain's political order.

Fortunately, Edward is able to redeem himself. *Waverley* has
plenty of adventure, but it is also very much about the character's
growth from romantic dreamer to a serious and sensible young
man. This maturation includes realizing, through a series of tragic
events, that his irresponsible behavior has caused serious pain to
others. He laments, "O, indolence and indecision of mind! if not in
yourselves vices, to how much exquisite misery do you frequently
prepare the way!"[30] He also matures through reflection, which
marks a contrast with the desultory, unfocused manner of thinking
he had developed during his adolescence. This helps Edward
"acquir[e] a more complete mastery of a spirit tamed by adversity,
than his former experience had given him; and . . . he felt himself
entitled to say firmly, though perhaps with a sigh, that the romance
of his life was ended, and that its real history had now commenced."[31]
With the epiphany that his life's romantic stage was at and end and
its "real history" beginning, Waverley gains the wisdom to exercise
prudence and good judgment, finally overcoming his desultory
education.

Renouncing an Uprising, Preserving the Past

Perhaps the most conservative element of *Waverley* is its tone regarding social and political change. The novel was published as Britain and its many European allies were nearing the end of their long wars against Napoleon and Revolutionary France. The French Revolution had first sent European powers into a tumult nearly a generation before, so it's little wonder that Scott would be reluctant to celebrate an attempt to overthrow a monarch, even if that king were replaced by a fellow Scot whose ancestors had once reigned. Scott's deep aversion to abrupt change—in Waverley novels and his works of nonfiction—justify Kirk's claim, quoted at the beginning of this chapter, that Scott "makes the conservatism of Burke a tender and living thing."

We learn of Edward's own feelings about such radical change after he has resigned his commission but has not yet joined the Jacobites. At this point, he feels "inexpressible repugnance at the idea of being accessary to the plague of civil war." After all, James II had "justly forfeited" his right to the throne, and had been succeed by a series of monarchs who "had reigned in peace and glory over Britain, sustaining and exalting the character of the nation abroad, and its liberties at home." These generations of peace and prosperity raised the basic question: "was it worth while to disturb a government so long settled and established, and to plunge a kingdom into all the miseries of civil war. . . ?"[32] The answer to that question for the wavering Waverley is no—until it is yes—and then, finally, no again.

A conservative may instinctively sympathize with the Jacobites because the Stuarts arguably had the better claim to the throne. And Catholics are likely to resent the effort to keep the throne open only to Protestants and all the restriction of Catholic rights, and rites, that entailed. But Edward's initial antipathy for the uprising is prudential and pragmatic. Two prominent scholars of Scottish literature frame the issue this way:

> In Scott's view, the Glorious Revolution in Scotland and England had curbed the tyranny of the old regime's unfettered monarchy by locating the decisive power in parliaments whose members were elected by property-owning gentlemen. For Scott, this arrangement not only restrained arbitrary royal power, it also offered a bastion against the dangerous innovations proposed by radicals and democrats.[33]

If Scott, who was fond of using epigraphs for the chapters of later novels, could have applied a quotation from a twentieth-century thinker, he may have been drawn to this definition by English political theorist and philosopher Michael Oakeshott: "The man of conservative temperament believes that a known good is not lightly to be surrendered for an unknown better."[34]

One of the fascinating elements of *Waverley*, however, is that despite its suggestion that Edward makes the wrong decision in joining the Jacobite cause, Scott conveys undeniable sympathy for the Highlanders fighting against the Hanoverian establishment.[35] Barton Swaim of the *Wall Street Journal* thinks the novel is "enduringly relevant" because of "Scott's ability to find sense and decency and intelligence on both sides of a deadly struggle. . . . [He] shows us the virtues and essential reasonableness of two sides implacably opposed to each other in an ancient conflict—each determined to defeat and ruin the other, so deep is their mutual loathing."[36] In particular, Scott emphasizes the loyalty and honor of the Highlanders. In one powerful scene, a Highlander proposes that a judge who has just sentenced a Highland chief to death should only exile the prisoner and instead execute six lesser members of his clan. When his proposal elicits laughter in the courtroom, the Highlander, "looking sternly around," says: "if they laugh because they think I wad not keep my word . . . I can tell them they ken neither the heart of a Hielandman, nor the honour of a gentleman."[37]

Similarly, Fergus notes that although the English fancy themselves the more advanced people, Jacobite leaders were subject to execution, which had not always been the case in Scotland. This change, he sarcastically explains, "is one of the blessings, Edward, with which your free country has accommodated poor old Scotland—her own jurisprudence, I have heard, was much milder."[38] With this complex evocation of the virtues and vices of Jacobites and Hanoverians alike, Scott introduced what the historian Arthur Herman calls "a key ingredient of the modern consciousness, a sense of historical detachment."[39] At the same time, Scott's depiction of Highland honor and loyalty is in keeping with a nationalist strain that runs throughout his work, the sense that although Scotland may be better off by becoming more like the rest of Britain, certain admirable manners and customs have been lost. He makes that claim explicit in the novel's final pages, when he says of the Highlanders:

> This race has now almost entirely vanished from the land, and with it, doubtless, much absurd political prejudice; but, also, many living examples of singular and disinterested attachment to the principles of loyalty which they received from their fathers, and of old Scottish faith, hospitality, worth, and honour.[40]

Many of those shortcomings and strengths are illustrated over the course of *Waverley*, so the reader, too, understands the significance

—positive and negative—of their disappearance. As Oakeshott noted, "there is no such thing as an unqualified improvement."[41]

Scott's interest in depicting the values of the Highlanders is also emblematic of the act of commemoration that runs throughout Scott's work, and which he makes explicit in the postscript to *Waverley*. If, as Matthew Continetti of the American Enterprise Institute has suggested, "the job of a conservative is to remember," then a driving force behind *Waverley* is a conservative one.[42] Scott explains that his sight was set on "preserving some idea of the ancient manners of which I have witnessed the almost total extinction" and "tracing the evanescent manners of" Scotland.[43] It is worth nothing that Scott is using the word *manners* in a different sense than we explored in the previous chapter; here, it's the now archaic sense of (as Samuel Johnson defined it) "general way of life, morals, habits."[44] These manners illustrate the values and priorities of a people. The existence of a universal human nature does not preclude significant variations in the particular expressions of that nature, and many of those variations are manifest in manners and customs. As such, they speak volumes about a culture. If you don't believe me, take Burke's word for it:

> Manners are of more importance than laws. Upon them, in a great measure, the laws depend. The law touches us but here and there, and now and then. Manners are what vex or sooth, corrupt or purify, exalt or debase, barbarize or refine us, by a constant, steady, uniform, insensible operation, like that of the air we breathe in. They give their whole form and colour to our lives. According to their quality, they aid morals, they supply them, or they totally destroy them.[45]

Capturing such details of a culture, then, help us understand the people—their virtues and vices, their admirable qualities and their shortcomings—more fully.

Scott acts on this impulse to preserve "some idea of these ancient manners" because of the enormous changes experienced in Scotland since the Jacobite uprising of 1745–46. These changes, "though steadily and rapidly progressive, [have], nevertheless, been gradual; and, like those who drift down the stream of a deep and smooth river, we are not aware of the progress we have made until we fix our eye on the now-distant point from which we set out."[46] (The abrupt changes inflicted by an uprising or revolution is something else entirely.) These changes, which he calls "progress" in that passage, arose as a result of the aggressive British response to the uprising— what Scott calls "the destruction of the patriarchal power of the Highland chiefs, and the abolition of the heritable jurisdictions of the Lowland nobility and barons, [and] the total eradication of the Jacobite party." Economic changes are important, too, and he identifies the role played by "the gradual influx of wealth, and extension of commerce . . . to render the present people of Scotland a class of beings as different from their grandfathers, as the existing English are from those of Queen Elizabeth's time."[47] That comparison is truly remarkable: the Scots of the early nineteenth century, Scott suggests, had changed more since 1746 than their English counterparts had changed since the late-sixteenth or early-seventeenth centuries. It is not revolutionary change, but it is extraordinary change, and in *Waverley*, Scott sought to convey what had been lost.

As much as Scott seeks to preserve and praise elements of Highland culture, Edward has an important epiphany that underscores his own separateness from it, and its ultimate incompatibility with what Britain was becoming. As the Jacobites prepare for battle against (by coincidence) the English regiment to which Edward had been attached, the young man hears familiar accents, recognizes the English dialect, and sees the standard under which he had marched. The familiarity contrasts with the side for which he now fought:

> It was at that instant, that looking around him, he saw the wild dress and appearance of his Highland associates, heard their whispers in an uncouth and unknown language, looked upon his own dress, so unlike that which he had worn from his infancy, and wished to awake from what seemed at the moment a dream, strange, horrible, and unnatural. "Good God," he thought, "am I then a traitor to my country, a renegade to my standard, and a foe . . . to my native England!"[48]

Edward finally understands that as an Englishman, his ultimate loyalties are not in the Highlands. They are with his home, with the traditions and government that shaped him, and which he was foolish to abandon, no matter how seductive his days of Highland "romance" had been. According to the author and critic Joseph Bottum, Scott depicts a Scotland that "is thick with things properly demanding emotion," such as "family, historical continuity, oaths, royalty, the dramatic scenery of an untamed countryside," whereas the modern world that Edward eventually embraces is "disenchanted."[49] On the contrary, though, Edward's disillusionment with the Jacobites is based in part on his understanding that, apart from the wild landscape, the England in which he had grown up, and the modern world to which he returns, offers all of those "thick" qualities—plus the advantage of being familiar to him.

Scott's attitude toward the past has been interpreted in very different ways by some of his most prominent readers. The philosopher Isaiah Berlin saw in Scott's sympathetic vision of the past what we might now call cultural relativism. Berlin believed that Scott painted "very attractive and slightly hypnotic pictures of [past] ages" that made them look "equally good if not better" than the modern. What's more, this implicit "notion of compatibility, of plurality of ideals, each of which has its own validity, becomes part of the great battering-ram which Romanticism employs against the notion of order, against the notion of progress, against the notion of perfection, classical ideals, the structure of things."[50] If it strikes you as incongruous to perceive Scott as a vandal attempting to knock down the walls of order and structure, that makes two of us. A fair reading of the Waverley novels gleans that Scott indeed brought forward virtues of bygone days, but not at the expense of "the structure of things." Rather, he depicts how the past helped build that very structure.

On the other hand, the Romantic essayist William Hazlitt claimed that the Waverley novels were successful because they make the past seem appalling. They "carry us back to the feuds, the heart-burnings, the havoc, the dismay, the wrongs and the revenge of a barbarous age and people—to the rooted prejudices and deadly animosities of sects and parties in politics and religion, and of contending chiefs and clans in war and intrigue. . . . As we read, we throw aside the trammels of civilization, the flimsy veil of humanity."[51] Beneath Hazlitt's smirking overstatement lies the important observation that even as readers are entertained by the misanthropy of the past, they recognize the sympathy, restraint, and civility of the present. Scott's greatness is probably found somewhere between Berlin's and Hazlitt's readings. He seeks to re-create the past in both its greatness and its gore, not to diminish our age but to show his contemporaries how they arrived where they were, how far they had progressed—and what they may have lost along the way. In the process, he (returning to Newman's phrasing) "silently indoctrinat[es]" readers "with nobler ideas."

Before leaving the world of eighteenth-century British uprisings, it's worth considering, all-too-briefly, one more element of *Waverley* that makes it remarkably relevant for our non-monarchical age. Yes, the novel's plot revolves around an eighteenth-century conflict over the rightful king of Britain. And yes, like most of Scott's novels, the hero is a member of the landed gentry. But Scott's novels always feature important characters of other classes and walks of life. In *Waverley*, for example, there is a very touching scene involving the death of the son of one of Everard Waverley's tenants, who had been in the regiment Edward abandoned. Edward is also aided in his adventures by an endearing "poor simpleton" named Davie Gellatley.[52] Scott's novels touch on the worth of the highest and lowest ranks of British life. This is why G. K. Chesterton declared, "Of all these nineteenth century writers there is none, in the noblest sense, more democratic than Walter Scott," who more than anyone else represented "the idea of the dignity of all men."[53]

Scott wrote more than two dozen novels after *Waverley*—even as he continued to write poems, histories, and essays. His achievement and influence are truly astonishing, so it's appropriate that his bust adorns the front of the Library of Congress, alongside figures like Demosthenes, Dante, and the American novelist whose work we will examine next.

Chapter Four

Utopian Delusions—Nathaniel Hawthorne, *The Blithedale Romance* (1852)

In 1971, John Lennon released his best-known solo song, "Imagine," with its memorable chorus: "You may say I'm a dreamer / But I'm not the only one." Its verses implore listeners to, among other things, "Imagine no possessions / I wonder if you can."[1] A year later, the American band Steely Dan recorded a song called "Only a Fool Would Say That," which some listeners hear as a wry rebuttal to Lennon. In addition to verses that include a reference to "a man with a dream" and a call to "imagine," the chorus runs: "I heard it was you / Talkin' 'bout a world where all is free / It just couldn't be, and only a fool would say that." It would be an overstatement to call Steely Dan conservative (even if they do an awful lot of longing for days gone by), but those lyrics capture a sentiment that is central to conservativism.

It's not that we conservatives don't want to give peace a chance, as Lennon would urge elsewhere; it's that we tend to be skeptical of sweeping claims about human perfectibility. We distrust—or should distrust—politicians who promise policies that are sure to bring about a future of uniform peace and hope. We recognize that efforts to achieve universal harmony inevitably devolve into the use of steel blades, brass knuckles, and iron curtains. Our skepticism is in keeping with the Judeo-Christian belief that we live in a fallen world. "The cast of American conservative thought is profoundly antiutopian," American political philosopher Frank Meyer observed in the 1950s.[2] That remains true.

Back in the mid-twentieth century, American conservatives expressed this anti-utopian skepticism with an imperative coined by William F. Buckley Jr.: "Don't immanentize the eschaton." Buckley's catchy if oddball phrase, based on an essay by the German-American philosopher Eric Voegelin, refers to the Gnostic belief that it is possible to establish a heaven on Earth; according to political columnist and author Jonah Goldberg, the phrase warns against "trying to make what is reserved for the next life part of the here and now."[3] The most obvious—and pernicious—version of this utopian thought is Marxism, which in its various forms has led to the death of millions of people around the world in the name of a workers' paradise. If you want a utopia, you need to break a few eggs. But as Thomas More would tell you, *utopia* means *no place*. The idealized visions of alternative worlds and modes of government are impossible to realize on earth.

Conservatives are temperamentally averse to utopianism in large part because we see it as an unrealistic break from tradition, an unreasonable preference for the abstract and untested over the wisdom and experience of the ages. This conservative attitude should not be confused with an aversion to all change. As Edmund Burke insisted even as he condemned the French Revolution, "a state without the means of some change is without the means of its conservation."[4] The problem is that utopian visions tend be built on the belief that human nature can be perfected or fundamentally altered. Thomas Sowell offers a helpful way of understanding these competing outlooks by distinguishing between the constrained vision, which corresponds to how conservatives tend to see the world, and the unconstrained vision, which aligns with the progressive social perspective. The unconstrained vision is characterized by "the conviction that foolish or immoral choices explain the evils of the world—and that wiser or more moral and humane social policies are the solution." On the other hand,

> the constrained vision sees the evils of the world as deriving from the limited and unhappy choices available, given the inherent moral and intellectual limitations of human beings. For amelioration of these evils and the promotion of progress, they rely on the systemic characteristics of certain social processes such as moral traditions, the marketplace, or families.[5]

The unconstrained vision—that which would immanentize the eschaton—denies the flaws and limitations that the constrained vision sees as inherent. According to the constrained vision, our institutions can make the best of our shortcomings by directing them toward productive ends or playing them off of each other. Perhaps this is why the one great break from history that American conservatives embrace—the American Revolution and its charting documents—has been successful: as we saw in our discussion of *Rasselas*, the Constitution in particular recognized and accounted for the lesser angels of our nature in constructing a government with checks and balances, with ambition counteracting ambition.

A Farmer's Life for Me

The failure of a utopian scheme, the shortcomings of the unconstrained vision, is the subject of Nathaniel Hawthorne's haunting and humorous *The Blithedale Romance*, a novel loosely based on the author's own participation in a socialist agricultural commune called Brook Farm. Hawthorne joined the commune at West Roxbury, located about a dozen miles from Boston, in the spring of 1841. He initially enjoyed his time there—the early mornings and long days of labor in the fields—but eventually grew frustrated when, contrary to his expectations, he was unable to find free time or adequate focus to write. He left the farm that November. As the novelist Henry James observed of the community, "There must have been in the enterprise a good deal of a certain freshness and purity of spirit, of a certain noble credulity and faith in the perfectibility of man."[6] Biographer Brenda Wineapple explains that this idealism was another reason Hawthorne didn't last with the project: "With all his goodwill toward Brook Farm, he did not share [the] faith in a human nature free of envy or avarice or evil. . . . [He] didn't for a moment assume people were basically good."[7]

Hawthorne would wait more than a decade before gleaning his experience on the farm for fictional material. In the meantime, he published several short story collections and two novels, including *The Scarlet Letter*. When Hawthorne did finally publish *The Blithedale Romance* in 1852, he included a preface that insisted on a distance between the novel and the author's actual experiences on Brook Farm. Hawthorne explained that although "he ha[d] occasionally availed himself of his actual reminiscences" for the sake of realism, the work itself was a "fancy-sketch," and the setting of the socialist commune a place "where the creatures of his brain may play their phantasmagorical antics."[8] In other words, while there was certainly overlap between truth and fiction, it would be a mistake to read *The Blithedale Romance* as a straightforward and unambiguous account of Hawthorne's experiences with the commune. As Henry James quipped, "The Brook Farm community left no traces behind it that the world in general can appreciate; I should rather say that the only trace is a short novel, of which the principal merits reside in the qualities of difference from the affair itself."[9]

Hawthorne presents *The Blithedale Romance* as the recollections of its narrator, a middle-aged bachelor named Miles Coverdale, of his time with an agrarian commune called Blithedale. Coverdale, an aspiring poet, joins the commune one April (like Hawthorne) and over the course of several months develops conflicted attitudes toward both the project and several of the other community members. One reason *The Blithedale Romance* is such a rich novel is that Hawthorne is too good a novelist to make it primarily about ideas. The novel's drama depends on the complex relationships between several of the other members of the community: there is Zenobia, a proud, wealthy, and beautiful proto-feminist, based on the historical figure Margaret Fuller, who lived at Brook Farm while Hawthorne was there; the philanthropist Mr. Hollingsworth, with whom Coverdale develops an antagonistic friendship; and Priscilla, a frail girl who arrives at the farm and attaches herself to Zenobia. There are also intriguing characters outside of the farm, including the Veiled Lady, a mysterious figure who purportedly possessed "many of the privileges of a disembodied spirit."[10]

Coverdale and the other members of the commune have ambitious aims for their project—nothing short of what he calls "the reformation of the world."[11] Early in the novel, he explains the idealism that inspired their participation in the socialist experiment in terms that underscore a shared frustration with traditional ways of life and a desire to start a fresh world: "We had left the rusty iron frame-work of society behind us. We had broken through many hindrances that are powerful enough to keep most people on the weary tread-mill of the established system, even while they feel its irksomeness almost as intolerable as we did." What's more, the community had a missionary zeal to it, as the participants' purpose was "to give up whatever we had heretofore attained, for the sake of showing mankind the example of a life governed by other than the false and cruel principles, on which human society has all along been based."[12] By Coverdale's account, the people of Blithedale saw themselves as trailblazers, the hardy few with the courage to cast aside the flawed ways of the past and start anew.

Elsewhere, Coverdale expresses a vision in which the reform he and his friends undertake is part of a global tectonic shift—literally:

> It was impossible . . . not to imbibe the idea that everything in nature and human existence was fluid, or fast becoming so; that the crust of the earth in many places was broken, and its whole surface portentously upheaving; that it was a day of crisis, and that we ourselves were in the critical vortex. Our great globe floated in the atmosphere of infinite space like an unsubstantial bubble.[13]

Coverdale sees the project at Blithedale as specially positioned to transform human society, to break from traditional human institutions and establish an entirely new relationship with both society and the natural world. His vision of radical change includes a disregard for America's founding documents: "We did not greatly care—at least, I never did—for the written constitution under which our millennium had commenced."[14] He recognizes a similar energy in Zenobia, who "made no scruple of oversetting all human institutions, and scattering them as with a breeze from her fan."[15]

The relationship between Coverdale, Zenobia, Hollingsworth, and Priscilla is often described in terms that imply their inseparability, occasionally with negative implications—including the many times they are referred to as a "knot." There is also a whiff of free love to the project: the community "seemed to authorize any individual, of either sex, to fall in love with any other, regardless of what would elsewhere be judged suitable and prudent."[16] It may be too much to call the characters hippies, but it wouldn't be far off, either, as the project resists traditional morals and norms. These imprudent love affairs inflict a heavy emotional toll on the characters.

Still, it would be a mistake to interpret the novel as an attack on socialism in particular. In his preface, Hawthorne disavows any attempt "to illustrate a theory, or elicit a conclusion, favorable or otherwise, in respect to Socialism."[17] It is also worth noting that while the novel does poke fun at the characters' idealism, it would be foolish to compare their venture with later, more ambitious—and tyrannical—communist ventures. This utopian project is not comparable to the Soviet Union. Indeed, there is something distinctively American about Blithedale: it's a group of like-minded individuals creating a community based on shared beliefs and aims. It is also entirely voluntary and—hooray!— privately funded. (The original Brook Farm was a joint stock company, meaning it relied on investors like Hawthorne.) At the risk of overstatement, I'll even say that it's precisely the kind of community organization that so impressed Alexis de Tocqueville during his visit to the United States a decade before Brook Farm. The problem isn't with the project in general. The problem is that it's driven by a utopian vision.

And very early on, it becomes clear that the community's naïve utopian dreams ignore the truths of human nature.

Love for Labor, Lost

An early test of the experiment's idealism occurs during the first meal with Silas Foster, a local man who has been hired to manage the farm and train the others. It's a culture clash, what Coverdale calls "the first practical trial run of our theories of equal brotherhood and sisterhood," as it threw together "people of superior cultivation and refinement" with "unpolished companions." But the level-headed Foster is the only experienced farmer in the group, and he frequently punctures Coverdale's inflated sense of purpose. When Coverdale pretentiously envisions the "blazing windows" of the farmhouse on a cold night as a "beacon-fire . . . for humanity," Foster points out that "the blaze of that brush-wood will only last a minute or two longer." The reader may join Coverdale in wondering "whether he meant to insinuate that our moral illumination would have as brief a term."[18] If so, he'd have been onto something. Coverdale anticipates the labor that awaits him as a soul-elevating proposition, the transcendental benefits of which will obscure the fatigue induced by toil. Befitting a project that he foresees as "Paradise, indeed!", it will be a religious experience:

> While our enterprise lay all in theory, we had pleased ourselves with delectable visions of the spiritualization of labor. It was to be our form of prayer, and ceremonial of worship. Each stroke of the hoe was to uncover some aromatic root of wisdom, heretofore hidden from the sun. Pausing in the field, to let the wind exhale the moisture from our foreheads, we were to look upward, and catch glimpses into the far-off soul of truth.[19]

Note Coverdale's admission that at the outset, all they had was "theory"—their venture is not based on any empirical experience, which is one reason their hopes are dashed. The theoretical and pagan vision of rural labor seems beautiful, but it is remarkably naïve and even condescending. As Coverdale acknowledges, "Matters did not turn out quite so well as we anticipated."[20]

For one thing, Coverdale falls ill almost immediately and has to spend several days in bed instead of out in the field. The illness shows him that he may be unprepared for the physical rigors of the project before him, and he "seriously wished . . . that the reformation of society had been postponed about half-a-century, or at all events, to such a date as should have put my intermeddling with it entirely out of the question." The funny phrasing aside, he harbors serious doubts about his involvement in the project at all—why should he want to change society when, as he reflects, "it had satisfied me well enough" by providing a life of comfort and relative ease? In his exaggerated regret, he even fears that his farming will deprive a real farmer of sustenance: "Was it better to hoe, to mow, to toil and moil amidst the accumulations of a barnyard; to be the chambermaid of two yoke of oxen and a dozen cows; to eat salt beef, and earn it with the sweat of my brow, and thereby take the tough morsel out of some wretch's mouth, into whose vocation I had thrust myself?"[21]

The spiritualized farmwork he and his companions anticipate never arrives. Quite the contrary—rather than elevating their thoughts, their experience with farming brings them down to the ground: "Our thoughts . . . were fast becoming cloddish. Our labor symbolized nothing, and left us mentally sluggish in the dusk of the evening."[22] The dispiriting effects of their labor convinces Coverdale that "intellectual activity is incompatible with any large amount of bodily exercise. The yeoman and the scholar—the yeoman and the man of finest moral culture, though not the man of sturdiest sense and integrity—are two distinct individuals, and can never be melted or welded into one substance."[23] Any fan of Wendell Berry's novels or Robert Burns's poetry will find fault with that conclusion, but Coverdale is at least right to recognize the absurdity of his idealized vision of farming.

Coverdale grows so jaded that he laughs at visitors to the

commune who admire its work. By then, his "enthusiasm had insensibly been exhaled together with the perspiration of many a hard day's toil"; he scorns the idealism demonstrated by what he calls "these longing proselytes" who, after all, hold the view of manual labor that Coverdale entered with: "they gave us credit for imbuing the ordinary rustic occupations with a kind of religious poetry, insomuch that our very cow-yards and pig-sties were as delightfully fragrant as a flower garden."[24] Sometimes "these lay enthusiasts snatch up a hoe . . . and set to work with a vigor that perhaps carried him through about a dozen ill-directed strokes" and quickly discover that they had underestimated the difficulty of the labor they had admired: "I seldom saw the new enthusiasm that did not grow as flimsy and flaccid as the proselyte's moistened shirt-collar, with a quarter of an hour's active labor under a July sun."[25] The wonderful imagery aside, it's remarkable that Coverdale does not express more sympathy for these visitors, given how similar their experience is with his own—his dismissive attitude indicates Coverdale's lack of self-awareness. Where he had once believed the farm would be a beacon-fire for humanity, now he pokes fun at those who are still inspired by the commune. Still, Coverdale's point is not that rural labor is without merit or value; rather, it's that the difficulty of such labor deserves much more respect than it receives from outsiders.

Although Coverdale sheds his idealism regarding the potential for farming to elevate his soul, he clings to the promise of this "rich experience" to reform humanity. He expresses the utopianism of the project forcefully when he describes how the Blithedale Bunch views the past:

> Altogether, by projecting our minds outward, we had imparted a show of novelty to existence, and contemplated

it as hopefully as if the soil, beneath our feet, had not been fathom-deep with the dust of deluded generations, on every one of which, as on ourselves, the world had imposed itself as a hitherto unwedded bride.[26]

The beautiful language of this passage is one reason it's so remarkable. The image of soil "fathom-deep with the dust of deluded generations," with its forceful alliteration, is particularly powerful. More substantively, Coverdale expresses at once the sense of uniqueness that he and his peers nurture—the "show of novelty" that they perform—and the ignorance that this sense of superiority implies. The farmers are oblivious to the fact that their predecessors—and their predecessors' predecessors—had similarly seen themselves as bringing something entirely new to the world, which like a virgin bride awaits the consummation of their success. Coverdale the narrator knows something that Coverdale the idealist does not, and that is what the Book of Ecclesiastes tells us: "There is nothing new under the sun."

During a tense conversation with the more pessimistic Hollingsworth, Coverdale holds out hope that "in due course of ages, we must all figure heroically in an Epic Poem."[27] Always skeptical about Blithedale's prospects, Hollingsworth complains to Coverdale about "what a wretched, unsubstantial scheme is this, on which we have wasted a precious summer of our lives" and asks whether he "seriously imagine[s] that any such realities as you, and many others here, have dreamed of, will ever be brought to pass?"[28] Coverdale's response conveys his sadder and wiser attitude, acknowledging that "when the reality comes, it will wear the every-day, common-place, dusty, and rather homely garb that reality always does put on. But . . . . our highest anticipations have a solid footing on common sense."[29]

A Dangerous Monomaniac Not Named Ahab

Hollingsworth is the greatest skeptic about the Blithedale project, and perhaps the novel's most complicated character. He is not a likeable character, yet he is generally insightful about Blithedale and its personalities. Early on, for example, he observed that "Miles Coverdale is not in earnest, either as a poet or a laborer."[30] This understanding of the people around him is one reason he is such an effective manipulator, so it's important to take him seriously when he intuits that Coverdale "only half believe[s]" in even his most idealistic expressions. Coverdale's rival for the affections of Zenobia and Priscilla, but also a friend who nurses him during illness, Hollingsworth is perhaps the most articulate spokesman against the Blithedale project. In a wonderful narrative move, Hawthorne has this unlikeable character deliver the truth about what the utopians seek to accomplish.[31] He declares to Coverdale, "I see through the system. It is full of defects,—irremediable and damning ones!—from first to last, there is nothing else! I grasp it in my hand, and find no substance whatever. There is not human nature in it."[32] So why does Hollingsworth waste his time at Blithedale? Because he wants it to fail so he can use the land for his own purposes.

Hollingsworth's own pet project is prison reform. Coverdale describes Hollingsworth's plan as a "rigid and unconquerable idea,—a scheme for the reformation of the wicked by methods moral, intellectual, and industrial, by the sympathy of pure, humble, and yet exalted minds, and by opening to his pupils the possibility of a worthier life than that which had become their fate."[33] It is difficult to see how this could possibly be a bad thing, or an ideal any more naïve than the utopian vision of the Blithedale farmers. Yet Coverdale "saw in his scheme of philanthropy nothing but what was odious." The very idea that the "great black ugliness of sin" could be "transmut[ed] into virtue"—that is, that criminals could be reformed—is too idealistic for Coverdale.[34]

Some of Coverdale's skepticism is no doubt plain old jealousy. Hollingsworth is able to win the attention and admiration of Zenobia and Priscilla, much to the narrator's frustration: they barely give him the time of day "while Hollingsworth, by some necromancy of his horrible injustice, seemed to have brought them both to his feet!"[35] But his distrust is well-founded, because Hollingsworth has ulterior motives for befriending the women. Roger Scruton proposed that "if friendship has a basis it is this: that a person may desire the company of someone for whom he has no specific purpose."[36] Or in the words of Michael Oakeshott, "the relationship of friend to friend is dramatic, not utilitarian; the tie is familiarity, not usefulness."[37] Seen in this light, Hollingsworth is not truly friends with the novel's other characters. He demonstrates a totalitarian approach to personal relationships, insisting on socio-political agreement as a prerequisite for what he considers friendship. In an argument with Coverdale he asks, "How can you be my life-long friend, except you strive with me toward the great object of my life?"[38]

The danger of Hollingsworth's obsession with criminal reform is not that it is necessarily a dangerous and quixotic dream, but that it warps his character and makes him use and manipulate people, caring about them only insofar as they can help him realize his purpose. Hollingsworth himself is aware of this character flaw, at one point admitting that "the most marked trait in my character is an inflexible severity of purpose."[39] This is a milder version of Coverdale's assessment that Hollingsworth "had taught his benevolence to pour its warm tide exclusively through one channel; so that there was nothing to spare for other great manifestations of love to man, nor scarcely for the nutriment of individual attachments, unless they could minister, in some way, to the terrible egotism which he mistook for an angel of God."[40] Hollingsworth's philanthropy descends into a misanthropic attitude toward anyone who does not share his vision. Coverdale concludes that his erstwhile friend's single-minded vision, his "prolonged fiddling upon one string," drove him mad.[41]

It's impossible to resist comparing Hollingsworth to one of his literary peers, Captain Ahab from *Moby Dick*, published the year before *The Blithesdale Romance* by Hawthorne's friend Herman Melville. That novel's narrator—let's call him Ishmael—describes the whale "as the monomaniac incarnation of all those malicious agencies which some deep men feel eating in them, till they are left living on with half a heart and half a lung."[42] Ahab's obsession distorts his perspective and deforms his moral intelligence. His single-minded quest for the elusive whale that maimed him (I apologize for the spoilers, but you have had more than 150 years to read the novel) leads him to make decisions that endanger himself and his crew. His peg leg, like Hulga's in Flannery O'Connor's short story "Good Country People," represents an absence, a lacking in his humanity.

The sources of their monomania differ—and Hollingsworth's obsession certainly seems more productive and positive than Ahab's—but Coverdale notices that Hollingsworth's obsession turns him into something "not altogether human": "This is always true of those men who have surrendered themselves to an overruling purpose. It . . . grows incorporate with all that they think and feel, and finally converts them into little else save that one principle. . . . They have no heart, no sympathy, no reason, no conscience."[43] In Hollingsworth's case, "even godlike benevolence has been debased into all-devouring egotism," and an admirable sympathy descends into misanthropy.[44]

Unfortunately, the force of Hollingsworth's personality enthralls Zenobia. Coverdale gets a glimpse of this pernicious effect early, when Hollingsworth gives Zenobia a "stern and reproachful" glance and, their eyes meeting, he "began his influence on her life." Coverdale is surprised to see the woman "of whose haughty spirit I had been told so many examples—absolutely changed color, and seemed mortified and confused," and amends her behavior to suit his preferences.[45] His sway over her is evident during a conversation about the relationship between the sexes. Zenobia declares "that, when my sex shall achieve its rights, there will be ten eloquent women, where there is now one eloquent man." She condemns the silence into which women are forced, "the mistrust and disapproval of the vast bulk of society throttles us, as with two gigantic hands at our throats!"[46] Her evocative simile likens the subjugation of women to physical abuse. Even readers with conservative attitudes regarding traditional marriage and the relationship between the sexes are likely to be startled by Hollingsworth's response. While acknowledging that woman "is the most admirable handiwork of God, in her true place and character," he insists that true place and character is quite limited to "man's side." Away from there, "woman is a monster—and, thank Heaven, an almost impossible and hitherto unimaginable monster—without man, as her acknowledged principal!"[47] Coverdale is amazed to see that after these assertions, even strong-willed and independent Zenobia "looked humbled" and replied, "be it so."[48]

Later in the novel, when Hollingsworth rejects her affections, Zenobia is inconsolable. She confides to Coverdale that if he were to write a poem about her, it's moral should be "a very old one . . . There are no new truths, much as we have prided ourselves in finding some."[49] That could very easily serve as a lesson of Blithedale, where the reformers' ambitions fall apart in the face of the realities of human nature and human passions. Like Coverdale, Zenobia recognizes the futility of their cause, and she has grown "sick to death of playing at philanthropy and progress," and she mocks their "effort to establish the one true system. . . . It was, indeed, a foolish dream!"[50] Readers will recognize that Zenobia's general reaction in the futility of their utopianism is justified. But one reason this work is so compelling is that because Zenobia's despair is a reaction to the cruelty and monomania of Hollingsworth, it's easy to sympathize with her despite her attraction to toppling "all human institutions."[51] That becomes especially true when we see the tragic finality of her extreme reaction.

Beyond Blithedale: A Glimpse of "Earth's Holocaust"

Before leaving transcendental New England, I want to briefly recommend another work by Hawthorne, a fable called "Earth's Holocaust." This short work shares themes with *The Blithedale Romance*, but takes an even more surreal approach by presenting the narrative as something like a fairy tale, complete with a first sentence that begins "Once upon a time." The story's unnamed narrator describes a bonfire in which the people of the world decide to cast the abundant "worn-out trumpery" that has accumulated over the ages.[52] In goes the "all the rubbish of the Herald's Office," such as titles, honors, and symbols of monarchy; weapons and ammunition; books, pamphlets, and papers; liquor, coffee, tea, and tobacco; and Christian—Catholic and Protestant alike—symbols and artifacts, including crosses, communion tables, and various "priestly garments."[53] Each set of items thrown into the fire elicits a protest from a different onlooker who seeks to explain what will be lost with the objects. For example, a man who objects to burning privileges and honors warns that the "fire is consuming all that marked your advance from barbarism, or that could have prevented your relapse thither."[54] But not all of the arguments are compelling, as when a drunk warns that with the loss of booze will come the loss of companionship. The unevenness of these objections contributes to the ambiguity of the fable about the urge for reform.

At the fable's end, though, a mysterious figure reassures despondent witnesses of the bonfire that these efforts at reform are doomed to fail. "There is one thing" that must be thrown into the fire for the changes the reformers seek, and that is "the human heart itself."[55] Without that spiritual and moral purification, this figure explains, humanity is destined to regress to "the old world yet!" The figure who articulates this advice could very well be the Devil himself—another instance of an otherwise sinister and untrustworthy character dispensing wisdom, like Hollingsworth in *Blithedale*. The narrator sees the wisdom in the mysterious figure's point. He muses: "The Heart—the Heart—there was the little, yet boundless sphere, wherein existed the original wrong, of which the crime and misery of this outward world were merely types." To reform the intellect is one thing; lasting change requires one to "purify that inner sphere"—a much more difficult and uncertain process than chucking objects onto a fire or, for that matter, creating a sustainable commune.[56] The conservative philosopher Russell Kirk interprets the story as an illustration of "the substance of Hawthorne's resolute conviction; that moral reformation is the only real reformation; that sin always will corrupt the projects of enthusiasts who leave sin out of account; that progress is a delusion, except for the infinitely slow progress of conscience."[57] Like *The Blithedale Romance*, then, "Earth's Holocaust" is a warning to utopians who seek to make Heaven on Earth.

Taken together, the tales convey distinctively conservative instincts. Reform is possible, and there are enough instances to see that societies can improve over time. But clean breaks from the past are neither possible nor desirable, and those who seek them are doomed to be disappointed. Former vice president Kamala Harris likes to urge audiences to "see what can be, unburdened by what has been."[58] While I appreciate the alliteration of the second clause, the expression itself conveys a quixotic desire to cast off the past—and wrongly implies that "what has been" is necessarily a burden. Coverdale and his fellow utopian farmers lived to see these false conceptions dispelled.

None of this should be interpreted to mean that conservatives eschew the entire notion of improvement. The next novel's title character develops ambitious plans to build better, more stable lives for his people—better lives firmly grounded in their shared traditions and pasts.

Chapter Five

Personal Purpose and National Identity— George Eliot, *Daniel Deronda* (1876)

T he first thing you'll notice about George Eliot's final novel is that it is not short. It is a Victorian novel, after all, and those are known for being as long as a gas line during the Carter administration. In an age like ours, dominated by bite-sized discourse, a nearly-seven-hundred–page work can be intimidating. It requires a level of focus that's rare these days. I can only assure you that if you overcome that initial fear (or tendency toward distraction), you will be rewarded enormously. This is a rich and enriching, heartening and disturbing, funny and tragic work. It features several unforgettable characters (including a couple who are so evil, you wish you *could* forget them) as well as big ideas about duty, marriage, national identity, and even the establishment of a Jewish state.

In other words, it grapples with serious ideas, befitting of an author who had started her career as a philosopher. But it's an unforgettable novel because it teems with remarkable and compelling characters. If that sounds like a lot for a single novel, you can understand why it's so long.

Unconventionally Conservative

Mary Anne (or, as she later spelled it, Marian) Evans was born in the West Midlands of England in 1819. A devout Christian in her youth—her first publication was a religious poem—before she stopped professing Christianity in the early 1840s, her earliest books were translations of philosophical and theological works; she also edited a liberal quarterly before eventually publishing fiction in the mid-1850s and assuming the *nom de plume* of George Eliot. Her first novel, *Adam Bede*, was published in 1859; her sixth and best-known, *Middlemarch*, was completed in 1872. Even as Eliot worked on that masterpiece, she began preparations for her next great work by studying Jewish thinkers, learning Hebrew, and keeping notebooks on matters related to Judaism. Eliot's research for the project, as the great scholar of Victorian Britain Gertrude Himmelfarb puts it, "consisted of a massive work of research into Jewish learning and lore."[1] In a recent biography of the novelist, Clare Carlisle contends that Eliot's study of Kabbalah, a school of Jewish mysticism, was an enormous influence, and calls *Daniel Deronda* "a Kabbalistic novel."[2]

In addition to her eschewal of organized religion, other elements of Eliot's life may make her seem an unlikely inclusion among books for conservative readers. The most obvious is her long-term relationship with the philosopher George Henry Lewes, a married father of four. Unable to divorce his wife (who was herself having an affair with a married man) for legal reasons, Lewes lived with Eliot regardless. "It was a rather free and easy circle in which Eliot moved in these years," wrote Himmelfarb, yet "there was nothing free and easy in the domestic life of Lewes and Eliot—theirs was a proper and entirely monogamous marriage, all but in name."[3] She even took her non-husband's last name. When Lewes died, Eliot went on to marry a long-time acquaintance, but that marriage ended when she died less than a year later. Eliot had an exalted view of the institution. As she wrote to one acquaintance who was soon to be married, "The very possibility of a constantly growing blessedness in marriage is to me the very basis of good in our mortal life."[4] So while Eliot's romantic life was certainly unconventional and in some ways radical, Himmelfarb justifiably contends she held "a cultural and social as well as a political conservatism," and that while one of her characters "might be a model for a latter-day feminist[,] Eliot quite definitely was not."[5]

This conservatism is manifest in the title character of her most ambitious novel, *Daniel Deronda*. The impressive young man is, according to the novel's omniscient (and very entertaining) narrator, "fervidly democratic in his feeling for the multitude, and yet, through his affections and imagination, intensely conservative; voracious of speculations on government and religion, yet loath to part with long-sanctioned forms which, for him, were quick with memories and sentiments that no argument could lay dead."[6] Broad-minded and open to change, but jealous of tradition and the past. There are worse ways to be.

We first encounter Daniel in a casino in continental Europe, watching a beautiful young woman play roulette. (The rest of the novel does not sound this much like a James Bond movie.) Unbeknownst to the reader yet, this attractive girl, Gwendolen Harleth, has fled England after learning terrifying news about the man she had hoped to marry. Suddenly, across the table she notices this handsome stranger giving her what she later calls "the evil eye."[7] From there, her luck sours. Not only does she begin losing in roulette (though she keeps doubling her bets), but when she returns to her hotel room, she finds a letter from her mother informing her that their family's finances are in shambles. Distraught, and needing money to return home, Gwendolen pawns a necklace—only to have it returned to her almost immediately and anonymously, though both she and the reader suspect it was Deronda.

The memorable opening pages establish the personalities of the novel's central figures. Gwendolen is daring, confident, impulsive; Daniel is moralistic, sympathizing, and generous. Although the opening scene gives the impression that the ensuing novel will focus on their relationship, that is not the case. The two characters share the stage infrequently and the novel traces the very different courses their young lives take, the disparate decisions and discoveries they make, and the distinct duties they perceive for themselves.

Duty and the Spoiled Child

Conservatives like to rhapsodize, rightly, about both liberty and personal responsibility. By the former, we refer to the privileges of being independent from other people or institutions; by the latter, we mean the consequences of that independence, which means either being held accountable for our actions or, except for extreme cases, not relying on the state for help. We also speak of the related, but distinct, concept of duty: what we owe other people, the community, institutions, and even the nation. If personal responsibility is self-directed, duty is other-directed. It confirms our relationship to those people and things around us. It's helpful to think of duty in the context of Roger Scruton's claim that "conservatism starts from a sentiment that all mature people can readily share: the sentiment that good things are easily destroyed, but not easily created."[8] Duty is often about the middle way between destruction and creation, focusing on the maintenance of what we have been given or what we have made. By binding us to others, it helps us recognize what is beyond us and understand our place in a broader community.

The characters of *Daniel Deronda* understand the importance of duty, at least enough to pay it lip service. They're often discussing the duties to which they are bound or searching for such a duty, but the two central characters have obstacles blocking them from realizing those commitments. For Gwendolen, the great obstacle to her broader sense of purpose is her solipsism; Daniel suffers from the virtue of remarkable powers of sympathy.

Gwendolen may have her share of flaws, to put it kindly, but she is a fascinating character: superficial, self-absorbed, and spoiled, yet charming, attractive, and pitiable. Clare Carlisle calls her Eliot's "most compelling heroine"[9] and Christopher Hitchens recognized her as "a central character of uncommon depth and versatility. One is forever being impressed by the resources of this young woman, as she confronts the inescapable dilemma of all Victorian heroines—her marriageability."[10] From the moment we see her, through Daniel's perspective, we're unsure what to make of her. The novel's first sentences are questions about her appearance and personality: "Was she beautiful or not beautiful? and what was the secret of form or expression which gave the dynamic quality to her glance? Was the good or the evil genius dominant in those beams?" Daniel concludes it is "probably the evil."[11] Even her "green and silver" attire calls evil to mind, reminding some onlookers of a serpent.[12] Yet even this apparent aversion to virtue is for show, part of Gwendolen's desire not "to express herself virtuously so much as cleverly—a point to be remembered in extenuation of her words, which were usually worse than she was."[13]

If Gwendolen is guilty of any single vice, it is her—how to put this nicely—robust sense of her own worth. Early in the novel, after she learns that her family has suffered financial ruin, she finds solace in the undeniable fact of her own beauty:

> And even in this beginning of troubles, while for lack of
> anything else to do she sat gazing at her image in the

growing light, her face gathered a complacency gradual as the cheerfulness of the morning. Her beautiful lips curled into a more and more decided smile, till at last she took off her hat, leaned forward and kissed the cold glass which had looked so warm. How could she believe in sorrow?[14]

She manages to keep her chin up, if only because she knows it's a beautiful chin. This moment of narcissism demonstrates her confidence as well as her shallowness. She will find that it is no match for greater challenges she faces later.

As selfish as Gwendolen is, she at least has a vague sense of obligations beyond herself, though she struggles to fulfill them. After her family's financial losses, she considers it her duty "to get a little money" for her mother, which is one way she rationalizes her decision to marry the cad pursuing her, Henleigh Mallinger Grandcourt.[15] She is also prodded in this direction by her uncle, Mr. Gascoigne. When she first plays hard-to-get with Grandcourt, he warns her, "You have a duty here both to yourself and your family" to take the courtship more seriously.[16] And although he has heard unpleasant rumors about Grandcourt's past, Gascoigne insists that the prospects of a match, and the wealth that the match would bring, "almost takes the question out of the range of mere personal feeling, and makes your acceptance of it a duty."[17] He envisions that marriage will provide her a sense of purpose beyond herself, "a new fountain of duty and affection," as well as money and power that "may be used for the benefit of others. These considerations are something higher than romance."[18] Gascoigne's rationale is not necessarily wrong; the problem is that he assumes this general principle applies in a marriage with a man as sinister as Grandcourt.[19]

Gwendolen has a more reliable adviser in Daniel Deronda. After their first encounter in Geneva, she grows to rely on Daniel because he is especially perceptive at identifying her duty, or at least her best courses of action. When she despairs about her marriage, he challenges her to find a duty beyond herself, to elevate above her characteristic solipsism and "look on other lives besides your own. . . . Try to care about something in this vast world besides the gratification of small selfish desires."[20] In another conversation, Daniel implicitly contrasts Gwendolen with the woman he loves (more about her soon), whom he describes as "capable of submitting to anything in the form of duty."[21] There are hints, though, that after another tragedy strikes that she recognizes spheres beyond herself, and in particular a duty to her mother and sisters, "to be kind to them all." She asks Daniel, "Is that the best I can do?" His reply is profound:

> I think so. . . . Looking at your life as a debt may seem the dreariest view of things at a distance; but it cannot really be so. What makes life dreary is the want of motive, but once beginning to act with that penitential, loving purpose you have in your mind, there will be unexpected satisfactions—there will be newly-opening needs—continually coming to carry you on from day to day. You will find your life growing like a plant.[22]

By committing herself to a greater cause, Gwendolen may find meaning and purpose in her own life. Now, we saw in the last chapter how a single motive can become an all-consuming and destructive obsession. But there is a selflessness in what Deronda advises, a sense of humility absent from Hollingsworth in Hawthorne's novel.

Daniel's Duty

When Daniel tells Gwendolen about the importance of finding a purpose beyond herself, he's speaking from experience. He too struggles, but in his case from extremely powerful sympathetic abilities. (He would have gotten along with Evelina and Orville had he been born in the previous century.) The narrator describes his "subdued fervor of sympathy, an activity of imagination on behalf of others, which did not show itself effusively, but was continually seen in acts of considerateness that struck his companions as moral eccentricity."[23] An early indication of this sympathetic power is when he redeems Gwendolen's necklace for her. We see it again through a backstory of his college years, when he sacrifices his own college studies to help an ailing classmate, and again when he rescues a girl from drowning herself in the Thames. In the latter case especially, the sympathy has remarkable benefits for himself: he and the girl, a Jewish singer named Mirah, fall in love. On other occasions, however, this "many-sided sympathy. . . threatened to hinder any persistent course of action." The narrator warns us that there is a legitimate danger to the excesses of this apparent virtue: "A too reflective and diffusive sympathy was in danger of paralyzing in him that indignation against wrong and that selectness of fellowship which are the conditions of moral force."[24] Daniel is aware of this danger and therefore "longed for . . . either some external event, or some inward light, that would urge him into a definite line of action, and compress his wandering energy."[25] That event or light arrives when he discovers the truth about his parentage.

Daniel has developed doubts whether the man who raised him, a kindly country gentleman named Sir Hugo, is his father. The uncertainty of his family background makes Daniel feel rootless. "Many of us complain that half our birthright is sharp duty," the narrator explains; "Deronda was more inclined to complain that he was robbed of this half."²⁶ But after rescuing Mirah, he determines to help her find the family from which she has been separated, and in the process encounters a community of Jews in London. He is also called to the continent to meet, for the first time, his mother. She reveals to him that she is Jewish but abandoned her heritage because her father had been so domineering about it. Her revelation, however, gives Daniel the sense of duty, the destiny, he had lacked: "I consider it my duty—it is the impulse of my feeling—to identify myself, as far as possible, with my hereditary people, and if I can see any work to be done for them that I can give my soul and hand to, I shall choose to do it."²⁷ His sense of purpose satisfied (even if the ultimate achievement of that purpose remains very much in doubt), Daniel's restless sympathies are stilled, and his sympathetic connections to those outside of this purpose, including Gwendolen, weaken.

There are smaller duties sprinkled throughout the novel, ones that may not bring pleasure or a sense of a higher purpose, but are required based on connections and relations. Because of his close relationship to her, Daniel feels a sense of duty to tell Gwendolen of his decision to marry Mirah and leave England. Mirah and her brother feel a sense of duty to care for their repugnant father even though he abandoned them and lives a dissolute life. These are duties the responsible person fulfills without regard for any reward or higher sense of self. What's more, Eliot is sophisticated enough to represent occasions when a perceived duty is misguided or shortsighted. When one of Gwendolen's peers, a young woman named Catherine Arrowpoint, is told by her parents that "where duty and inclination clash, she must follow duty," she replies that some people use "the sacred word duty" as "a name for what they desire any one else to do."²⁸ Identifying one's duty correctly is as difficult as actually carrying it out. And as we've already seen,

Gwendolen's uncle, Mr. Gascoigne, is guilty of the misapplication of "the sacred word duty" by consistently encouraging his niece to marry Grandcourt.

Let's turn to why that was such bad advice.

Like a Horse and Carriage

Generally speaking, it is good to find a spouse who shares your values—someone whose expectations from marriage and life match your own. Shared goals will help you sail the matrimonial vessel toward the sun-filled horizon and navigate the dangerous shoals and rocks on which even the most capable lovers occasionally wreck.

An important exception to this rule is when what you share is a desire to dominate your spouse. Unfortunately, that's exactly what Gwendolen and Grandcourt have in common. Gwendolen's vision of marriage is disordered and selfish, based on control rather than reciprocity. What she wants from a husband is simple: servility and subservience. She believes a wife can do as she pleases if "she [knows] how to assert herself."[29] The marriage she imagines with Grandcourt is not from any fairy tale:

> She was thinking of him, whatever he might be, as a man over whom she was going to have indefinite power; and her loving him having never been a question with her, any agreeableness he had was so much gain. Poor Gwendolen had no awe of unmanageable forces in the state of matrimony, but regarded it as altogether a matter of management, in which she would know how to act.[30]

Matrimony as management—how romantic! If many naïve lovebirds are guilty of reducing marriage to endless bliss, free of acrimony and antagonism, Gwendolen commits the opposite mistake of reducing successful matrimony to steady administration in service of one's own power. Certainly, the convenience of marrying Grandcourt is a major factor in her decision—particularly because it would return her family to financial stability. But her fatal mistake was in "accept[ing] Grandcourt solely as the man whom it was convenient for her to marry, not in the least as one to whom she would be binding herself in duty."[31] There's that d-word again—but Gwendolen misses it.

In the process, Gwendolen overlooks her duty to somebody else—somebody to whom her new husband has duties, too. During an especially haunting scene early in the novel, a woman named Lydia Glasher reveals an awful secret to Gwendolen: years ago, she left her husband to have an affair with Grandcourt, who fathered her four children before abandoning her—and them. Her husband has since died, and she believes Grandcourt should marry her and make her son his heir. Gwendolen seems to agree and promises, "I will not interfere with your wishes."[32] When her family faces financial straits, though, Gwendolen reneges on this vow.

It would be an understatement to say that the marriage between Gwendolen and Grandcourt is an unhappy one. Her plans to control him are frustrated by his overpowering desire to tyrannize her. Even when she rejects his initial advances, his resolve strengthens because "to be worth his mastering it was proper that she should have some spirit."[33] If she didn't have spirit, what was there for him to break? Gwendolen's resistance to his control appeals to his sadistic tastes and even his competitive instinct, as he "meant to be master of a woman who would have liked to master him, and who perhaps would have been capable of mastering another man."[34]

The narrator often describes Grandcourt's desire to control Gwendolen in terms that dehumanize her: that "his strongest wish was to be completely master of this creature" makes clear that he perceives her more as a trophy than a woman or partner.[35] Similarly, after she accepts his marriage proposal, he gloats that "she had been brought . . . to kneel down like a horse under training for the arena."[36] Elsewhere, the narrator compares his treatment of her to "govern[ing] a difficult colony": that is, violent and cruel.[37] Marriage makes Grandcourt happy precisely because it gives him more power, "new objects to exert his will upon."[38] During one argument, he insists that because she has married him, she "must be guided by [his] opinion."[39] It isn't enough for Gwendolen to be "his to do as he liked with"—he is determined to "make her feel it also."[40] The cruelty is the point. Grandcourt's and Gwendolen's wishes to control each other are enough to make one mourn with the narrator, "ah, piteous equality in the need to dominate!"[41] It is indeed their union's only form of equality. If the reader is initially reluctant to sympathize with a character as selfish, superficial, and spoiled as Gwendolen, Grandcourt's disgusting treatment of her is likely to challenge that bias.

Few readers today need to be warned about only marrying someone for whom you feel some semblance of affection, and the power that Grandcourt wields over Gwendolen—by the nature of her limited options as a young English woman in the mid-nineteenth century—is hard to imagine today. But neither character has any interest in marriage as a partnership or union, and their mutual emphasis on control and mastery is antithetical to the compromise and mutual sacrifice necessary for a happy marriage.

National Identity and "Separateness"

Perhaps the storyline that makes *Daniel Deronda* especially compelling to the modern reader is Daniel's discovery of his

Jewishness. As I mentioned above, learning of this lineage gives Daniel the sense of purpose he had lacked. He explains to Gwendolen:

> The idea that I am possessed with is that of restoring a political existence to my people, making them a nation again, giving them a national center, such as the English have, though they too are scattered over the face of the globe. That is a task which presents itself to me as a duty; I am resolved to begin it, however feebly. I am resolved to devote my life to it.[42]

In short, he becomes a Zionist—a remarkable plot twist for a novel that was published more than twenty years before the first Zionist Congress of 1897.

Daniel is inspired to "restor[e] a political existence" for the Jewish people by two men. The first is Mirah's brother, Mordecai, from whom Daniel first hears expressions of Zionism. Speaking to a group of philosophically minded friends, Mordecai declares that "looking towards a land and a polity, our dispersed people in all the ends of the earth may share the dignity of a national life which has a voice among the peoples of the East and West."[43] Mordecai's vision for Jews is what he calls "separateness" that is possible when Jews assume "the character of a nationality."[44] Only the refuge of a nation can ensure the survival of Jews. The second inspiration for Daniel's sense of purpose is his grandfather. Although his mother had rejected her Jewish identity, Daniel is drawn to his grandfather's notion that "the strength and wealth of mankind depended on the balance of separateness and communication," as well as the fear that his fellow Jews were "losing themselves among the Gentiles."[45] Daniel's development as a character is secured when he declares, "my first duty is to my own people, and if there is anything to be done toward restoring or perfecting their common life I shall make that my vocation."[46]

In an essay Eliot wrote shortly after publishing *Daniel Deronda*, she mused on the significance of national identity. She observed the common knowledge that "the preservation of national memories is an element and a means of national greatness, that their revival is a sign of reviving nationality, that every heroic defender, every patriotic restorer, has been inspired by such memories and has made them his watchword."[47] These national memories are a source of pride for peoples around the world, including the English. Expatriates in distant lands find solace in them because they provide a "sense of special belonging which is the root of human virtues."[48] What she is referring to here may fairly be called nationalism, a term that has accumulated negative connotations since Eliot's lifetime, in large part because of the world wars that cut long scars across the twentieth century. Among those on the Right who have recently warned against nationalism is the columnist and author Jonah Goldberg, who called it "an unfettered mystical claim about abstract concepts like 'the people' or 'the nation'—ill-suited for a multiethnic, religiously and culturally diverse liberal democratic nation grounded in a republican constitution."[49] For Roger Scruton, nationalism was "a belligerent ideology that looks for a source of government higher than the routines of settlement and neighbourhood."[50]

But many other conservatives view it with something like Eliot's more positive perspective. Rich Lowry and Ramesh Ponnuru of *National Review* endorse the kind of "benign nationalism" that "can be a healthy and constructive force" and includes "a sense of belonging, allegiance, and gratitude to" one's country.[51] Although William F. Buckley Jr. is said to have distinguished between nationalism (a vice) and patriotism (a virtue), Irving Kristol proclaimed at the end of the twentieth century that "the three pillars of modern conservatism are religion, nationalism, and economic growth."[52] And it is even possible to be wary of nationalism *per se* while agreeing with the general point about the importance of national identity. Scruton celebrated "national loyalty," which he called "the *sine qua non* of consensual government in the modern world" because it "places before the citizen's eyes, as the focus of his patriotic feeling, not a person or a group but a country. This country is defined by a territory, and by the history, culture and law that have made that territory ours."[53] Elsewhere, Scruton contrasts the specificity of national identity with cosmopolitanism, or the citizenship of the world attitude that people who fly United Nations flags espouse:

> It would be the height of folly to reject the "we" of nationality in favor of some global alternative or some fluctuating community in cyberspace. The task is not to surrender to globalization but to manage it, to soften its sharp edges, so that our attachments and loyalties can still guide us in exercising the thing that defines us, which is the sovereignty of the people, in a place of their own.[54]

"A place of their own"—this is a crucial component of national identity, and it gives Daniel a sense of purpose when he discovers his Jewish ancestry.

In the essay in which Eliot had discussed nationalism, she suggested that one reason Jews are so often disparaged by "the prejudiced, the puerile, the spiteful, and the abysmally ignorant" is that although they are dispersed among other peoples around the world, they have retained a "separateness, or what we may call the organised memory of a national consciousness."[55] But how long could that last? She speculated that Jews were either "destined to complete fusion with the peoples among whom they are dispersed, losing every remnant of a distinctive consciousness as Jews," or find a more stable way to secure separateness. She wondered:

> are there in the political relations of the world, the conditions present or approaching for the restoration of a Jewish state planted on the old ground as a center of national feeling, a source of dignifying protection, a special channel for special energies which may contribute some added form of national genius, and an added voice in the councils of the world?[56]

This "center of national feeling"—what Scruton called "a place of their own" and Daniel described to Gwendolen as "a national center"—is Daniel's final purpose. With Mirah and Mordecai he pursues the creation of a Jewish state to realize his "grandfather's notion of separateness with communication."[57]

As you can imagine, some critics accuse Eliot of promoting an imperial mindset. The influential post-colonial theorist Edward Said protested Eliot's depiction of Jews as "European prototypes so far as colonizing the East."[58] Susan Meyer of Wellesley College suggests that the novel's narrator "advocates the Jewish colonization of Palestine."[59] The problem with this line of criticism is that colonists do not return to their homeland; they leave their homeland and go to territory to which they are not indigenous. If their colonial enterprise fails, they return to their home country. But as the poet and critic Adam Kirsch explains, Israel "has no mother country obligated to defend it, or to accept millions of refugees if it falls."[60] The Hamas attacks against Israel on October 7, 2023, are a painful reminder that Eliot's explications of the rationale for a Jewish state remain salient. So are the protests in support of the attacks, and against the existence of a Jewish state, that have been held on the campuses of American universities and in cities around the world.

It's crucial to understand, though, that in *Daniel Deronda*, Eliot was not just making a point about Jewish national identity; she was also arguing the case for the distinct identities of other nations, including England. The concept of "separateness and communication" does not apply only to Jews among Gentiles: as quoted above, Daniel's grandfather believed "the strength and wealth of *mankind* depended" on it [emphasis added]. The peoples of all nations must strike the balance between their national identities and the ability to commerce with other nations. Ruth Wisse, professor emerita at Harvard, explains that Eliot "was worried about the degree to which the English were losing the content of their Englishness, were losing their love for England, their connection to the land, their own idea of their own past, and present, and future."[61] To take just one example, the novel opens in a cosmopolitan setting, with Gwendolen squandering money at a casino in Germany, surrounded by "distant varieties of European type."[62] In this moment, we see what the scholar Marc E. Wohlfarth calls "a sorry picture of a baneful cosmopolitanism, with uprooted [English and European] individuals drifting in and out of international spas and casinos." Jews, by contrast, "have remained true to their identity."[63] Eliot elevates what professor of English Aleksandar Stević calls "the virtues of national purity . . . against the alienating effects of cosmopolitanism" and intimates that Daniel's search for a Jewish national center might offer a way for the English to secure their own national identity.[64] Wisse offers a similar interpretation, suggesting that "because they were in so much greater danger than other peoples . . . the Jews would perhaps be able to show the way of how a people could liberate itself and reclaim its sovereignty."[65]

What's more, through a speech by Mordecai, Eliot also makes a connection between the Zionist vision and the American founding:

> only two centuries since a vessel carried over the ocean the beginning of the great North American nation. The people grew like meeting waters—they were various in habit and sect—there came a time, a century ago, when they needed a polity, and there were heroes of peace among them. What had they to form a polity with but memories of Europe, corrected by the vision of a better?[66]

Individual expressions of nationalism will differ according to the histories and traditions of nations, so American nationalism—its notion of "separateness but communication"— emphasizes different qualities than the English and Jewish variations. Americans are not an ancient people. They are at least the descendants of people who left their homelands—European homes initially, but many more since; they do not seek to return to one, like Daniel, Mirah, and Mordecai. Our separateness entails an embrace of the ideals that make the United States exceptional, the ideals of the Founding, including the equality of men and the government's role in protecting certain unalienable rights. It entails recognizing and embracing the virtuous qualities and principles, the manners and customs, that distinguish America and help Americans flourish.

The balancing principle of "communication"—that is, engagement with other nations—is a source of tension among conservatives today. Should this communication entail helping other nations—including Israel—that are fending off autocratic, tyrannic, or terrorist forces? Or do conservatives prefer a more isolationist approach, a more limited sense of communication? Does communication mean policies that encourage free trade, or does a protectionist, tariff-ridden trade policy strike the right balance between communication and separateness? What's more, in a pluralistic democracy like the United States, this balance of separateness and communication also has applications for the various religious, ethnic, and national backgrounds of the citizens. To flourish as a nation, we must nourish our common American values and principles—yet we will also continue to cherish the traditions, customs, and manners of our ancestral lands and practice the faiths of our fathers. These questions, though they seem a long way from *Daniel Deronda*, are natural modern-day extensions of some of the ideas the novel raises about nationalism, along with its provocative depictions of duty and matrimony.

The next novel we'll look at considers similar themes. In *My Ántonia*, Willa Cather considers assimilation—the opposite of separateness—in the context of the American immigrant experience, and offers us a more positive vision of marriage and family than Gwendolen was able to experience.

Chapter Six

Imagining the American Dream—Willa Cather, *My Ántonia* (1918)

I first became aware of the political valence of Willa Cather's work when I was in college, through a provocative essay by the critic Joan Acocella titled "Cather and the Academy." Acocella surveyed the landscape of Cather criticism and observed that both the Left and Right had the habit of seizing on her novels for political or ideological ends. In the case of the Left—primarily represented by literary scholars—Cather's life and works were most notable as expressions of feminist and (eventually) lesbian points of view. "No tree can grow, no river flow, in Cather's landscapes without this being a penis or a menstrual period," Acocella half-joked.[1] The Right, on the other hand, has tended to embrace Cather for her political conservativism—as expressed in both the form and content of her art, as well as her life (she was no fan of the New Deal, for example). Similarly, during her lifetime she received praise from other outlets for her sympathetic depiction of Catholics. (More about that later.)

For these conservative readers, whom Acocella dubs "affirmativists," Cather is a great (and, Acocella implies, naïve) celebrator of the American Way. Her moniker for this school is an apt one: consider biographer James Woodress's claim that *My Ántonia* "ends on an affirmative note."[2] Acocella wryly writes, "With

94

friends like these, it was not hard for Cather to find enemies." Acocella's argument boils down to something like "a pox upon both their houses," which is unfortunate, I believe, because (as you may not be surprised to learn, given her appearance in this book about great novels for conservatives) in fact the affirmativists have the better argument, at least when it comes to *My Ántonia*, her 1918 novel about a pioneer childhood in Nebraska.[3] This isn't to say that Cather presents a simple vision or flinches from presenting the harsh side of pioneer life and immigration. Rather, she emphasizes the virtues of hope, diligence, and discipline—particularly through Ántonia, whom Woodress describes as "both the Madonna of the Wheat Fields and the symbol of the American westering myth."[4] It is a rhapsodic, elegiac, and often tragic story of pioneers in Nebraska early in its statehood, a beautifully written work about the wonder and promise of the American landscape, and the opportunities that this nation offers its people, newcomer and native alike.

Cather was born on December 7, 1873, in Franklin County, Virginia, right across the border from West Virginia (and not far from where Patsy Cline would be born about sixty years later), the oldest of seven children. Her parents were fourth-generation Virginians, but when she was nine years old, they decided to leave the rolling mountains of the Shenandoah for the plains of Nebraska, settling in the small farming community of Red Cloud. After attending the University of Nebraska-Lincoln, Cather lived in Pittsburgh and then New York City, but stayed abreast of the families and friends she knew from childhood, and mining her experiences on the plains for some of her greatest novels.

Although Cather was recognized as a great novelist in her time (she won the Pulitzer Prize in 1923), she tends to be underappreciated today. One reason may be that she wasn't as glamorous as major writers who followed her. "No genius ever looked less like one, according to the romantic popular view," posited short-story writer Katherine Anne Porter.[5] The novelist Tom Perrotta observes that she is "far less alive in the American cultural imagination than contemporaries like Hemingway and Fitzgerald."

> She's frumpy and rural; they're dashing and cosmopolitan. They ushered in the Jazz Age, reinventing literature and helping to transform American society, forging myths of masculinity and reckless youth that haven't faded, while she remained stubbornly turned toward the past, nostalgic for her prairie childhood, increasingly uncomfortable with the country that emerged after World War I and with the literary modernism that defined the era. But that image doesn't do justice to the complexity of Cather's life or to the magnitude of her achievement.[6]

Paradoxically, even if she is less revered than those near-contemporaries, her work endures precisely because she eschewed literary trends. "Freud had happened," Porter explains, "but Miss Cather continued to cite the old Hebrew prophets, the Greek dramatists, Goethe, Shakespeare, Dante, Tolstoy, Flaubert, and such for the deeper truths of human nature, both good and evil."[7] In the specific case of *My Ántonia*, she did this by attending to relatively undramatic and quotidian events. Biographer James Woodress explains:

> the story would be made up of little, everyday happenings for the most part, for such events made up the bulk of most people's lives. It would be the other side of the rug, the pattern that is not supposed to count. There would be no love affair, no courtship, no marriage, no broken heart, no struggle for success. . . . The result was the creation of a

novel that gives the impression of real autobiography rather than fiction.[8]

Cather also had bold ambitions for her title character. A friend recounted that Cather visited her while working on the novel and, taking a jar full of flowers and scented stock and placing it on a bare table, she explained: "'I want my heroine to be like this—like a rare object in the middle of a table, which one may examine from all sides.' She then adjusted the lighting so that it streamed through the jar. 'I want her to stand out—like this—like this—because she is the story.'"[9] And that story tells of the challenges Ántonia endured to flourish in the United States.

Cather based Ántonia on an immigrant she knew from her childhood in Red Cloud named Annie Sadilek Pavelka. Some of the more tragic events in Ántonia's life correspond to those in Pavelka's, and according to one biographer, "the story of Annie's father's suicide was one of the first stories [Cather] had heard in Nebraska."[10] But although Ántonia is the novel's main character, she is not its central consciousness. That would be Jim Burden, a childhood friend of Ántonia who recounts his life in Nebraska and the fate of the people he grew up with. He left Nebraska to attend Harvard and stayed in the northeast for his career, but he still often thinks of his childhood. Cather begins the novel with a frame narrative in which Cather describes an encounter on a train with Jim. The two travelers recount their shared past in the Nebraskan plains of the late-nineteenth century and catch up on their lives since, and we gain valuable insight into Jim's character: "As for Jim, disappointments have not changed him. The romantic disposition which often made him seem very funny as a boy, has been one of the strongest elements in his success."[11]

In his telling of the story that follows, Jim certainly demonstrates some of his "romantic disposition," as when he says of the farmgirls he grew up with, "if there were no girls like them in the world, there would be no poetry"—a beautiful bit of hyperbole.[12] And as another character says, "the trouble with you, Jim, is that you're romantic."[13] It's almost enough to make you feel like you're back in the Scottish Highlands with Edward Waverley, though Jim can't blame his romantic excesses on old novels. He's romantic about the Nebraska landscape, the people he grew up with, and especially Ántonia Shimerda, the oldest daughter of a family of Bohemian (as in from Bohemia, a region in Czechoslovakia; not hippie) immigrants.

Becoming Nebraskan

Like Cather herself, Jim left Virginia as a child (in his case, unlike Cather's, because his parents have died) and moves to Nebraska to live with his grandparents in a small, fictional town called Black Hawk (clearly based on Cather's home of Red Cloud). He's accompanied by Jake Marpole, "one of the 'hands' on my father's old farm under the Blue Ridge."[14] Jim's departure from Virginia is difficult. There's the landscape, for one thing: "I had never before looked up at the sky when there was not a familiar mountain ridge against it." More than that, though, there's the personal loss inherent in leaving where he'd lived with his parents, whom he believed "would still be looking for me at the sheepfold down by the creek, or along the white road that led to the mountain pastures." On the way to Nebraska, he "felt erased, blotted out."[15] But soon what the frame-story's narrator called Jim's "personal passion [for] the great country" becomes evident in the transcendent descriptions of the Nebraska plains that run throughout the work. Jim's first impression of the prairie testifies to the significant differences between his old home in the Shenandoah and his new one on the plains: "As I looked about me I felt that the grass was the country, as the water is the sea.

The red of the grass made all the great prairie the colour of wine-stains, or of certain seaweeds when they are first washed up. And there was so much motion in it; the whole country seemed, somehow, to be running."[16]

Burden frequently weaves in biblical imagery into his descriptions of the land, as in his description of his first fall in Nebraska:

> As far as we could see, the miles of copper-red grass were drenched in sunlight that was stronger and fiercer than at any other time of the day. The blond cornfields were red gold, the haystacks turned rosy and threw long shadows. The whole prairie was like the bush that burned with fire and was not consumed. That hour always had the exultation of victory, of triumphant ending, like a hero's death—heroes who died young and gloriously. It was a sudden transfiguration, a lifting-up of day.[17]

Burden is loosely allusive here, slipping quickly from the burning bush of the Old Testament to the day's "sudden transfiguration," which evokes the transfiguration of Christ on Mount Tabor.[18] Both metaphors elevate the specific landscape of the Nebraska plains into the realm of the universal or eternal—and, perhaps, suggest the presence of grace within the landscape, its role in shaping the human soul. In addition to the biblical imagery, Cather uses classical references to place her subject matter in the context of a broader tradition. The presence of the Roman poet Virgil looms large: a line from his celebration of rural life, the *Georgics*, serves as the novel's epigraph, and he is the subject of Jim's college studies. Like the *Georgics*, Cather's novel attends to man's labor with the land—or, as Woodress proclaims, "what Virgil did for his native place, Cather also was doing for Nebraska—putting it on the literary map."[19] As another scholar puts it, "like Virgil's poem [*My Ántonia*] transcends mere local color by emphasizing the eternal beauty of creative life on the rich earth."[20]

Elsewhere, Jim recalls a stunning vision he witnessed as a teenager. At the end of an idyllic afternoon with Ántonia and two other girls, they "saw a curious thing" as the sun set in a cloudless Nebraska sky:

> Just as the lower edge of the red disk rested on the high fields against the horizon, a great black figure suddenly appeared on the face of the sun. We sprang to our feet, straining our eyes toward it. In a moment we realized what it was. On some upland farm, a plough had been left standing in the field. The sun was sinking just behind it. Magnified across the distance by the horizontal light, it stood out against the sun, was exactly contained within the circle of the disk; the handles, the tongue, the share—black against the molten red. There it was, heroic in size, a picture writing on the sun.

The arresting image—it's so evocative, the people behind an edition of the novel used it as the basis of its cover design—demands close attention. It's universal and "heroic," but also ephemeral, fleeting. The plough itself is briefly transfigured into something awe-inspiring and sublime, a machine so quotidian and common in this farming community that it can be overlooked—yet it can also be elevated into something sublime and seemingly eternal.

Soon enough, their "vision disappeared; the ball dropped and dropped until the red tip went beneath the earth. The fields below us were dark, the sky was growing pale, and that forgotten plough had sunk back to its own littleness somewhere on the prairie."[21]

When former Republican senator Ben Sasse—a native of Cather's

Nebraska—said that her "sketches open up entire worlds," this could be what he had in mind.[22] And the passage certainly buttresses the mid-twentieth century critic Lionel Trilling's assessment that "few modern writers have been so successful with landscape."[23]

Although Cather often celebrates natural beauty, she's not blind to the dangers that the landscape poses. The novel's farmers toil in the field to scrape by—they could have warned Miles Coverdale how difficult Blithedale would be. The winters torment them. Ántonia's father kills himself shortly before Christmas, driven to despair by the harsh conditions and his failures as a farmer. And The Eden of Nebraska has its own serpent. One afternoon with Ántonia, Jim encounters a large rattlesnake—"not merely a big snake, I thought—he was a circus monstrosity." Before the rattler can strike at them, Jim bashes it with his spade. Initially sickened by the act, Jim soon "began to feel proud of [the snake], to have a kind of respect for his age and size. He seemed like the ancient, eldest Evil. Certainly his kind have left horrible unconscious memories in all warm-blooded life."[24] Ántonia meanwhile, is proud of Jim: "You is just like big mans," she tells him in her still-broken English. And although Jim admits that he became less impressed by the event as he grew older, the episode hints at the biblical sweep of the landscape before them, its potential to form souls, for better or worse.

It is a paradox of great art that proper attention to the specific and particular can convey universals.[25] Cather was a "provincial" artist, as Katherine Anne Porter acknowledged—"and all true art is provincial in the most realistic sense: of the very time and place of its making, out of human beings who are so particularly limited by their situation, whose faces and names are real and whose lives begin each one at an individual unique center."[26] Journalist and essayist H.L. Mencken recognized something similar when he explained that Cather's novels tell "not only the story of poor peasants, flung by fortune into lonely, inhospitable wilds; there is the eternal tragedy of man."[27]

The landscape is beautiful, and it is dangerous; it is a vehicle of grace and a source of death. But, as Jim discovers, it is not constant.

The Conformation of the Land

Every weekday for more than three decades, listeners to Rush Limbaugh's radio show heard a bass line and guitar riff leading into the host's familiar voice. Unless they were classic rock nerds, they might not have known that El Rushbo's de facto theme song was taken from a song called "My City Was Gone" by The Pretenders, about lead singer and songwriter Chrissie Hynde's return to her childhood home of Akron after an extended absence:

> I went back to Ohio
> But my city was gone
> There was no train station
> There was no downtown

She finds that her old haunts and neighborhoods have disappeared; they were "pulled down" and even "reduced to parking spaces." Shopping malls loom where farms once flourished. The "pretty countryside" has been paved over "by a government that had no pride."[28] Limbaugh explained that he used the song not only because it was catchy, but because he liked the irony of a song with lyrics that were "the antithesis of what they thought I was. . . . You know, I'm big time conservative; I support real estate development. Here I'm choosing as a theme song a song that rips them to shreds."[29] There's another reading of the song, though, one that challenges Limbaugh's interpretation of it as a sort of anthem for progressive economic policy. John J. Miller of *National Review* ranks the song among the greatest conservative classic rock songs because "the lyrics also display a Jane Jacobs sensibility against central planning and a conservative's dissatisfaction with rapid change."[30] Where Limbaugh hears a protest against real-estate development, Miller hears a Burkean lament.

The difference between Limbaugh's and Miller's interpretations doesn't just have to do with their readings of the song, but of their understandings of conservatism and the concept of creative destruction. That term is often used to refer to the changes wrought by economic change and innovation. Economic development is good—but it also imposes enormous changes that can upend families, customs, and ways of life. This fact is one reason many members of the so-called New Right view corporations with more skepticism than previous iterations of American conservatives.

I take this road trip from Nebraska to Ohio because comparing Hynde's experience in Akron is an instructive contrast with an important moment in *My Ántonia*. When Jim returns to Red Cloud after many years away, he is struck by the changes around him—but unlike Hynde, who was "stunned and amazed" by what she saw, Burden sees improvement and prosperity:

> The old pasture land was now being broken up into wheat-fields and cornfields, the red grass was disappearing, and the whole face of the country was changing. There were wooden houses where the old sod dwellings used to be, and little orchards, and big red barns; all this meant happy children, contented women, and men who saw their lives coming to fortunate issue.[31]

There's more to this remarkable passage, but before I continue quoting, I want to dwell on the marvelous phrase *fortunate issue*. This term for the fruits of one's labors is open to multiple interpretations: does *fortunate* here refer to luck or to prosperity? *Issue* most likely means "outcome" or "result," but there's also the relevance of a more obscure meaning, the act of flowing out—as in, their prosperity involves an act of flowing out, of giving, of creating goods for others to enjoy. Additionally, it also has connotations of reproduction, which analogizes the prosperous farm as something akin to an off-spring (which reminds us also of the "happy children" signified by the prosperity Burden describes). Whichever interpretation of this phrase one accepts, these changes in the landscape are the hard-won products of a lifetime of work.

Jim further describes this success as the cooperation of nature and man and perceives continuity even in these remarkable changes:

> The windy springs and the blazing summers, one after another, had enriched and mellowed that flat tableland; all the human effort that had gone into it was coming back in long, sweeping lines of fertility. The changes seemed beautiful and harmonious to me; it was like watching the growth of a great man or of a great idea. I recognized every tree and sandbank and rugged draw. I found that I remembered the conformation of the land as one remembers the modelling of human faces.[32]

We saw in Scott's *Waverley* the dangers of radical and sudden change—Edward recognized that for all of his personal grievances with the Hanoverian regime, the abrupt, violent move to unsettle the status quo would do more harm than good. What we see in this passage, to the contrary, is that the change in Red Cloud is change in keeping with its source. The land is both fertile and recognizable. The changes are consonant with the past. The phrase "conformation of the land" is especially provocative: its primary suggestion is a reference to the land's shape, but there is also the suggestion of the land conforming to the will of the families who farmed it. That Jim would be impressed by these surroundings and changes conforms to one of the first things we learn about him in the introduction: "He loves with a personal passion the great country through which his railway runs and branches. His faith in it and knowledge of it have played an important part in its development."[33] Jim successfully develops the country's land because of the intense personal connection he has with it, and the love he feels for it.

Many readers have identified in Cather's work, including *My Ántonia*, a sharp sense of loss. Trilling wrote in an ambivalent analysis of her novels that "Cather shares the American belief in the tonic moral quality of the pioneer's life; with the passing of the frontier she conceives that a great source of fortitude has been lost."[34] Similarly, Joseph Epstein observes that Cather "laments the passing of the old order." Cather prepares us for that sense of loss with the novel's epigraph: *Optima dies . . . prima fugit.* From the Roman poet Virgil's *Georgics*, which I mentioned earlier, it means *the best days . . . flee first.* Importantly, though, as Epstein also notes, Cather's "lamentation [is] crowned by celebration."[35] One of the things *My Ántonia* celebrates most emphatically is the success of many of its immigrant characters.

A Notion of Immigrants

In his final speech as president, Ronald Reagan said that America leads the world "because, unique among nations, we draw our people—our strength—from every country and every corner of the world. And by doing so we continuously renew and enrich our nation."[36] Much has changed since Reagan made those remarks, and immigration policy has been a source of intra-conservative division for decades. What's more, the legality of immigration is never an issue in Cather's work; in the novel's late-nineteenth century setting, there was no Border Patrol and few restrictions to enforce. Too often the phrase "we're a nation of immigrants" becomes a case for porous borders, as if Americans must not protect what Reagan called "the challenge to our sovereignty" posed by illegal immigration.[37] But even as most conservatives now put much-needed emphasis on securing our borders, we still celebrate the contributions made by law-abiding newcomers to the United States because they personify the opportunities open to the hard-working and industrious. Their successes illustrate the opportunities that the American way of life makes possible for the hard-working and industrious.

Cather captures these contributions and the work and sacrifice they entail beautifully in *My Ántonia*. As Joseph Epstein, one of Cather's most articulate admirers, proclaims, "The peculiar feeling of displacement and yet dignity that accompanies the immigrant experience in America is on display nowhere more vividly than in the novels and stories of Willa Cather."[38] She does not present it as a simple or easy experience, but for Ántonia and many of her peers, it is a rewarding one.

A significant obstacle the Shimerda family faces in their new home is that their Catholic faith sets them apart from the Protestants around them. Cather, an Episcopalian, is often mistaken for a Catholic, no doubt in part because of the sympathy she expresses for Catholic immigrants in *My Ántonia*. (Another major reason is her powerful depiction of Catholic clergymen in *Death Comes for the Archbishop*.) The most vivid example of this occurs after Ántonia's father kills himself. His son, at prayer, is described as "deeply, even slavishly, devout"[39]—harsh phrasing that corresponds to centuries of anti-Catholic prejudice. The supposed slavishness of Catholics, for example, was feared to be an impediment to their participation in a democracy. But soon another Catholic relative of Mr. Shimerda, Anton Jelinek (the cousin of Ántonia's future husband), arrives and impresses Jim's family with his demonstrations of belief. Jim concedes, "it was impossible not to admire his frank, manly faith."[40] Jim's grandparents are notably tolerant when it comes to Catholic immigrants. After Mr. Shimerda makes the sign of the cross, the grandfather assures young Jim that "the prayers of all good people are good."[41] And after Shimerda's suicide, Jim's grandmother is so upset when the Norwegian church wouldn't bury him in their yard that she vows to establish "an American graveyard that will be more liberal-minded."[42]

Not that there aren't plenty of grumblers. "My God!" shouts a tramp when he sees the many immigrants around him, "so it's Norwegians now, is it? I thought this was Americy [*sic*]."[43] And the Burden's farmhand Jake, after an unpleasant encounter with Ántonia's brother, grumbles that "these foreigners aren't the same. You can't trust 'em to be fair."[44] Jim was also frustrated by the prejudice that the young immigrant girls like Ántonia faced in Black Hawk:

> I thought the attitude of the town people toward these girls very stupid. All foreigners were ignorant people who couldn't speak English. There was not a man in Black Hawk who had the intelligence or cultivation, much less the personal distinction, of Ántonia's father. Yet people saw no difference between her and the three Marys; they were all Bohemians, all "hired girls."[45]

Mr. Shimerda's suicide demonstrates that not all immigrants to the United States find prosperity or happiness. Perhaps the most haunting immigrant characters are Pavel and Peter, who have traveled from

Ukraine. The story of why they left their homeland is horrifying: one winter night, they were traveling by sled with a wedding party when a pack of wolves begins pursuing them. Peter and Paul drove the sled carrying the bride and groom and determined that they only way to save themselves was to shed weight. They threw the newlyweds to the wolves. (This is based on a story that Cather heard growing up, not realizing that it was a well-known folk tale.) The two were shunned by their village and eventually out of Europe, their story following them wherever they went. They found little happiness in America.

Yet the immigrant success stories are many: Ántonia and her husband, Anton, an immigrant from Bohemia; Lena Lingard, an immigrant from Norway; and Tiny Soderball, from parts unknown. Jim celebrates that, despite the prejudices his friends faced during their early days in Black Hawk, he was able to "see my country girls come into their own. . . . To-day the best that a harassed Black Hawk merchant can hope for is to sell provisions and farm machinery and automobiles to the rich farms where that first crop of stalwart Bohemian and Scandinavian girls are now the mistresses."[46] The immigrants enjoyed this success in part because of what Jim calls "family solidarity," as the daughters sent the money they earned to their family.[47] Not all of these immigrant girls continued that "family solidarity," but Ántonia certainly did.

Affirming the Family

One reason Ántonia is so admirable is that she's resilient and strong. When called upon, she works long days and seasons in the fields. She faces two great personal tragedies and overcomes them both through her resilience, as well as help from her neighbors: the death of her father and the abandonment of her suitor, who left her to raise their child on her own. After these episodes, there are frequent references to her working and looking like a man. It's hard to blame feminist scholars for making hay of these references, which certainly conflict with conventional gender roles. But this strength does not make her unfeminine or unwomanly, as the conclusion of the novel demonstrates. Her strength is one manifestation of an important part of Cather's vision, which Porter describes this way: "to reverence that indispensable faculty of aspiration of the human mind toward perfection called, in morals and the arts, nobility."[48]

The most moving part of the novel—the part that, whenever I read it, seems to bring a lot of dust particulates into the room that trigger allergic reactions in my eyes—occurs when Jim, on a business trip through Nebraska, visits Ántonia's new home to see her for the first time in twenty years. She and her husband, Anton, have nine children, in addition to her first out of wedlock. As when she was much younger, everyone around her adores her. Her family, Jim notices, "seemed to feel the same pride in her, and to look to her for stories and entertainment as we used to do."[49] The passages in which Jim interacts with Ántonia's children are some of my favorite in the novel, as they realistically depict the ways of large families. The children are not only proud of their mother: "Clearly they were proud of each other, and of being so many."[50]

Jim, who has an unhappy marriage, sees that Ántonia and Anton "seemed to be on terms of easy friendliness, touched with humour." Their relationship is complementary, as their similar names would imply, and Jim infers that "she was the impulse, and he the corrective."[51] But the relationship has required sacrifice, and particularly from Anton: a city-lover more used to carefree living, "his wife had managed to hold him here on a farm, in one of the loneliest countries in the world," because he "had been made the instrument of Ántonia's special mission. This was a fine life, certainly, but it wasn't the kind of life he had wanted to live." Ántonia explains to Jim that her husband worked hard to "make it as good for me as she could," and he now looks forward to the companionship of his maturing sons.[52] Their relationship makes it clear that Ántonia is the vital force in the marriage and far from downtrodden or passive. Jim recognizes in Ántonia another emblem of the eternal and the universal. Like the plough left in the field, the heroic qualities of pioneer life meet in her:

> She lent herself to immemorial human attitudes which we recognize by instinct as universal and true. I had not been mistaken. She was a battered woman now, not a lovely girl; but she still had that something which fires the imagination, could still stop one's breath for a moment by a look or gesture that somehow revealed the meaning in common things. She had only to stand in the orchard, to put her hand on a little crab tree and look up at the apples, to make you feel the goodness of planting and tending and harvesting at last.[53]

This passage's reference to Ántonia picking apples, in addition to a nearby observation in which Jim sees "a rich mine of life, like the founders of an early race," recalls the Edenic qualities of the Nebraska they inhabit. But Ántonia is not cast out, despite her missteps and difficulties. Her Eden becomes the site of her redemption.

Jim's admiration for Ántonia's marriage and family is remarkable in part because her fate is so different from his own. The frame-story's narrator tells us early on that Jim has no children, and hints that he's in an unhappy marriage. "I do not like his wife," this narrator admits. "She is handsome, energetic, executive, but to me she seems unimpressionable and temperamentally incapable of enthusiasm.

Her husband's quiet tastes irritate her, I think. . . . She has her own fortune and lives her own life."[54] This is nobody's idea of marital bliss. In other ways, though, Jim's adult life sounds quite enviable, particularly in its wealth and the opportunities for travel it provides. He's even able to visit Ántonia's home village in Czechoslovakia, and she eagerly hears his description of it. Their destinies—their decisions—took them in very different directions, but both directions are crucial to the formation of the nation.

Indeed, it would be a mistake to interpret *My Ántonia* as celebrating only domestic life. Other female characters find happiness and prosperity choosing different paths than the title character. (This is also the case in Cather's preceding novel, *The Song of the Lark*, about a female writer who forsakes marriage for the sake of her art.) Cather biographer Janis P. Stout rightly identifies what she calls "the novel's subtext of alternative lives for women."[55] Such alternative lives are exemplified by Jim's friends Tiny and Lena, both of whom have successful careers away from home—Lena as a dressmaker in Lincoln, Tiny as an innkeeper in Alaska, and then both in San Francisco. Stout is also on the right track when she contends that Cather

> understands in a way that Jim does not the cost of Ántonia's life and the lives of women in general, and she sees alternatives. . . . She sees the reassuring vitality and stability offered by women such as Ántonia, who takes as her vocation the nurturance of others, or essentially the emptying of the self, but she also sees the validity and the dignity of choices that mean the expansion of the self.[56]

Along these lines, nobody could reasonably argue that Cather ignores the troubles and difficulties of Ántonia's life, and pioneer or immigrant life more broadly, even in the novel's generally "affirmative" final chapters. One reason the novel's conclusion doesn't slide into schmaltz is that a good deal of the final pages recount the murder/suicide of a notorious couple in Black Hawk. As Woodress puts it, "Cather escapes [sentimentality] by her usual juxtaposition of contrasts; in this case good and evil are alternated. Jim Burden's golden memories are constantly being interrupted by the sterner realities."[57]

Nonetheless, the novel's emphasis is on Ántonia's happiness and the joy she has found in her life at home while raising a large family. Yes, it's possible that Jim the Romantic overstates his case when he calls her "the mine of life."[58] But she is indeed a source of much life, both in herself and through her children, and in her farming. This is part of what makes *My Ántonia* a deeply conservative novel about the complexity of the American dream, the reality of individual agency, and the rewards of hard work and sacrifice. It's easy to understand why Bradley Birzer of Hillsdale College calls Cather "the most American of American authors."[59]

Chapter Seven

A Life in Bloom—Zora Neale Hurston,
Their Eyes Were Watching God (1937)

W hen Zora Neale Hurston published what is now her best-known novel, some major literary figures complained about the work's depiction of black characters. Ralph Ellison, eighteen years before he published *Invisible Man*, complained that *Their Eyes Were Watching God* "was not addressed to Negro readers, but to a white audience that had recently 'discovered' the Negro in its quest to make spiritual readjustments to a world in transition."[1] Alain Locke, a major figure in the Harlem Renaissance movement and an erstwhile supporter of Hurston's, charged the novel was too full of "entertaining pseudo-primitives whom the reading public still loves to laugh with, weep over and envy."[2] And the novelist Richard Wright, writing for the communist journal *New Masses*, claimed that Hurston resorted to stereotypical depictions of black people, a "minstrel technique that makes the 'white folks' laugh. . . . In the main, her novel is not addressed to the Negro, but to a white audience whose chauvinistic tastes she knows how to satisfy."[3]

Fast-forward to the 1970s, when Hurston—who died in poverty in 1960—was rediscovered by a new generation of African-American writers and admirers. Alice Walker—author of the Pulitzer Prize–winning novel *The Color Purple*—tracked down Hurston's unmarked

113

grave and provided a headstone. "Her work had a sense of black people as complete, complex, undiminished human beings and that was crucial to me as a writer," Walker has said of Hurston.[4] Oprah Winfrey and Quincy Jones produced a made-for-TV film based on *Their Eyes Were Watching God*, starring Halle Berry. Novelist and short-story writer Edwidge Danticat has called Hurston one of her favorite authors.[5] A major biography of Hurston was written by the black essayist Valerie Boyd. Esteemed literary scholar Henry Louis Gates Jr. has written extensively about her and edited a collection of her non-fiction. Contrary to the condescending critiques doled out in the 1930s, Gates concludes that "race pride permeates everything she writes."[6] The passage of time and the shifting of political opinions and contexts have changed the conventional wisdom among black intellectuals and public figures about Hurston's greatness.

More recently, a number of writers—including, but not only, right-of-center thinkers—have recognized the prominent conservative elements in Hurston's thought. "She was more eccentrically self-directed than many of her fans today realize," explains author and linguist John McWhorter, "a fervent Republican who would be at home today on Fox News and whose racial pride led her to some unorthodox conclusions."[7] McWhorter surmises that Hurston "would almost certainly have considered Clarence Thomas' politics praiseworthy along with those of Tom Sowell and Shelby Steele, and by my reading she would have seen Malcolm X as a rabblerouser with no concrete program and felt similarly about Jesse Jackson."[8] That last conjecture is from a piece titled "Why the National Review Would Have Loved Zora Neale Hurston" and appropriately enough, *National Review* has praised her work in recent years. Roger Clegg observes that she "reminds us that it is not a foreign concept for an African American to have conservative sensibilities and take conservative positions."[9] "Hurston was a gradualist," explains journalist Dwight

Garner. "Her conservatism shows up in her instinctual wariness of the New Deal, which she viewed as governmental overreach."[10] She was an American patriot and an anti-communist who wrote, "The [Communist] party is a Society of the Dead, soulless zombies, but even the living-dead have no place among the living people."[11] In one of her best known remarks, she rejected victimhood:

> I do not belong to the sobbing school of Negrohood who hold that nature somehow has given them a low-down dirty deal and whose feelings are all hurt about it. Even in the helter-skelter skirmish that is my life, I have seen that the world is to the strong regardless of a little pigmentation more or less. No, I do not weep at the world—I am too busy sharpening my oyster knife.[12]

That last phrase suggests she's preparing for better things, equipping herself for the opportunity and prosperity that await her. Elsewhere, Hurston addressed racism with confident humor: "Sometimes, I feel discriminated against, but it does not make me angry. It merely astonishes me. How *can* any deny themselves the pleasure of my company! It's beyond me."[13] McWhorter is certainly correct when he advises that "we have much to learn from someone who is—as quiet as the secret is kept—America's favorite black conservative."[14]

Rethinking Janie Crawford

Born in central Florida in 1891, Hurston grew up in Eatonville, the nation's first all-black incorporated town. She attended both Howard University and Barnard College as an undergraduate before studying ethnography at Columbia University. She wrote poems, plays, essays,

and stories, as well as ethnographic studies before publishing her first
novel in 1934, followed by a collection of black folklore the next year.
Two years later, she published the work for which she is best known.
Their Eyes Were Watching God is probably more familiar to American
readers than several of the other books I've included in this collection, as it is often required reading for many high-school students
around the country. I include it here both because people who
attended school before the 1990s may be less familiar with it, and
even those who have read it may be unfamiliar with Hurston's heterodox views and the book's more conservative implications.

    Their Eyes Were Watching Gods is the story of Janie Crawford, who
in the opening scene returns to Eatonville after a years-long absence.
When a friend asks where she's been, Janie tells her the story—not
just of where she's been, but how she got there, from childhood to the
present day. We learn the most formative influence on Janie's childhood was her grandmother, a former slave who was raped by her
master's son toward the end of the Civil War. Despite Nanny's efforts
to protect her own daughter, she too is raped and, after giving birth
to Janie, leaves her child to be raised by Nanny. After seeing Janie flirt
with a young man, her grandmother worries that she'll get herself in
trouble, so she marries the sixteen-year-old off to a much older man.
It's an unhappy match, and Janie runs off with an ambitious man
named Joe Starks. While—as we'll see later in this chapter—Joe Starks
is a remarkable man in many regards, he is not a good husband, and
Janie feels stifled and unfulfilled during their two-decade marriage.
After his passing, she marries a much younger man named Tea Cake,
who—though a very flawed spouse in his own right—shows Janie
freedom and love her other two husbands had not. She moves with
him to the Everglades, where they live until their marriage ends in
tragedy. Accused of murdering Tea Cake, Janie is found not guilty and
returns to Eatonville.

It's a marvelous novel, the masterwork of an author who was unafraid to express heterodox attitudes about race that are consistent with what conservatives continue to believe about individual responsibility and the dangers of victimhood. Yet although conservatives have become vocal in their celebration of Hurston's life and political writings, they have been relatively quiet about this novel. Perhaps that's because since the novel began receiving renewed critical attention in the 1970s, it has often been interpreted as a groundbreaking work of feminism, a quest narrative in which Janie voyages through different towns and marriages on a journey culminating in a romantic relationship that allows her to express her individuality and autonomy. According to Walker, "Janie Crawford . . . refuses to allow society to dictate behavior to her."[15] It's easy to see support for such a reading in one of the novel's most beautiful passages, in which a young Janie has a rapturous vision of love—and sex—as she watches bees go about their business:

> She was stretched on her back beneath the pear tree soak-
> ing in the alto chant of the visiting bees, the gold of the sun
> and the panting breath of the breeze when the inaudible
> voice of it all came to her. She saw a dust-bearing bee sink
> into the sanctum of a bloom; the thousand sister-calyxes
> arch to meet the love embrace and the ecstatic shiver of the
> tree from root to tiniest branch creaming in every blossom
> and frothing with delight. So this was marriage! She had
> been summoned to behold a revelation. Then Janie felt a
> pain remorseless sweet that left her limp and languid.

The pseudo-orgasmic experience inspires the dream at the center of her youth: "Oh to be a pear tree—*any* tree in bloom!"[16] I say "dream" to connect to the novel's opening passage, which establishes the centrality of dreaming to the story that unfolds: women, unlike men, "forget all those things they don't want to remember, and remember everything they don't want to forget. The dream is the truth. Then they act and do things accordingly."[17] It is shortly after this vision that Nanny marries Janie off to her first husband, Logan Killicks, so that Janie can have "protection" after Nanny dies. But for Janie, the very thought of Logan "was desecrating the pear tree," an insult to her ideal of love.[18] Janie enters her first marriage hoping to realize her dream of the pear tree and wondering, "Did marriage end the cosmic loneliness of the unmated? Did marriage compel love like the sun the day?"[19] She soon learns, and as Gwendolen Harleth could have told her, the answer is an emphatic no. Although Janie tells Nanny, "Ah want things sweet wid mah marriage lak when you sit under a pear tree and think," she finds that is not to be with Killicks: "Janie's first dream was dead, so she became a woman."[20] Such details certainly give credence to a feminist reading of the novel.

On the other hand, contra a straightforward feminist reading, Janie is not unhappy because she is forced to comply with standard gender roles—she's unhappy because Killicks seeks to subvert those roles by demanding that she work with him outside. She protests by insisting on separate spheres for husband and wife: "Youse in yo' place and Ah'm in mine." In a twist that undermines the modern stereotype of the controlling husband, he demands, "'Tain't no use in foolin' round in dat kitchen all day long. . . . You ain't got no particular place. It's wherever Ah need yuh."[21] Yes, the marriage is an unpleasant patriarchy—but the patriarchy wields its power by frustrating her desire for conventional gender roles.

Before long, Janie is wooed away by a man named Joe Starks, who appeals to her desire for conventional marital roles: "You ain't got no business cuttin' up no seed p'taters neither. A pretty doll-baby lak you is made to sit on de front porch and rock and fan yo'self and eat p'taters dat other folks plant special just for you." His courting offered "a far horizon. He spoke for change and chance."[22] But her marriage with him, though much longer than her first (which she technically never ends), is also unhappy. Joe is a controlling and jealous man who subjects Janie to the most extreme version of a traditional marriage. When she is asked to deliver a speech, Starks forbids it: "Ah never married her for nothin' lak dat. She's uh woman and her place is in de home." This treatment "took the bloom off things."[23] Starks further insists that she stays inside the store they run together and forbids her from socializing with the community on the porch outside; he makes her cover her long hair in public; he's resentful when she dazzles townspeople with her oratorical abilities. He beats her and insults her—and she often insults him in return. In these ways, her marriage with him generally supports the feminist reading of the novel, as "he wanted her submission and he'd keep on fighting until he felt he had it." She eventually "wasn't petal-open anymore with him" and there is little sense of tragedy or loss when he finally dies, leaving her a wealthy widow. [24]

While Janie's marriage with Tea Cake is happier than her previous two, it's hardly a chapter from a feminist handbook. Shortly after the wedding ceremony, Tea Cake absconds with money that Janie had pinned inside her shirt "just to be on the safe side"; Janie is worried senseless until Tea Cake finally returns from a gambling spree.[25] This episode makes clear that if he's her knight in shining armor, the chainmail is rusty. As Tea Cake sees it, Janie "aims tuh partake wid everything"—yet Tea Cake insists that they never spend the money she has in the bank and "eat whatever mah money can buy yuh and wear de same. When Ah ain't got nothin' you don't git nothin.'"[26] And while it's easy to conclude that a sign of Janie's independence is that she's able to leave the house, she only works outside in "the muck" picking beans because Tea Cake "gits lonesome out dere all day 'thout" her and asks her to join him.[27] A sweet sentiment, to be sure, but not quite a sign of her liberation from a husband. That is confirmed when Tea Cake beats her in a jealous rage but explains to his friends that "Janie is wherever *Ah* wants tuh be. Dat's de kind uh wife she is and Ah love her for it."[28]

Early in their marriage, Janie imagines that Tea Cake "could be a bee to a blossom—a pear tree blossom in the spring," but by the time they're married the love she feels for him is "self-crushing."[29] Yet that loss of self is good—because of it, Janie's "soul crawled out from its hiding place."[30] The intensity of her love for her new husband is paradoxical in that it destroys who she had been and conjures a new sense of herself. Tea Cake eventually proves himself worthy of these feelings in the act of self-sacrifice that leads to his death. But it's hard to reconcile the complexities of their relationship with a straightforward feminist reading. This is not to suggest that the novel presents an uncomplicated *conservative* vision of traditional matrimony. Far from it. But as independent as Janie is, she is not quite the paradigm-breaking, social-construct-defying, patriarchy-destroying force that influential interpretations would suggest. Or, as literary scholar Shawn E. Miller puts it, "Janie is more dynamic than we have previously realized, and that her final triumph has more to do with her mastery of conventional marriage than with her escape from it."[31]

Eatonville's Little Napoleon

Apart from his role as Janie's second husband, conservatives may be interested in the character of Joe Starks for his political ambition and the important questions about self-governance that his power raises. Hurston loosely based him on the historical figure of Joe Clarke, a former slave who became the first mayor of the all-black town in which Hurston was raised. According to Hurston biographer Valerie

Boyd, "Booker T. Washington, perhaps the era's greatest advocate of black enterprise, observed that in black-governed towns like Eatonville, 'individuals who have executive ability and initiative have an opportunity to discover themselves and find out what they can do.'"[32] At his best, the fictional Joe Starks represents the fulfillment of black freedom, the promise of self-government for the descendants of slaves. At his worst, he signifies the domineering hand of small-scale tyranny.

When Janie and Joe arrive in Eatonville, he immediately expresses his disappointment with what he finds—"God, they call this a town? Why, 'tain't nothing but a raw place in de woods."—and his desire to improve it. When he learns the town doesn't have a mayor, an exchange ensues that raises provocative questions about the relevance of government:

> "Ain't got no Mayor! Well, who tells y'all what do do?"
> "Nobody. Everybody's grown. And then again, Ah reckon us just ain't thought about it. Ah know Ah ain't." . . .
> "No wonder things ain't no better," Joe commented. "Ah'm buyin' in here, and buyin' in big."[33]

Once elected mayor, Starks begins improving the town. When they install a streetlight, the mayor uses the occasion to deliver a speech to instill pride in the accomplishment: "Dis occasion is something for us all tuh remember uh our dyin' day. De first street lamp in uh colored town."[34] But his domineering approach to governance breeds resentment. When he "forced through" the construction of a drainage ditch in front of the store he owned, the townspeople "murmured hotly about slavery being over, but every man filled his assignment." There's a hint of corruption here, not just with the implication of forced labor, but also in the fact that Joe himself stands to benefit the most from the drainage right outside of his shop. And there's a hint of tyranny when he throws a resident out of town for stealing some of his cane. Even the appearance of his home reinforces this sense of superiority, as it's designed to look like the home of the region's prominent white families, making "the rest of the town [look] like servants' quarters surrounding the 'big house.'"[35] Again, the implication is that he's more like a slave master than a mayor.

Despite these grumblings, "there was something about Joe Starks that cowed the town. . . . he had a bow-down command in his face, and every step he took made the thing more tangible."[36] Or, as one character puts it eloquently: "Some folks needs thrones, and ruling-chairs and crowns tuh make they influence felt. He don't. He's got uh throne in de seat of is pants."[37] This complex relationship between the governing and the governed is best expressed by the narrator: "They bowed down to him . . . because he was all of these things, and then again he was all of these things because the town bowed down."[38] And after he dies, the people show their enduring respect for him with an elaborate and well-attended funeral signifying that "the Little Emperor of the cross-roads was leaving Orange County as he had come—with the out-stretched hand of power."[39] Starks is by no means a model ruler (and certainly not a good husband), but there is virtue in his ambition for the town, and his behavior raises questions about corruption and political power that conservative readers are likely to find especially intriguing.

Janie C. and Booker T.

We saw in the quotation that began this chapter how Hurston challenged what she called the "sobbing school of Negrohood," or the attitude toward race that emphasizes victimization and subordinates agency. Elsewhere, she praised a meeting in Florida of the Statewide

Negro Defense Committee, in which "nobody mentioned slavery, Reconstruction, nor any such matter. It was a new and strange kind of Negro meeting—without tears of self-pity."[40] In today's terms, her heterodox attitudes about race sound more like Jason Riley of the *Wall Street Journal* than Nikole Hannah-Jones of the *1619 Project*. *Their Eyes Were Watching God* is not primarily focused on race, but when it does address the issue head-on, what it says is complex and varied. On the one hand, it makes no bones about the effects of racism, including slavery. Nanny and her daughter, Janie's mother, are both raped by white men. Nanny observes, in what can be interpreted as a classic expression of what has become known as intersectionality: "Honey, de white man is de ruler of everything as fur as Ah been able tuh find out. . . . De nigger woman is de mule uh de world so fur as Ah can see."[41] Similarly, Tea Cake experiences the novel's most obvious racist episode when, after a hurricane destroys their community, he is conscripted by white men to help bury corpses the storm has left behind. All the corpses are put in a mass grave, but the white ones get coffins while the black ones are just sprinkled with lime and thrown in. Tea Cake ironically observes, "Look lak dey think God don't know nothin' 'bout de Jim Crow law."[42]

At the same time, there are also episodes that complicate a straightforward opposition between black and white characters. For one thing, Janie spends her early years with white children, unaware of racial difference between herself and them. In Eatonville, during a conversation about Starks, one person observes, "Us colored folks is too envious of one 'nother. Dat's how come us don't git no further than us do. Us talks about de white man keepin' us down! Shucks! He don't have tuh. Us keeps our own selves down."[43] The novel also complicates a simple black/white binary toward the end, when Janie stands trial for murder. There, most of the black people believe that she's guilty, while she is supported by a group of white women who are watching the trial, as well as the jury of twelve white men who find her not guilty. After the trial, in an ironic inversion of Nanny's claim about the state of black women, one black man reminds the others, "you know whut dey say 'uh white man and uh nigger woman is de freest thing on earth.' Dey do as dey please."[44] The powerful episode challenges simple preconceptions of white racism and black victimhood.

The novel's most interesting conversation about race is easy to miss, but it speaks volumes about Hurston's attitude regarding black progress. In the Everglades, a light-skinned black woman named Mrs. Turner takes a special liking to Janie because of their similar skin tones. (The feeling is not mutual.) Mrs. Turner looks down on their neighbors—and Tea Cake—because of their darker skin and different features. "You got mo' nerve than me," she tells Janie. "Ah jus' couldn't see mahself married to no black man. It's too many black folks already. . . . Ah can't stand black niggers."[45] She resents their behavior and habits, "Always singin' ol' nigger songs! Always cuttin' de monkey for white folks. If it wuzn't for so many black folks it wouldn't be no race problem."[46] And because she has "white folks' features in mah face," she resents that she's "lumped in wid all de rest. It ain't fair. Even if dey don't take us in wid de whites, dey oughtta make us uh class tuh ourselves."[47] The narrator explains that Mrs. Turner "didn't cling to Janie" as an individual; instead, "she paid homage to Janie's Caucasian characteristics as such."[48] She is, as scholar Rosemary Hathaway puts it, "the most vehemently . . . race-conscious character in the novel."[49] But her consciousness sounds more like shame than pride.

Mrs. Turner sparks the most surprise from Janie when she denigrates a major black historical figure. Hoping to pair her brother with Janie (despite Janie's marriage), Mrs. Turner boasts that he "read uh paper on Booker T. Washington and tore him tuh pieces!" Janie expresses wonder at this attitude toward Washington, the activist and founder of the Tuskegee Institute in Alabama:

> "Booker T.? He wuz a great big man, wusn't he?!"
> "'Sposed tuh be. All he ever done was cut de monkey for white folks. So dey pomped him up. But you know whut de ole folks say 'de higher de monkey climbs de mo' he show his behind' so dat's de way it wuz wid Booker T." . . .
> "Ah was raised on de notion dat he wuz uh great big man," was all that Janie knew to say.
> "He didn't do nothin' but hold us back—talkin' 'bout work when de race ain't never done nothin' else. He wuz uh enemy tuh us, dat's whut. He wuz uh white folk's nigger."
> According to all Janie had been taught this was sacrilege so she sat without speaking at all.[50]

Hathaway has noted that this exchange has "received very little critical attention," even though it is "crucial to an understanding of the political nature of the novel."[51] From Mrs. Turner's point of view, Washington is what we would now call an Uncle Tom—a black person who is more interested in winning the favor of powerful whites than advancing the cause of his race. It's the kind of complaint one is liable to hear today about any black Republican or conservative.

How could Washington have earned such scorn from Mrs. Turner? After all, as I quoted earlier this chapter, Hurston's biographer called Washington "perhaps the era's greatest advocate of black enterprise." A look at one of his most controversial speeches will clarify what's at stake. In 1895, speaking at the Cotton States and International Exposition in Atlanta, Washington encouraged the white audience to hire black workers, and urged Southern blacks to develop practical skills. If the first thirty years after slavery had focused on political gains, Washington believed it was time that those interested in the progress of black Americans should focus on industry and job skills rather than "a seat in Congress or the state legislature." Washington argued that black citizens, having been only recently freed from slavery, were better off realizing economic goals than political ambitions. "It is important and right that all privileges of the law be ours," he said, "but it is vastly more important that we be prepared for the exercise of these privileges." To that end, he also urged black Southerners to take advantage of the opportunities in their region rather than moving to the North. The central metaphor is that when in need of water, don't ask others to send a bucket to you, but "cast down your bucket where you are. . . . Cast it down in agriculture, in commerce, in domestic service, and in the professions[.]"[52]

For Washington, work was closely related to education and character. According to biographer Robert J. Norrell, Washington sought "to counter the belief that free blacks had declined in character and morality from the time of slavery." In his autobiography *Up from Slavery*, Washington provided what Norrell calls "proof of progress [through] blacks' emerging self-mastery. Unsanitary living habits, poor morality, and bad schools had been overcome with good educational opportunities. The Tuskegee campus demonstrated that blacks had learned how to work."[53] In Washington's own words, "while the Negro should not be deprived by unfair means of the franchise, political agitation alone would not save him, and that back of the ballot he must have property, industry, skill, economy, intelligence, and character."[54] This message was enormously popular. According to John McWhorter, "Thousands of boys were named after him. His name still brands public schools across America. Black people once had pictures of him in their homes in the same way they later had pictures of Martin Luther King Jr., and today have pictures of Barack Obama."[55]

But Washington's pragmatism had its share of critics, the most prominent of whom—W. E. B. Du Bois—expressed his disagreements more eloquently than Mrs. Turner. As economist and author Glenn C. Loury describes the differences between the two men, "Washington was a conservative advocate of a philosophy of self-help; Du Bois was a radical exponent of a strategy of protest and agitation for reform."[56] Although their differences are sometimes exaggerated, Du Bois charged that "Mr. Washington's programme practically accepts the alleged inferiority of the Negro races" and let white Americans wash their hands of any obligation to help blacks rise by "shift[ing] the burden of the Negro problem to the Negro's shoulders and stand[ing] aside as critical and rather pessimistic spectators."[57] This is likely what Mrs. Turner meant when she accused Washington of "playing duh monkey." Hathaway speculates that in the conversation between her and Janie, "Hurston may well be aligning *herself* with Washington here, because she too was accused by her contemporaries of 'cuttin' de monkey for white folks."[58] We've seen as much in the early reviews of *Their Eyes Were Watching God*.

What's more, although Janie stays quiet as Mrs. Turner denigrates Washington, Hurston herself praised and admired him. She visited the Tuskegee Institute in 1927 and "paid her respects at the grave of founder Booker T. Washington."[59] And after activist Marcus Garvey was convicted for mail fraud, Hurston contrasted his activism with Washington's:

> [Garvey] had taken the people's money and he was keeping it. That was how he had become the greatest man of his race. Booker T. Washington had achieved some local notice for collecting monies and spending it on a Negro school. It

had never occurred to him to keep it. Marcus Garvey was much in advance of the old school of thinkers.[60]

Washington here represents the "old school," a more legitimate, effective, and honest approach to the problem of race. Similarly, in an earlier novel, one of Hurston's characters declares, "Ain't never been two sho 'nuff smart mens in dese United States—Teddy Roosevelt and Booger T. Washington. Nigger so smart he at de White House. Built uh great big ole schools wuth uh thousand dollars, maybe mo'. . . . Du Bois? Who is dat? 'Nother smart nigger? Man, he can't be smart ez Booger T.!"[61] Hurston contrasted Du Bois and Washington in stark terms, focusing on the jealousy of the younger activist over the fact that Washington, "a graduate of Hampton Institute, had the world by the ears because of the success of Tuskegee, and his 'Dignity of labor' slogan." Hurston imagined the injustice Du Bois must have felt at seeing Washington's success:

> Washington had emerged from extreme poverty and [was] a Southerner. And though Du Bois was definitely brown of skin, and Washington the son of a White man, it is obvious that Du Bois could [not] conceive of such a person as rating higher than a Dr. of Philosophy from Berlin, to say nothing of ivied Harvard. . . . it is obvious that the cultured Du Bois could not think of Washington as anything but a field hand out of place.[62]

Although this may be not be a charitable representation of Du Bois's attitude, the important point is that it illustrates Hurston's preference for Washington. Adding intrigue to this conflict is that Hurston had worked with Du Bois early in her career, enjoying what biographer Valerie Boyd calls "a chummy correspondence" with him before becoming alarmed by "the esteemed editor's increasingly strident insistence that Negro art be both beautiful and propagandistic."[63] Considering Hurston's relatively light political touch in *Their Eyes Were Watching God*, it's easy to see how she might object to Du Bois's famous declaration, "I do not care a damn for any art that is not used for propaganda." That aversion to propaganda is one reason Janie's exchange with Mrs. Turner is so fascinating: it hints at some shortcomings with the woman's complaints about Washington, but *only* hints at them and leaves the reader to parse. Propaganda has no patience for parsing.

This overlooked passage has intriguing implications for present-day readers. The divergent perspectives between Washington and Du Bois—and by extension, Mrs. Turner and Janie—resonate in modern-day conversations about racial equality. Here again is Jason Riley:

> Since the 1960s . . . the Du Bois-backed focus of political integration has prevailed among black civil rights leaders. It crystalized under Martin Luther King, and several generations of blacks have come to believe that the only legitimate means of group progress is political agitation of the NAACP-Jesse Jackson-Al Sharpton variety. By this way of thinking, if you are more interested in black self-development than in keeping whites on the defensive, you're accommodating racism.[64]

And as a PBS description of Washington explains, "Booker T. today is associated, perhaps unfairly, with the self-help/colorblind/Republican/Clarence Thomas/Thomas Sowell wing of the black community and its leaders."[65] The use of "unfairly" in that sentence says it all: the people at PBS respect Booker T. and don't want him tainted by analogizing him with contemporary black Americans they don't like. But the fact is that the black conservatives they mention carry on the tradition of Washington's ideas—as did Hurston.

In an essay describing Hurston's influence on her own work, Alice Walker described the Zora who was her model:

> Zora Hurston, who went to Barnard to learn how to study what she really wanted to learn: the ways of her own people, and what ancient rituals, customs, and beliefs made them unique.
>
> Zora, of the sandy-colored hair and the daredevil eyes, a girl who escaped poverty and parental neglect by hard work and a sharp eye for the main chance.
>
> Zora, who left the South only to return to look at it again. Who went to root doctors from Florida and Louisiana and said, "Here I am. I want to learn your trade."
>
> Zora, who collected all the black folklore I could ever use.
>
> That Zora.[66]

Hurston was all of those remarkable and admirable things, to which we may fairly add admiration for the Zora who celebrated black enterprise and agency; who loved America and believed that the nation's black people were "a wing-footed people" and indelibly part of it; who both recognized the injustice of slavery, Jim Crow, and racism and rejected "the sobbing school of racial victimhood"; and who wrote a beautiful and moving novel that conveys the complexities of desire, marriage, prejudice, sacrifice, hope, and racial progress.

Chapter Eight

All the News That's Fit to Print (Up to a Point)—
Evelyn Waugh, *Scoop* (1938)

I t is the more or less unanimous belief among American conservatives that the mainstream news media is deeply, embarrass-
ingly, and undeniably biased. According to a recent poll con-
ducted by Gallup and the Knight Foundation, "Democrats express
significantly more trust in news organizations than Republicans.
Among Republicans, trust in news continues to decline. New data
show that more independents today report distrusting news than
ever previously reported."[1] This distrust often materializes itself in
disdain, particularly during political campaigns, when Republican
candidates express their animosity toward the opinions, priorities,
and storylines of what they alternately refer to as "lamestream
media," "corporate media," or "legacy media." As Ross Douthat puts
it, it's been clear since 2012 that "Republican voters will forgive a
multitude of sins, or else disbelieve in those sins' existence, for a
candidate who's eagerly, even zestfully at war with the establishment
media."[2] President Trump owes much of his success to his willingness
to wage that war.

Skepticism of the news media is less of a principle and more of a
habit or inclination, meaning it's more contingent than some of the
other issues explored in this book. It's theoretically conceivable that

some day, mainstream media outlets will be defined by their right-wing bias—though I'm not holding my breath. (Of course, many progressives think that's already the case.)

Bob Woodward and Carl Bernstein's Watergate reporting inspired generations of journalists to "speak truth to power" (to use the ungrammatical catchphrase beloved by progressive activists) and hold the powerful to account. In theory, these are noble goals. In practice, they tend to be applied selectively. I'm sure any conservative could identify approximately one million examples of egregious instances in which reporters held Republican politicians to much higher standards than their Democratic counterparts, or when they seemed particularly excited to serve up thin-gruel about conservatives as evidence of corruption or hypocrisy, while underplaying, ignoring, or even calling "misinformation" stories suggesting the same about left-of-center politicians. From Candy Crowley incorrectly fact-checking Mitt Romney during a presidential debate with President Obama to the credulous coverage of President Trump's supposed collusion with Russia to the similarly un-skeptical reporting on uncorroborated accusations of sexual assault by a Supreme Court nominee to the defense of former President Joe Biden's clearly deteriorating mental acuity and physical health, there is no shortage of reasons for conservatives to view the media with suspicion.

As immediate and serious as this skepticism of the media is on the right in the United States, it so happens that one of the best expressions of this skepticism is an eighty-five-year old English novel.

Getting the Scoop

When I started work on this book, I was certain that I'd include something by Evelyn Waugh, one of my favorite novelists—not that this is an eccentric opinion, as he's generally considered one of the twentieth century's greatest prose stylists. In his obituary for Waugh, William F. Buckley Jr. called him "a conservative, a traditionalist, a passionately convinced and convincing Christian, a master stylist routinely acknowledged, during the last decade, as the most finished writer of English prose."[3] The Modern Library's list of the one hundred best novels of the twentieth century includes three of his works, tied for the most by any writer. The conundrum for me was which Waugh to include. As I mentioned in the introduction, *Brideshead Revisited* is especially beloved by traditional Catholics and American Anglophiles like me; *A Handful of Dust* is one of the funniest tragic novels you'll ever read; *Put Out More Flags* is an underrated work that features one of the funniest cads in literature, the great Basil Seal; and if trilogies were fair game, I would have been tempted to include Waugh's marvelous World War II series, the Sword of Honour trilogy.

What sets Waugh's fourth novel apart is that it is simply the best in its class—no satires of the press remain as funny and relevant. The novel "is immortal," according to journalist and biographer Richard Brookhiser, "because Waugh had a low opinion of the press, which is never falsifiable."[4] Robert Hutton (another journalist—I guess we can trust some of them) explains that "eight decades after it was published, and after the industry has gone through two technological revolutions, [*Scoop*] remains the best description of UK journalistic life." As Hutton also points out, former Tory prime minister David Cameron kept a copy of the novel on his desk and notes that Boris Johnson's pre-Parliament career as a journalist resembles that of a character from *Scoop*.[5] Appropriately enough, Johnson recently recommended the novel for summer reading.[6] As undeniably English as this novel is, American readers will have no problems finding the humor and truth in its send-up of journalism. And while that is certainly the most prominent aspect of the novel, there are other elements that elevate this comic masterpiece.

Waugh based *Scoop* on two journalistic trips he made to the East African nation of Abyssinia, known today as Ethiopia (and which you may recall from this book's first chapter, though Samuel Johnson spelled it differently): in 1930, to cover the coronation of Haile Selassie, and again in 1935, to cover Benito Mussolini's invasion. In a preface for a later edition of the novel, Waugh recalled that "foreign correspondents, at the time this story was written, enjoyed an unprecedented and undeserved fame. . . . In Abyssinia I had served as the foreign correspondent of an English daily paper. I had no talent for this work but I joyfully studied the eccentricities and excesses of my colleagues."[7]

In the novel, Waugh created a stand-in for his outsiders' perspective in the character of William Boot, a young country gentleman who has the cushy gig of writing an obscure ("ignominiously sandwiched between Pip and Pop, the Bedtime Pets, and the recipe for a dish called 'Waffle Scramble'") bi-weekly nature column called Lush Places for the *Daily Beast*.[8] (If that name sounds familiar, it's because Waugh's fictional paper inspired the name of a real online news outlet.) William is not an ambitious writer: this modest column satisfies whatever literary inclinations he may have. He's worried, though, because in the draft of his most recent column, his sister had pulled a prank by altering the names of the animals he was describing. William fears that he'll be fired for this episode and is terrified when he receives a summons from Salter, the foreign editor, to visit him in London. It doesn't occur to him that there's been no blowback over his mistake because nobody cares enough about his column to complain about it. And Salter doesn't want to fire him—he wants to send him to an African nation called Ishmaelia to cover the possible onset of a civil war. That is, Salter *thinks* he wants to send William.

In fact, readers know that Salter has reached out to William in a case of mistaken identity. The man Salter is supposed to hire is a novelist named John Courteney Boot, who in the novel's first pages has contacted an influential friend for help securing a job that would get him out of the city to escape his girlfriend. (When I put it that way, it sounds like the premise of a *Seinfeld* episode.) The friend—named Mrs. Stitch (who also appears in Waugh's Sword of Honour trilogy)—appeals to the publisher of the *Daily Beast*, who gives Salter vague instructions that he wants "Boot." Salter contacts the first Boot who comes to mind: William. This hilarious, efficient, and understated depiction of professional bungling and confusion all happens in the novel's first 15 pages, and it's a marvelous demonstration of Waugh's deadpan wit: rather than signal the confusion for the reader's benefit by having the narrator remark something like, *Unfortunately, the editors had contacted the wrong person! They'd surely come to regret their sloppiness—or would they?*, Waugh leaves it to us to recognize the misunderstanding. What's more, this opening makes clear that the world of journalism is more arbitrary and disorganized than newspaper readers might wish to believe. That impression is reinforced when Salter, the foreign editor of a major newspaper, struggles to find Reykjavík on a map.

Ishmaelite Crisis!

To best understand the absurdities of the foreign correspondent racket, it helps to learn, as William did, the ins and outs of Ishmaelite politics. The narrator informs us that early visits from "various courageous Europeans" to Ishmaelia failed spectacularly, as they were "eaten, every one of them" and eventually European nations "decided that they did not want that profitless piece of territory; that the one thing less desirable than seeing a neighbour established there was the trouble of taking it themselves."[9] So much for the White Man's Burden. Instead, it became a constitutional republic ostensibly based on western norms and traditions, including three branches of government, "religious liberty, secular education, *habeas corpus*, free trade, joint stock banking, chartered corporations, and numerous other agreeable features."[10] That was the idea, anyway. What actually emerges is a type of benevolent monarchy under Jacksonian rule, featuring an annual tax-collection regime characterized by military marches into the jungles to collect "the spoils of the less nimble" (that is, people who aren't able to evade them). Snarks the narrator, "Under this liberal and progressive régime, the republic may be said, in some way, to have prospered."[11] But there are rumors of a possible civil war, which is why the *Daily Beast* and other European papers are desperate to send reporters there.

Waugh explained that when he wrote *Scoop*, "public interest had just been diverted from Abyssinia to Spain," and he "tried to arrange a combination of these two wars" for the novel.[12] In this case, the tension is based on what the narrator calls "a domestic row in the Jackson family," the most prominent clan in the nation.[13] The first president was a native of Alabama named Samuel Smiles Jackson. In Jackson's first two names, Waugh's first readers would have recognized a reference to a British self-help writer whose works include, well, *Self-Help*. The nation's current ruler is the first president's grandson, Rathbone Jackson. The Jacksons were held up by socialists around the world as emblems of the international worker.

The insurgent Fascist party is led by Smiles Soum, a minor minister and distant relation in the Jackson line. His White Shirt movement is based on the premise that Ishmaelia has been tainted by the black influence of the Jacksons. Everything wrong in the world and the nation could be attributed to the malign influence of that family: "Ishmaelites who were suffering the consequences of imprudence or ill-fortune in their financial or matrimonial affairs were the victims of international Jacksonism."[14] This context makes clear that, as the critic and journalist (not another!) Christopher Hitchens aptly notes, "We are in Absurdistan."[15]

Journalism for Dummies

With the threat of a civil war looming, "newspaper men flocked to Jacksonburg"—William Boot, columnist of Lush Places, among them.[16] William first experiences the nation's polarized political situation for himself when he seeks a passport. He has to visit two legations, as a rival to the officially recognized one has recently opened. At one, he encounters an ardently Afro-centric consulate general who praises the accomplishments of African civilizations over the centuries—including the pyramids, but also the discovery of America and the work of "the great Negro Karl Marx."[17] The rival consulate aligns itself with the Nazis and proudly identifies the Ishmaelite people as "pure Aryans . . . the first white colonizers of Central Africa."[18] As it turns out, these ardent advocates of Ishmaelite identity are themselves not actually from Ishmaelia.

As unfamiliar as Ishmaelia is, the field of foreign correspondence isn't much better. William is instructed before he sets out that the *Daily Beast* isn't just reporting on the war; it is doing what it can to generate a specific result. In other words, it has an agenda. When instructing William about his responsibilities, the paper's publisher, Lord Copper, tells him:

> Remember that the Patriots are in the right and are going to win. *The Beast* stands by them four-square. But they must win quickly. The British public has no interest in a war which drags on indecisively. A few sharp victories,

some conspicuous acts of personal bravery on the Patriot side and a colourful entry into the capital. That is *The Beast* Policy for the war. . . . We shall expect the first victory about the middle of July.[19]

It is one thing for a paper to have an editorial policy—clear positions that the paper takes on particular concerns or topics of the day. You can expect the *New York Times* editorial board, for example, to express a very different opinion about a tax cut or welfare program than the *Wall Street Journal*'s board. What Copper is expressing here is something different. He's making very clear to his new correspondent that the news he sends should support that policy, facts be damned.

Later, when William is remiss in sending reports home, he receives frustrated telegrams from the *Beast*: "LORD COPPER HIMSELF GRAVELY DISSATISFIED STOP LORD COPPER PERSONALLY REQUIRES VICTORIES STOP ON RECEIPT OF THIS CABLE VICTORY STOP CONTINUE CABLING VICTORIES UNTIL FURTHER NOTICE."[20] The paper's objective is not to report news, but to—as journalists today would say—create a narrative. That's why when William tells a friend that he doesn't have any news to send his paper, the friend advices, "for heaven's sake invent some."[21]

William Boot is guided along on his adventure by a veteran journalist named Corker, who gives invaluable insight into the superficial knowledge of the trade. "I used to think that foreign correspondents spoke every language under the sun and spent their lives studying international conditions. Brother, look at us!"[22] Corker is William's own personal journalism school, telling him "of the classic scoops and hoaxes . . . the innuendo and intricate misrepresentations, the luscious, detailed inventions that composed contemporary history." It is not a reassuring catalogue of events.

There's the reporter named Hitchcock who, "straddling over his desk in London, had chronicled day by day the horrors of the Messina earthquakes." And there's the American journalist Wenlock Jakes, who not only "scooped the world with an eye-witness story of the sinking of the *Lusitania* four hours before she was hit," but also helped shape the course of history with one of his stories. Falling asleep and missing his train stop on his way to cover a revolution, Jakes made the best of a bad situation by sending his paper a "story about barricades in the streets, flaming churches," and other horrors of war.[23] This breaking news surprised editors across Europe, who send correspondents of their own to cover the alarming news. But when they arrived to the site of the supposed revolution to find only disappointing peace, they made their own contributions to Jake's tall tale. This barrage of fake news caused a real panic, "and in less than a week there *was* an honest to God revolution under way." Corker caps off the moral of Jakes's Nobel Peace Prize–winning exploits by observing, "There's the power of the press for you."[24]

Late in the novel, one interested party observes to William, "It is seldom that [newspapers] are absolutely, point-blank wrong. That is the popular belief, but those who are in the know can usually discern an embryo truth, a little grit of fact, like the core of a pearl, round which have been deposited the delicate layers of ornament."[25] To that end, the novel abounds in phony scoops based on half-truths or mis-understandings. One correspondent reports a falsehood about a Soviet agent arriving to Ishmaelia. The story causes a stir in Europe, but rather than reply to the false story by printing the truth, the other reporters determine to go with it. Corker explains to William that running a counter-story would be "risky, old boy, and unprofessional. It's the kind of thing you can do once or twice in a real emergency, but it doesn't pay. They don't like printing denials—naturally. Shakes public confidence in the Press."[26] This is a hilarious damning of the press that feels all-too relevant today: the belief that the reputation of the press relies on standing by its mistakes rather than correcting them. And, like the absurd confusions of the novel's start, it is conveyed in Waugh's perfect deadpan style. Rather than having William reply to Corker to identify the absurdity of this approach, Waugh lets it linger, leaving readers to pick up on the problem themselves.

As comical as these journalist exploits are, one of Waugh's most famous contemporaries suggested the fiction wasn't far removed from fact. George Orwell, writing about his time covering the Spanish Civil War, sounds like he could be in conversation with William Boot:

> Early in life I had noticed that no event is ever correctly reported in a newspaper, but in Spain, for the first time, I saw newspaper reports which did not bear any relation to the facts, not even the relationship which is implied in an ordinary lie. I saw great battles reported where there had been no fighting, and complete silence where hundreds of men had been killed. I saw troops who had fought bravely denounced as cowards and traitors, and others who had never seen a shot fired hailed as the heroes of imaginary victories; and I saw newspapers in London retailing these lies and eager intellectuals building emotional superstruc-tures over events that had never happened. I saw, in fact, history being written not in terms of what happened but of what ought to have happened according to various "party lines."[27]

The fabricated conflicts, the denial of real battles, the distortions in the service of party interest—all of these details from Orwell's autobiographical account suggest that Waugh wasn't alone in his skepticism of English journalism in the 1930s. Later in this chapter, we'll see other instances of Orwell's ideas overlapping with Waugh's.

Back to Ishmaelia, where the government does the job the press corps won't, denying that there's a Russian mole and effectively killing the story in the process. But William, who has a contact in the British embassy, learns that while the details of the original story are incorrect, there is indeed a Soviet spy in Ishmaelia. The prospect of breaking this story excites William because he's convinced it could make a real difference—"his might be the agency which would avert or precipitate a world war; he saw his name figuring in future history books . . ."—but Corker once again advises him to keep his mouth shut. After all, Soviet mole stories were yesterday's news—and the original version, though false, was more compelling than the truth William offered.[28]

The final phony scoop in Ishmaelia is offered by a legendary journalist named Hitchcock, who once wrote a convincing but fabricated story about an earthquake he'd never seen. Hitchcock is a bit of a genius, the sort of con man that Waugh delights in depicting, like Basil Seal with a press badge. The press corps is thrown into turmoil when the *Daily Brute* (rival to Boot's *Beast*) runs a story by Hitchcock purportedly from the fascist capital of Laku. The only problem with the story: Laku doesn't exist. William, thanks to his embassy connections, knows that Laku is Ishmaeliate for *I don't know*, which was what a native told a boundary commissioner who asked the name of a landmark. When William conveys this information to Corker, he responds with characteristic faith in his profession, "Well, there is now, old boy."[29]

Hitchcock's story outrages the other reporters not just because it scoops them, but because a deal the foreign press had made with Ishmaelia's information and propaganda ministry has them all staying in Jacksonburg and only leaving with permission. Why was Hitchcock allowed to venture out while they were stuck in place? They hold a meeting to answer that question. Waugh presents the scene in passages of clipped dialogue that alternate between high-minded journalistic bromides (". . . gravely affecting our professional status . . .") and the braggadocio of brawlers ("Go on, sock me one and see what you get.") to illustrate the disparity between the press's sense of itself and its actual behavior.[30] Adding insult to injury, Hitchcock was elsewhere in Jacksonburg, hiding in a hut.

The novel's most important scoops belong to William himself. To avoid spoiling important plot twists, I'll refrain from specifying the precise nature of the first scoop and simply observe that he does not come about it through especially impressive investigative reporting or journalistic initiative, but because the woman he's seeing tells him something she heard in a bar. Based on these humble origins, Waugh presents William's work on the story as a mock epic: "with a single first finger and his heart heavy with misgiving, he typed the first news story of his meteoric career. . . . [This] was a moment of history—of legend, to be handed down among the great traditions of his trade."[31] In short, he'll be the sort of person Corker talks about to journalistic rookies, along with Hitchcock and Jakes, but he'll have the advantage of conveying true accounts. William's second big scoop also results from his connections, this time to his old college buddy at the consulate who tells him some details about the inner-workings of Ishmaelian politics.

While it's easy to chuckle at the irony of a character named William Boot failing to engage in any real shoe-leather reporting, it's also important to recognize that a reason William is able to land these stories is that, as an outsider, he's impervious to the groupthink that infects the more experienced foreign correspondents around him. While the other reporters, including Corker, are off on a wild goose chase to find the non-existent city of Laku, William's distance from their assumptions and beliefs allows him to avoid their mistakes and trip into the truth. But would these scoops be enough to keep from being fired by his editors at the *Beast*, whom he's kept waiting for stories? You'll have to find out for yourself. It is fair to say William returns to England to find himself regarded as a journalistic hero. When an aspiring journalist asks whether "it's a good way of training oneself—inventing imaginary news?," William replies, "None better."[32]

The sheer number of instances of dumb luck raises an important question: how much do we really control in our lives? How much agency do we possess? Not only do William's leads come through good fortune—his very commission to Ishmaelia results from the blind chance of people confusing him with another writer named Boot. There's another such lucky moment worth dwelling on. Because of his excellent reporting, William finds himself in danger and unable to make contact with London. He wonders, "am I still to be an exile from the green places of my heart? Was there not even in the remorseless dooms of antiquity a god from the machine?"[33] At that very moment, an airplane passes overhead and from it a man—someone we've encountered earlier in the novel, but whose identity was mysterious—descends to help William out of his scrape. Not quite *deus ex machina*, but pretty close. Not that Waugh makes a point of drawing readers to this joke; it's another instance of the novel's lack of laugh track to alert us when a joke's been made. Waugh trusts us to get it.

It's notable that the main target of Waugh's satire is not the political bias of reporters, but their laziness and groupthink—precisely the sorts of things that might lead to bias, but are nonetheless distinct from it. Additionally, to their great credit, the journalists in *Scoop* lack the self-righteousness that is common to many reporters and news organizations. They don't purport to be the last line between civilization and anarchy, democracy and tyranny, light and darkness. They're just lazy fools. And bad writers. Waugh once explained his approach to novel-writing by saying, "I regard writing not as an investigation of character but as an exercise in the use of language, and with this I am obsessed. I have no technical psychological interest. It is drama, speech, and events that interest me."[34] This emphasis on language may be one reason he enjoys poking fun at the writing of his characters. There's William, of course, and his mawkish accounts of country life, as well as Salter, who is somehow impressed by the writing:

> He's supposed to have a particularly high-class style: 'Feather-footed through the plashy fen passes the questing vole' . . . would that be it?"
> "Yes," said the Managing Editor. "That must be good style. At least it doesn't sound like anything else to me."[35]

The editor, unable to know good style when he sees it, concludes that what strikes him as unfamiliar must be good. Based on a later description of the paper's prose, that could make sense: "sub-editors busied themselves with their humdrum task of reducing to blank nonsense the sheaves of misinformation which whistling urchins piled before them."[36]

The jabs at modern writing Waugh throws in *Scoop* do not amount to a sustained criticism, but they anticipate the critique offered by Orwell eight years later in his classic essay "Politics and the English Language." In both works, bad writing and foolish (or worse) politics are closely connected. Orwell wrote that "the English language . . . becomes ugly and inaccurate because our thoughts are foolish, but the slovenliness of our language makes it easier for us to have foolish thoughts."[37] Orwell also warned against "worn-out metaphors which have lost all evocative power and are merely used because they save people the trouble of inventing phrases for themselves."[38] That's precisely the problem with the first draft of history that someone at the *Daily Beast* writes: "I have to denounce the vacillation of the government in the strongest terms . . . A *spark* is set to the *corner-stone* of civilization which will *shake* its *roots* like a *chilling breath*" (emphasis added).[39] As David Lebedoff observes, "There is one more thing that they both [Orwell and Waugh] saw coming, and no other portent could so terribly chill their hearts: the assault on language. . . . And the perversion of the English language that alarmed them in their own time has exceeded even their worst fears."[40]

Country Mice, City Mice

In addition to the send-up of journalistic pretensions, American readers will likely recognize the cultural gulf separating the London-based editors, especially Salter, and the country-based William. Salter's view of rural life reads like a parody of the American press corps' detachment from rural America. One of the first things we learn about Salter is that "his knowledge of rural life was meagre." His experiences during World War I were so traumatic that "if a psychoanalyst, testing his associations, had suddenly said to Mr Salter the word 'farm,' the surprising response would have been 'Bang,' for he had once been blown up and buried while sheltering in a farm in Flanders." What's more, Salter hilariously sees something distinctively foreign about the rural life:

> there was something unEnglish and not quite right about 'the country,' with its solitude and self-sufficiency, its bloody recreations, its darkness and silence and sudden,

inexplicable noises; the kind of place where you never
knew from one minute to the next that you might not be
tossed by a bull or pitch-forked by a yokel or rolled over
and broken up by a pack of hounds.[41]

Waugh's technique in this passage is wonderful. This series of nightmarish visions begins with what seems to me to be not a drawback
but a virtue: "self-sufficiency." (Solitude doesn't sound so bad, either.)
But to Salter, that strength seems little better than being gored by a
bull or mauled by dogs.

Salter endures the horrible fate of visiting William's country estate
at the end of the novel, and it goes about as horribly as he might have
feared. The train ride there includes passengers "who, instead of
slinking and shuffling and wriggling themselves into corners and
decently screening themselves behind newspapers, as civilized people
should when they traveled by train, had sat down squarely quite close
to Mr Salter . . . stared at him fixedly and uncritically and suddenly
addressed him on the subject of the weather in barely intelligible
accents."[42] As Sartre may have observed, Hell is friendly people on
mass transit. After this and other misadventures on the journey to
Boot Magna, he has dinner with William's family and feels as if "he
was in a strange country":

> These people were not his people nor their laws his. He
> felt like a Roman legionary, heavily armed, weighted
> with the steel and cast brass of civilization, tramping
> through forests beyond the Roman pale, harassed by
> silent, elusive savages, the vanguard of an advance that
> had pushed too far and lost touch with the base . . . or
> was he the abandoned rearguard of a retreat; had the
> legions sailed?[43]

The rural countrymen as "savages," the visitor from the capital endangered and perhaps lost forever—I'm not aware of any journalists who've been this blunt in their opinions of what is known as fly-over country, but it's easy to get a similar impression when they venture into rural Republican strongholds for stories about the white working class.

To be fair, this sense of foreignness is mutual, as William is an unreformed country creature who feels like anywhere away from home is "a foreign and hostile world," and that London is an "abominable city."[44] It's an attitude that remains constant at the end of the novel, too, when he adamantly refuses Salter's invitation to return to the city for an awards banquet. The city and the country seem irreconcilable. At the same time, there is the ironic humor of Salter fearing this excursion into an unfamiliar and dangerous place to visit William, who has returned from a much more dangerous journey into a legitimately foreign and dangerous land. Another ironic touch is that this country/city dynamic also plays out in Ishmaelia. Jacksonburg is the relatively bustling capital city, the only place where the reporters are allowed to be apart from the non-existent city of Laku. The country, meanwhile, remains blissfully unaware of the goings-on in the city, apart from the annual tax raids described above. The description of life outside of the capital recalls the detachment of Boot Magna from London: "In the remote provinces, . . . the Ishmaelites followed their traditional callings of bandit, slave, or gentleman of leisure, happily ignorant of their connexion with the town of which a few of them, perhaps, had vaguely and incredulously heard."[45]

I referred above to the White Man's Burden, the Victorian-era notion that it was the obligation of European nations to help civilize other nations by colonizing them. It's an overstatement to call *Scoop* a post-colonial novel (that is, a work that critiques the motives and consequences of Western imperialism), but a consistent source of comedy is the incompetence of European nations in Ishmaelia. The European nations seeking to gain a foothold in the country are more or less incompetent and oblivious to what the others are doing. What's more, the character who has the most power in the country is a financier named Baldwin who has significant financial stakes in making sure that Britain ensures neither German nor Russian interests control the nation. Baldwin hopes William will convey a message to his readers: "*Might must find a way.* Not '*Force*', remember; other nations use 'force'; we Britons alone use 'Might.' Only one thing can set things right—sudden and extreme violence, or, better still, the effective threat of it."[46] This remarkably cynical passage develops the novel's interest in journalistic techniques via Baldwin's parsing of the difference between *force* and *might*, but also hints at the arbitrary difference between the terms, as if Britain's sense of itself is slightly delusional or shallow. Baldwin helps William type a telegraph to the *Beast* that compares his accomplishments to those of two major figures in the expansion of the British empire, Cecil Rhodes and T.E. Lawrence—a comparison that can be interpreted either as fantasy on Baldwin's part, or deflation of the historical figures by Waugh.[47]

Modern readers are likely to be offended by some of the descriptions of black characters, but it's worth noting that the most vulgar expressions come from Corker, who is very clearly an idiot. And not only do the parallels between the country/city divides in England and Ishmaelia hint at surprising similarities between the two nations, but Waugh also balances references to bigamy among the Ishmaelites with having William's manipulative love interest, a German woman named Kätchen, interested in marrying William even though she already has a husband. For all of the light-hearted mockery of the media, *Scoop* also hints at provocative points about Western morals.

The general lightness of the novel's tone toward the media is also complicated by the darkness of the novel's final passage. There, William is back at his desk, composing another edition of Lush Places in his characteristically purple style: "maternal rodents pilot their furry brood through the stubble. . ." It's typically overwritten, but it suggests the security and safety that William feels back at Boot Magna. Yet sentences later, the narrator concludes the novel with an enigmatic variation of the same image: "Outside the owls hunted maternal rodents and their furry brood." William's scene is expanded, his naïve vision of the country broadened to display dangers he didn't recognize or chose to ignore, and which perhaps the "maternal rodents" don't see, either. I've always found this ending disconcerting. In one sense, it is a good depiction of the narrator's realism in contrast with William's naiveté. I also wonder, though, whether it's Waugh's way of hinting at something more sinister on the horizon, of a gathering danger and tragedy that would disrupt the comedy he could write in 1938, and with Britain's declaration of war on Germany in 1939. "This light-hearted tale was the fruit of a time of general anxiety and distress," Waugh wrote in his 1963 preface.[48] The final, heavy-hearted sentence seems to acknowledge that tension.

Our next novel depicts the period in Britain immediately following that "time of general anxiety and distress," as World War II draws to a close—but danger and evil lurk close to home.[49]

Chapter Nine

A Martyr Mystery—Muriel Spark,
The Girls of Slender Means (1963)

I n a 1963 essay assessing the characteristics of conservatism in
America, William F. Buckley Jr. considered the place of religious
belief. "Can you be a conservative and believe in God?" he asked.
The answer was easy enough: "Obviously." What about being a
conservative and *not* believing in God—is that possible? Another
softball for Buckley to crush out of the park: "the answer is, as
obviously, yes." Believer and atheist—there will be many of both in
conservative circles, as well as liberal ones. But that's not the same as
saying that all attitudes toward religious belief were compatible with
conservatism as Buckley understood it: "Can you be a conservative
and despise God and feel contempt for those who believe in Him? I
would say no."[1] The sneering cynic or the New Atheist of the early
2000s may hold some opinions in common with conservatives, but
their disrespect for both tradition and the belief in what Russell Kirk
called "transcendent moral order" prevents them from being truly
at home in conservatism.[2]

The same year Buckley asked these questions, a Scottish-born
novelist—not someone who ever identified herself as a conservative,
as far as I know—wrote a novel that demonstrates the kind of respect
or reverence for religious belief that continues to be an important

trait of conservative thought. The Scottish-born novelist Muriel Spark is not an obscure writer—she is widely considered one of the greatest novelists of the twentieth century—but I wish more people, especially more Americans, knew about her work. Over the course of her long career—she published twenty-two novels between 1957 and her death in 2006—Spark demonstrated a consistent interest in the influence of evil. As brief as they are (almost all of them are fewer than two hundred pages long), her darkly comic novels teem with schemers, blackmailers, murderers, and manipulators. This includes her most famous character, the eponymous teacher of *The Prime of Miss Jean Brodie* (played by the legendary Maggie Smith in the 1969 film adaptation), who manipulates her students toward the futures she imagines for them, with tragic consequences. Brodie is also an example of Spark's depiction of characters who see themselves as (to use Brodie's own phrasing) "above the common moral code."[3]

Many of Spark's novels, and especially her early ones, also deal explicitly with religious faith, an expression of her conversion to Catholicism. According to Spark scholar Robert E. Hosmer Jr., Spark understood that "human history, set within the context of a fallen world, is a battleground between the forces of good and evil for the control of souls; human existence is everywhere a struggle in which human beings do have the powers of choice and free will. Every one of Spark's novels is concerned, one way or another, to document this struggle."[4] Similarly, editor Rosemary Goring claims that Spark's "true focus . . . was the nature of salvation."[5]

Raised in Edinburgh by her Scottish Jewish father and English Anglican mother, Spark was welcomed into the Catholic Church in the early 1950s, joining the remarkable company of early- and mid-twentieth century Catholic converts among the British literati, along with Evelyn Waugh and Graham Greene (both of whom supported her writing). "I began to see life as a whole rather than as a series of disconnected happenings," she said of her conversion. "I think it was this combination of circumstances which made it possible for me to attempt my first novel."⁶ Perhaps this conversion helped Spark depict religious belief in a complex and unsentimental way, including in *The Girls of Slender Means*.

The title of *The Girls of Slender Means*, her seventh novel, refers to the women who lived in a London boarding called the May of Teck Club. According to the club's constitution, it "exists for the Pecuniary Convenience and Social Protection of Ladies of Slender Means below the age of Thirty Years, who are obliged to reside apart from their Families in order to follow an Occupation in London."⁷ The club is named after Queen Mary, who was known as May of Teck before she married George V in 1910, and it is based on a house in which Spark lived toward the end of World War II called the Helena Club. The girls in the house number about forty, including a handful of older, long-term residents who have been allowed to reside there beyond the usual age limit (and are not bashful about commenting on the behavior of their younger housemates). In a London that was shattered by German bombs, the May of Teck Club's house remains standing despite being "three times window-shattered since 1940, but never directly hit."⁸ A bomb had dropped in its yard but did not explode and was removed; one of the older residents insists that another unexploded bomb lurks in the back garden, but the residents dismiss that theory as an old maid's tale.

Most of *The Girls of Slender Means* is set in the summer of 1945, during the period in which the Allies have defeated the Germans but are still at war with imperial Japan. The work is bookended by celebrations: V-E Day, celebrating Germany's surrender in May of 1945; and V-J Day, celebrating Japan's surrender that August. This uncertain period establishes an atmosphere of tenuous and cautious promise during which the characters look forward to a new life without the threat of bombings or the austerity of war-time rations— but they are not entirely at peace, either, as the war echoes in the distant Pacific. In an early scene, the young women visit Buckingham Palace to celebrate victory over Germany, and "the next day everyone began to consider where they personally stood in the new order of things."⁹ It is a time of peace, promise, and potential during which the young discuss "the new future."¹⁰ Elsewhere, the narrator describes the girls in this time as "capable of accommodating quick happenings and reversals, rapid formations of intimate friendships, and a range of lost and discovered loves that in later life and in peace would take years to happen, grow, and fade."¹¹

We see glimpses of this maturation through Spark's expert and tantalizing use of flashforwards, one of her favorite narrative techniques. Spark weaves throughout brief conversations set in the early 1960s, in which one of the May of Teck girls—Jane, now a newspaper gossip columnist—calls her old housemates with news about a former admirer of theirs named Nicholas Farringdon:

"Oh rather. Has he turned up?"
"No, he's been martyred."
"What-ed?"
"Martyred in Haiti. Remember he became a Brother—"
"But I've just been to Tahiti, it's marvellous, everyone's marvellous. . . ."

With this sudden piece of information—conveyed, in this case, humorously through the sort of confused dialogue you find in Waugh's *Scoop*—Spark establishes the novel as a mystery of sorts. Nicholas has died—why? How? "You'll have to find out more through your grapevine," Jane's old friend tells her.¹²

Before long, another question emerges. In the central timeline of 1945, Nicholas is an aspiring writer and pseudo-anarchist—in other words, a pretentious young intellectual—who becomes obsessed with the young women in the May of Teck house. He spends much of the summer of 1945 sleeping with the most beautiful one, Selina Redwood and her "long unsurpassable legs."[13] Readers will wonder, how does he go from that carefree and rather unserious young man to a missionary who dies for his faith? We become less concerned with the cause and manner of his death than the cause and manner of his conversion. The novel becomes a particular kind of murder mystery; it's a martyr mystery.

We get no answers to that question until the end, and even then, they aren't entirely clear. What we know for sure is that in a notebook full of literary posing and pretense, Nicholas also made an insightful and prophetic observation: "a vision of evil may be as effective to conversion as a vision of good."[14] He wrote that before he experienced his own conversion, yet the reader is invited to apply the paradox to Nicholas's experience. But what was the evil that changed Nicholas? As Hosmer explains, "Muriel Spark's preoccupations with manipulation and the themes of good and evil, particularly with the presence of evil as a paradoxical moment of grace for conversion, finds full expression" in *The Girls of Slender Means*.[15]

Although the mystery of Nicholas's conversion and martyrdom is a central conceit of the novel, the girls themselves occupy center stage. "The inhabitants of the club are all sharply sketched and knowable," writes the critic Frank Kermode, but three of them receive particular attention from the narrator—and Nicholas.[16] The first is Jane herself, who works for a minor publishing house. Her unscrupulous boss has assigned her the job of identifying the weaknesses and insecurities of writers "to reduce [their] literary morale as far as possible" so the publisher can have a stronger hand during contract negotiations.[17] Jane first befriends Nicholas with this task in mind, as he has sent the firm a manuscript of aphorisms and insights titled *The Sabbath Notebooks*. Nicholas is on to their scheme but enjoys Jane's company regardless, in part because through her he learns more about, and gains access to, the May of Teck house.

Another preeminent girl in the house is Joanna Childe, the broken-hearted daughter of an Anglican rector who gives elocution lessons to her housemates. Her last name suggests immaturity, and its spelling befits her poetic bent. Spark's narrator gives many snippets of her lessons, which amount to a sort of greatest hits collection of English-language poems about beauty, death, and the overlap between them. These snippets floating in and out of the narrative cast a spell and contribute to the sense of the house's energy and bustle. Although most readers probably won't recognize all of them, an advantage of reading in the age of the internet is that you can track them down in a quick web search. But even in the fragmented manner in which they're presented, the accumulated quotations of Poe, Wordsworth, Shelley, Byron, and others help establish Joanna's melancholy character and imply an air of tragedy. Some of them also suggest sex and romance.[18] Consider a line that appears several times in the novel, from a poem by Alfred, Lord Tennyson: "Now sleeps the crimson petal, now sleeps the white." The last lines of the poem read, "So fold thyself, my dearest, thou, and slip / Into my bosom and be lost in me." (It was basically the nineteenth-century version of "I Melt with You" by Modern English.) Later, a recitation of Matthew Arnold's "Dover Beach"— "The Sea of Faith / Was once, too, at the full . . ."—relates to the novel's interest in the place of religious belief in the modern world. There are also frequent references to Gerard Manley Hopkins's *The Wreck of the Deutschland*, about the sinking of a German ship and the drowning of five Franciscan nuns on board, which foreshadows the tragedy of the novel's final act. Rosemary Goring aptly calls these poetic interludes "beads on the rosary of this contemplative and . . . savage story."[19] Joanna also happens to be the only character explicitly identified as a conservative voter, pulling the lever (or whatever they did in voting booths in London back then) for Winston Churchill in his losing campaign that year because of his party's stand for "a desirable order of life that none of the members was old enough to remember from direct experience."[20]

Finally, there is the alluring Selina, with whom Nicholas has a summer-long love affair. Selina is characterized primarily by her beauty, her sexuality, and—most of all—her preoccupation with poise. Twice a day, she recites a sort of creed known as the Two Sentences, "a simple morning and evening exercise prescribed by the Chief Instructress of the Poise Course which [she] had recently taken." In this secular prayer, Selina confesses: "Poise is the perfect balance, an equanimity of body and mind, complete composure whatever the social scene. Elegant dress, immaculate grooming, and perfect deportment all contribute to the attainment of self-confidence."[21] It's an odd routine that calls to mind the divine offices, which priests pray multiple times a day; in fact, the prayer-like aspect of Selina's routine is underscored when we learn late in the novel about a rector's habit of praying the psalms twice daily. But, as we will see, her ritual emphasizes not spiritual development, repentance, or praise, but the much more self-absorbed priorities of composure, appearance, and self-confidence. The habit underscores the selfishness for which Selina will distinguish—or shame—herself by the novel's end.

The girls live together in a "spacious Victorian" that had once been a private home.[22] On the ground floor is a busy recreation room, from which Joanna's poetic utterances float as she gives elocution lessons, as well as the drawing and dining rooms. Most of the girls—and all of the minor characters—share dorm rooms on the second floor, while more central characters like Joanna have their own rooms on other floors. On the fourth floor reside the five "most attractive, sophisticated and lively girls" (including Selina) who "were filled with deeper and deeper social longings of various kinds, as peace-time crept over everyone."[23] The bathroom of this floor once had a skylight that gave access to the rooftop, but it was bricked off for some scandalous reason or another. But restless girls of slender bodies—and access to margarine, soap, and other rationed goods that might double as lubricant—could still gain access to the roof through a narrow bathroom window. This is how Selina gets there for her trysts with Nicholas, who has access through the window of a neighboring building.

Living on strict rations, the girls count their calories and share their soap and coupons. They also share an elegant evening dress—a Schiaparelli, if you simply must know who they're wearing—given to one of the girls by a rich relative. A prized possession, the Schiaparelli provides them a little taste of sophistication and luxury during lean years and slender means.

Grace Notes

Selina's routine, with its emphasis on poise or physical grace, connects to the novel's recurring interest in the role and definition of divine grace. Selina's grace is superficial, associated primarily with proper conduct and appearance. But the concept of course also has a significance in Christian theology. Spark offers some sense of this meaning through what appear to be asinine, petty disagreements between two of the older tenants in the house. One of the older boarders, Collie (you might call her a boarder Collie), is similarly concerned with grace, but in a slightly more spiritual manner. She believes herself to be "growing in grace," but this growth is impeded by a quotidian frustration when one of the housemates forgets to clean up after herself in the kitchen.[24] Later, she waxes philosophical about "growing in grace" on matters of sex—meaning, it seems, not to be squeamish about talk of sex.[25] These obviously aren't the most theologically rich discussions, but they represent a more sophisticated perspective than Selina's.

The most important instance of grace in the novel is the conversion of Nicholas. In his manuscript *The Sabbath Notebook*, Nicholas articulates a budding understanding of grace:

> Everyone should be persuaded to remember how far, and with what a pathetic thump, the world has fallen from grace, that it needs must appoint politicians for its keepers, that its emotions, whether of consolation at breakfast-time or fear in the evening. . . .

One character reading this passage explains that its reference to falling from grace renders Nicholas anathema to the anarchists: "They chuck him out when he talks like a son of the Pope. This man is a mess that he calls himself an anarchist; the anarchists do not make all that talk of original sin, so forth; they permit only anti-social tendencies, unethical conduct, so forth."[26] They take their materialism straight, hold the spirituality. Given what we know about Nicholas during the summer of 1945, it is surprising to see him writing about grace in this manner—he doesn't strike us as a particularly thoughtful Christian before his conversion. But the intimation of a fall from grace in his notebook prefigures his newfound faith.

But what could Nicholas mean by grace in this context? It might be helpful to remember that as a Catholic convert, Spark inherited a richer understanding of grace than Selina espouses. The Catholic Church teaches that "Grace is *favor*, the *free and undeserved help* that God gives us to respond to his call to become children of God, adoptive sons, partakers of the divine nature and of eternal life."[27] Saint John Henry Newman, a convert from Anglicanism who was an enormous influence on Spark's conversion, describes the operation of grace this way:

> And if you are conscious that your hearts are hard, and are desirous that they should be softened, do not despair. All things are possible to you, through God's grace. . . . He gives grace by little and little. It is by coming daily into His presence, that by degrees we find ourselves awed by that presence and able to believe and obey Him.[28]

Newman prescribes praying before the Blessed Sacrament and offering short prayers over the course of the day. "These are the means by which," Newman explains, "with God's grace, [a believer] will be able in course of time to soften his heart—not all at once, but by degrees; not by his own power or wisdom, but by the grace of God blessing his endeavour."[29] Selina is right to think that exercises—something like prayer—can help her grow closer to grace, but her sense of grace is far too superficial. My point is not that Nicholas spent his free time reading Newman's sermons, only that his understanding of grace is in keeping with the same tradition.

It's tempting to agree with one character's diagnosis that Nicholas is "a mess." There's his anarchism, for starters, which misunderstands political power and underestimates the power of institutions. In his manuscript, Nicholas declares the British "do not need a government" and that "Parliament should dissolve forever."[30] He recognizes the value of some institutions, but purely as totems or symbols of tradition and continuity rather than as vehicles of any political authority:

> We could manage very well in our movement towards a complete anarchist society, with our great but powerless institutions: we could manage with the monarchy as an example of the dignity inherent in the free giving and receiving of precedence and favour without power. . . We do not need institutions with power. The practical affairs of society could be dealt with locally by the Town, Borough, and Village Councils. . . . We can be ruled by the corporate will of men's hearts alone. It is Power that is defunct, not as we are taught, the powerless institutions.[31]

It's a hybrid form of anarchism that hedges its bets out of recognition for the importance of institutional steadiness and continuity. This brief passage, though, raises important questions about the nature of institutions—and of human nature. Regarding the former: can an institution be great if it lacks any power? On what other terms does one evaluate the strength of an institution if not its power—political, moral or cultural? His vision that practical affairs can be managed at the local level may seem like a right-of-center American's dream, but it's undermined by Nicholas's naïve belief in the ability to "rul[e] by the corporate will of men's hearts alone."[32] As we will see, Nicholas's epiphany involves a fuller understanding of men's hearts.

Dignity and Poverty

A related element that makes Nicholas come across as a bit of a "mess" is his preoccupation with the girls of the May of Teck Club. While his sexual attraction to Selina is understandable (if misguided), he also sees in the club "a poetic image that teased his mind and pestered him for details." To him, it stands "as a microcosmic ideal society" and he elevates it for its "beautiful heedless poverty." This seems like precisely the sort of idealized vision held by Miles Coverdale and skewered by Hawthorne in *The Blithedale Romance.* For their part, the girls themselves don't seem to share his view of their poverty, which the narrator explains "any sane girl would regard only as a temporary one until better opportunities occurred."[33] Nicholas is even surprised when Selina fails to "share with him an understanding of the lovely attributes of dispossession and poverty, her body was so austere and economically furnished."[34] His desire for her blinds him to her superficiality.

Yet the novel is not entirely dismissive of Nicholas's perspective. In fact, it is wryly endorsed in the book's first sentence: "Long ago in 1945 all the nice people in England were poor, allowing for some exceptions."[35] It isn't that poverty makes the people of England nice, or that prosperity would corrupt them. Instead, poverty was a shared trait that did not diminish the virtue or dignity of the people themselves. It also helps that Nicholas is reflective enough to recognize the unrealistic nature of his view of the club and that "he was imposing upon this society an image incomprehensible to itself."[36] At the same time, the narrator suggests there is some truth to Nicholas's vision, even if the girls themselves don't see the virtue of their poverty; "his ideal of the place . . . was a miniature expression of a free society, that it was a community held together by the graceful attributes of a common poverty. He observed that at no point did poverty arrest the vitality of its members but rather nourished it."[37] Or as Nicholas thinks to himself, "Poverty differs vastly from want."[38] The final impression we have of Nicholas, during his missionary work in Haiti, is his positive image of Jane as the representation "of all the May of Teck establishment in its meek, unselfconscious attitudes of poverty."[39]

These details help explain why, as Rosemary Goring puts it, "only Nicholas had the full measure of what was going on in the May of Teck, and the wider world beyond."[40] What's more, it is notable that Nicholas has the conviction of his beliefs—his very presence in Haiti, where he is killed, testifies to the sincerity of his perception of the dignity inherent in all people, including the materially impoverished.

Being in It Together

The novel's most dramatic moments raise compelling questions about the relationship between individuals and the community. Writing in the midst of the COVID-19 pandemic and its government lock-downs, when two weeks to stop the spread sprawled into shuttered cities and the assurance that "we're all alone together," George F. Will referred to a passage from *The Girls of Slender Means* to illustrate the siren song of collectivism. The girls enjoy what Will calls the "culmi-nation of wartime solidarity" at Buckingham Palace on V-E Day, but then (quoting Spark) "'began to consider where they personally stood in the new order of things.'" Will emphasizes, "Yes, *personally*. After wartime's necessary collective exertions, a solidarity that has been obligatory during danger was undesirable as normality." He closes the column with the warning that "nostalgia for a time when society was fused by the heat of war or some other crisis is not a permanent basis for a free and open society."[41] It's an important warning, especially now that we have a better understanding of the repercussions that the bizarre form of government-enforced communal isolation inflicted on many Americans.

Spark herself experienced the power of that sense of community when she traveled aboard a troopship from Rhodesia to England in early 1944. According to biographer Martin Stannard, the thirty women on board "were stacked four-deep in bunk beds and instructed to remain fully dressed in case of a German attack. The possibility of sinking was with them at every moment. By way of a joke, dark trousers were recommended to deflect the attention of sharks."[42] Spark would recall of that mortifying experience, "It was indeed a dangerous journey. But it is curious how a sense of danger diminishes in proportion to the number of people who participate in the risk. On this, as on other occasions during the war, being 'in it together' took the edge off fear."[43] To that end, Spark's novel also illustrates the dangers of the opposite inclination, the instinct toward excessive individualism during a time of crisis. Selina commits an act of such selfishness during the crisis that it inspires Nicholas to make a sign of the cross when he witnesses it, the first step in his conversion and eventual martyrdom.

Spark's Flair

Before turning to the novel's remarkable crescendo, I want to dwell on one of my favorite things about *The Girls of Slender Means*, and one of the elements that makes it (and all of Spark's novels, for that matter) eminently re-readable: Spark's remarkable style. Like the seductive Selina, Spark's novels are slim and economical—but unlike Selina, Spark's work is deep, rich, and layered. Goring aptly describes it as a "deceptively lightly-told meringue of a tale" in which "the layers of enfolded meaning are abundant and complex. A single reading is not sufficient to glean everything that is being suggested or revealed."[44]

A major ingredient to this richness is the detached and occasionally cruel tone of her omniscient narrator. Here is how the narrative voice describes the girls of slender means themselves: "As they realized themselves in varying degrees, few people alive at the time were more delightful, more ingenious, more movingly lovely, and, as it might happen, more savage, than the girls of slender means."[45] This sharp description invites the reader closer with sweet words—and then suddenly inserts and twists the blade. You might say that the narrator is as delightful, ingenious, lovely, and savage as the girls themselves. A comparably great moment is when the narrator says that Jane, throughout her life, had "incorrectly subscrib[ed] to a belief that she was capable of thought—indeed, was demonstrating a capacity for it."[46] Ouch! For his part, Nicholas is cuttingly described as "the disappointing son of a good English family."[47] Before you conclude that this tone is too mean to be admired, remember that Jane Austen's narrators often call characters stupid. Nonetheless, moments like this led the novelist Anthony Burgess, when naming *The Girls of Slender Means* one of the ninety-nine best novels of the post-war era, to observe that "Muriel Spark, safe with her theological certainties, withholds compassion."[48] There are certainly moments where this may be the case, and it is also true that throughout her fiction, Spark depicts moments of sudden, deadly violence that can seem callous. Yet the final chapter of *The Girls of Slender Means* is an exercise in compassion, as Nicholas mourns and meditates upon the tragic death of a major character. I think the critic A.L. Kennedy offers a more helpful understanding of the author's attitude:

> Spark is not misanthropic; she punishes hubris, not humanity. Pretense, unkindness, self-deception and our inability to understand our own unimportance in the larger world are her targets, and under them runs a sense that there are better ways: gentleness, relationships based on mutual regard, perspectives that approach eternity.[49]

This attitude becomes most apparent in a section of the novel that best reflects Spark's stylistic mastery.

Before I discuss that, though, let me keep you in suspense by discussing another element of Spark's style that helps her establish suspense, which is her use of flashforwards. As I mentioned earlier, the novel frequently jumps from the central timeframe of 1945 to 1963, during Jane's phone conversations about Nicholas's death. She also uses this technique to excellent effect in *The Prime of Miss Jean Brodie*, which provides glimpses into the present life of a central character even as most of the novel is about her childhood. We may ask ourselves, in our best David Byrne impression, well—how did she get there? Spark explained that she used that device, known as prolepsis, because "to give the show away in a strange way, strange manner, creates suspense more than the withholding of information does."[50] Novelist Gabriel Josipovici suggests that Spark's use of this technique may have roots in her interest in Scottish border poetry, in which it is "a powerful contributor to the sense of doom and inevitability."[51] It's a compelling speculation—she wrote in her memoir that as a child, "the steel and bite of the ballads, so remorseless and yet so lyrical, entered my literary bloodstream, never to depart."[52]

Spark's stylistic and narrative abilities shine during the remarkable climax of *The Girls of Slender Means*, a chapter-long set-piece depicting a disaster that destroys the May of Teck Club and causes a tragic death. (In the interest of avoiding spoilers, I'll be as vague as possible in recounting this scene.) It is a masterpiece of storytelling that blends humor, suspense, pathos, and tragedy and also draws on diverse elements of the plot that Spark has carefully, but subtly, established over the course of the novel. The Russian playwright and short-story writer Anton Chekhov famously advised that if you're going to have a gun on the wall at the start of a play, it had better be fired later. In *The Girls of Slender Means*, Spark hangs many guns on the wall, yet the reader hardly notices them at all until they all fire in the masterful climax. As many times as I've read the novel (that's not bragging—it's short!), I still find myself anxious as I read this chapter. I must balance the compulsion to speed through the narrative and discover what happens next with the competing impulse to slow down and luxuriate in Spark's remarkable story telling and style.

Here's what happens: a major disturbance forces the girls to leave the house, and the girls on the fourth floor—including Selina, Joanna, and Jane—are trapped. Firefighters are on their way to batter open the trapdoor, but time is running out. The house deteriorates around and below them. Joanna, frantic, recites a Psalm. During the height of this drama, Spark makes the reader hang in suspense even longer as the narrator takes a step back and glances at:

> all sorts and conditions of human life in the world at that particular moment, when in London homing workers plodded across the park, observing with curiosity the fire-engines in the distance, when [one character] was sitting in his flat at St. John's Wood trying, without success, to telephone to Jane at the club to speak to her privately, the Labour Government was new-born, and elsewhere on the face of the globe people slept, queued for liberation-rations, beat the tom-toms, took shelter from the bombers, or went for a ride on a dodgem at the fun-fair.[53]

It's a remarkable reminder that the girls' drama occurs in the context of a much larger one, as well as a poignant glance at the spreading peace that the girls may not live to experience. In the meantime, Selina is able to pass her slender body through the narrow bathroom window and to the safety of a neighboring roof—yet she returns, poised and graceful as ever, to slide back into the bathroom and put herself back in harm's way. For a moment—and only a moment—we (along with Nicholas) think we may be witnessing the sort of heroism that unites people during crisis. We are disappointed. And disturbed.

A major character dies in this scene, and Nicholas is changed by what he sees. Hosmer explains that "in an epiphany atop a burning building, [Nicholas] has a searing vision of evil sufficient to move him toward conversion."[54] It's not the last vision of evil, though, and readers may disagree as to whether that vision alone is "sufficient" to inspire his conversion. In the V-J Day celebration that concludes the novel, after a long and emotional denouement, Nicholas witnesses another moment of surprising cruelty, an act of sudden and silent violence. Helpless to do anything to stop the act—which nobody else in the massive crowd sees—Nicholas can only make a futile gesture that signifies both his frustration as well and his newfound maturity, his departure from the age of literary pretentions and manipulative dishonesty. The Scottish journalist Alan Taylor interprets the novel's concluding violence as Spark's way of "saying that well, the war may be ended, but human kind will go on being evil come what may."[55] There is truth in this interpretation, as it corresponds to our earlier discussions of enduring human nature. On the other hand, it is important to recognize the nobility of Nicholas's conversion. His response to what he sees on the roof of the May of Teck Club and at the V-J Day celebration do not convince him that he can change human nature, but that the message of grace is necessary given the shortcomings of that nature. A tragic element of this novel is that Spark helps readers solve the mystery of Nicholas's conversion; his acquaintances from that transformative time do not.

The Girls of Slender Means is a haunting story of conversion, the presence of evil, and the meaning of grace. Its characters, in London in the final days of World War II, are hopeful for the return of peace to their war-weary land. The novel we turn to next is set far from London, but its characters harbor similar hopes amid cycles of dysfunctional governments and violent regimes.

Chapter Ten

Civilization without Victimhood—V. S. Naipaul, *A Bend in the River* (1979)

I n 1991, the Trinidadian-born and Oxford-educated novelist V. S. Naipaul delivered a speech that reflected his optimistic vision of Western culture's influence on the rest of the world, a vision that recognizes its fallibility but emphasizes its virtues—the opposite of the attitude that dominates contemporary conversations. Naipaul recounted becoming aware, when he moved from Trinidad to England, that he was part of a "larger civilization" that expanded far beyond his Caribbean home.[1] He possessed, for example, historical and cultural knowledge from various backgrounds and had "been granted the ideas of inquiry and the tools of scholarship." This was his first glimpse of what he called "our universal civilization." He gradually recognized other elements of it, including the more challenging or double-edged aspects of "ambition, endeavor, individuality." He saw the power of Christian moral teaching as well as "the idea of the pursuit of happiness," which is "an elastic idea" that encompasses "the idea of the individual, responsibility, choice, the life of the intellect, the idea of vocation and perfectibility and achievement."[2]

Naipaul acknowledged that the universal civilization had "for at least three centuries a racial taint." But he explained that since World War II, there has been an "extraordinary attempt of this civilization to accommodate the rest of the world, and all the currents of that world's thought." Even those who disdain these cultural traits do so with an "unconscious contradiction" of relying on its scientific and economic advancements. By the time Naipaul delivered that speech, he had been exploring these ideas for some time, including in his remarkable 1979 novel *A Bend in the River*. A fascinating and disturbing account of a young man's experience in a postcolonial African nation, *A Bend in the River* illustrates the perils of reflexive anti-Western sentiment, depicts the dangers of a victim mentality, and warns of the thin barrier separating civilization from terror.

Out of Post-Colonial Africa

Vidiadhar Surajprasad Naipaul was born to a Hindu Indian family in the then-British colony of Trinidad in 1932. He won a national scholarship to attend Oxford, and although he did not perform particularly well there, he did earn the praise of an Anglo-Saxon professor named J.R.R. Tolkien.[3] He stayed in England after graduation, found work in London, and began writing fiction. His early works were set in Trinidad, and by the early 1960s, with the success of *A House for Mr. Biswas*, he was a major literary figure. After that work, though, he began to explore other nations and people, and his works took on a darker, less comic tone.

Naipaul based *A Bend in the River* on his experiences traveling through Africa. In 1966, he was writer-in-residence at Makerere University in the newly independent Uganda. Naipaul's biographer, Patrick French, explains that at this point, "optimism among Europeans and Americans about Africa as the emerging continent was high, and Makerere University seemed like a beacon of progress in the region, staffed largely by white expatriates who felt proud to be building a new nation while atoning for the wrongs of the colonial era. [Naipaul] was an anomaly."[4] He was an outlier not only because he was not driven by white guilt, but because he tended to be more skeptical of post-colonial regimes. What Naipaul saw in Uganda justified that skepticism. Shortly after his arrival at Makerere University, the nation's prime minister overthrew the president and eventually established a dictatorship. Journalist Patrick Marnham explains that while many Westerners and progressives applauded the new leader, "Naipaul immediately saw him for what he was, a brutal despot, and was angered by the African experts' ready endorsement of the new regime."[5] Naipaul understood that change was not necessarily progress.

Uganda was one of many formerly colonized nations that won independence after World War II, along with India, Pakistan, Algeria, Kenya, Trinidad and Tobago, Zimbabwe, Sudan, and others. (The movement did not begin after WWII, of course, as Mahatma Gandhi was leading non-violent resistance against British rule of India decades earlier.) The anti-colonial movement grew as an intellectual movement in the 1960s, shortly before Naipaul began writing about it, particularly with the publication of Frantz Fanon's *The Wretched of the Earth* (1961). "At the level of individuals," Fanon wrote, "violence is a cleansing force. It frees the native from his inferiority complex and from his despair and inaction; it makes him fearless and restores his self-respect."[6] This is the language of violent decolonization that you can still hear today.

Naipaul, "uninhibited by liberal guilt or complexes [as] he watched post-colonial Africa with pitiless lucidity," swam against this tide.[7] David Pryce-Jones, a senior editor at *National Review* as well as a friend of Naipaul's, describes the novelist as "conservative in the best sense, on the watch for causes and consequences. Critics of the Western mind—of whom there are plenty—could hardly believe that someone from his background had drawn conclusions quite the opposite of theirs."[8] As the 1970s wore on, more people saw the wisdom of his perspective. Patrick French frames the context well:

> A rising disillusion with the post-colonial project in many countries led to Vidia being projected as the voice of truth, the scourge who by virtue of his ethnicity and his intellect could see things that others were seeking to disguise. Why were so many African countries ruled by thieves? Why was Iran having an Islamist revolution? What had become of the gracious optimism of the 1960s and 1970s?[9]

Nonetheless, Naipaul was scorned by academics "even while his books were put on college reading lists."[10] Several years after the publication *of A Bend in the River*, Edward Said, one of the most influential postcolonial theorists, sneered that Naipaul had "allowed himself quite consciously to be turned into a witness for the Western prosecution," and that he perpetuates "the tritest, the cheapest and the easiest of colonial mythologies about wogs and darkies," and "specialize[s] in the thesis of self-inflicted wounds, which is to say that we 'non-Whites' are the cause of all our problems, not the overly maligned imperialists."[11] Said framed Naipaul as "a third worlder denouncing his own people, not because they are victims of imperialism, but because they seem to have an innate flaw, which is that they are not whites."[12] As we'll see, a fair reading of *A Bend in the River* does not support such a charge, but Said's claims provide a sense of how Naipaul outraged opposing intellectuals and activists.

Other liberals have recognized the value of Naipaul's perspective. In the final days of his presidency, Barack Obama told the *New York Times*, "there are writers who I don't necessarily agree with in terms of their politics, but whose writings are sort of a baseline for how to think about certain things — V. S. Naipaul, for example." Obama mused of Naipaul's work:

> I think about his novels when I'm thinking about the hardness of the world sometimes, particularly in foreign policy, and I resist and fight against sometimes that very cynical, more realistic view of the world. And yet, there are times where it feels as if that may be true. So in that sense, I'm using writing like that as a foil or something to debate against.[13]

Sounding a similar theme, Geoffrey Wheatcroft has posited that Naipaul "is certainly no liberal, and herein lies his importance. . . . It has been said that the real purpose of conservatism is to keep liberals honest, and the purpose of pessimistic anti-liberal writers is to tell us that life is not so simple and so benign as we would like to assume."[14] This aversion to easy solutions and an awareness of the enduring presence of barbarism are central to *A Bend in the River*. The urgency and relevance of his work became particularly evident after the terror attacks of September 11, 2001, and it's no coincidence that Naipaul won the Nobel Prize for Literature later that year.

Tides of History

The narrator of *A Bend in the River*, whom we know only as Salim, belongs to a Muslim family that emigrated from India two generations before to settle along the eastern coast of Africa in a land that had first been colonized by Arabs and was now governed by Europeans. Salim senses another change afoot and fears what lies ahead for himself and his family. In the novel's opening sentence, he declares both his ambition and a dark, Hobbesian view of humanity: "The world is what it is; men who are nothing, who allow themselves to become nothing, have no place in it."[15] On separate occasions, two prominent conservative writers have told me that this sentence is about as conservative a statement there is, because the opening clause insists that one must take the world on its own terms. But I wince at that opening phrase, which has become shorthand for dismissing a problem. "Hey doctor, you removed the wrong organ!" "Oh well, it is what it is." Or as Tony Soprano would put it, "What are ya gonna do?" Still, I see the point these friends are making: understanding the world's limits tempers the utopian impulse. Still, it's the second half of the sentence that really matters. That one insists on individual agency and rejects victimhood. This is what matters to Salim throughout the novel.

Salim's sense of helplessness on the coast and fear of impending political changes that may doom his family point toward what Jeremy Carl of the Claremont Institute calls "the thin veneer of civilization over humanity's inherent savagery" that is so important to Naipaul's fiction.[16] A symbol for the delicate state of civilization appears when Salim recalls watching his aunt on his family compound, where "the thin white washed wall . . . protected her so little. She was so vulnerable—her person, her religion, her customs, her way of life. The squalling yard had contained its own life, had been its own complete world, for so long. How could anyone not take it for granted? How could anyone stop to ask what it was that had really protected us?" This vision of the wall helps Salim foresee the end of his family's way of life and his need to strike out on his own, that "I could be master of my fate only if I stood alone." Establishing the novel's recurrent water imagery, Salim perceives his family as subject to two "tide[s] of history." The first had swept them to the coast in the first place. But "now . . . another tide of history was coming to wash us away."[17] He resolves to act before it could.

An opportunity arises for him when an acquaintance named Nazruddin returns to the coast from running businesses in an unnamed nation located in the interior of the continent. Since recently achieving independence from Europeans, this nation been convulsed in "wars and killings,"[18] which is why Nazruddin has left, though he still has businesses and holdings there. Recognizing Salim's restlessness in his stifling environment, Nazruddin offers him the shop he had left behind, along with this important advice: "What you must always know is when to get out."[19] Salim accepts the offer. Neither the town nor its country are named, but the novel's setting is generally understood to be Stanleyville, also known as Kisangani, in the Congo—or as it would have been known at the time of the novel's publication, Zaire.[20]

When Salim arrives, he finds that the town "had been destroyed, had returned to the bush."[21] Independence had brought distinct problems, unleashing "all the accumulated anger of the colonial period, and every kind of reawakened tribal fear." Salim hears reports of "casual killings over many months by soldiers and rebels and mercenaries, of people trussed up in disgusting ways and being made to sing certain songs while they were beaten to death in the streets."[22] Shops were poorly stocked, food was scarce, and gas and electricity were hard to come by. Salim is especially struck by the ruins: a ruined monument, a ruined suburb that "sun and rain and bush had made . . . look old, like the site of a dead civilization."[23] Meanwhile, back on the coast, there is an uprising and the old Arab families must flee, including Salim's own.

The Imperfect Pure Man

One of the people Salim gets to know early in his time at the bend in the river is a Belgian missionary named Father Huismans. A remnant of the nation's cast-off colonial presence, Father Huismans is an imperfect but impressive character. He has lived in the town for years and nurtures a deep interest in African cultural artifacts, occasionally venturing deep into the jungle to collect masks and carvings that he brought back to the town and stored in the lycée (the old colonial school) for preservation. Salim gradually sees Huismans "as a pure man" and takes comfort in his presence, yet he also describes the priest as aloof and "self-absorbed." Despite the priest's deep knowledge of African religion and culture, his interest never seemed to extend to "Africans in any other way; he seemed indifferent to the state of the country."[24] Father Huismans always considered himself as a European witnessing the death of old Africa, but he did not seem to believe that made him superior to the non-Europeans with whom he lived, and he saw it as his duty to preserve what remained—not only of old Africa, but of the European presence too. That is why, with no sense of contradiction, he collected junk from the peak of the colonial era, such as "pieces of old steamers and bits of disused machinery from the late 1890s."[25] Huismans perceives the town, and Africa, in broad historical terms, and "saw himself as part of an immense flow of history."[26] (There's that water imagery again . . .)

Father Huismans's historical vision is best represented in the priest's appreciation of an inscription for an old monument at the town's dock: *Miscerique probat populos et foedera jungi.* As Huismans explains to Salim, the motto is an adaptation of a passage from Virgil's *Aeneid*, which he translates as "he approves of the mingling of the peoples and their bonds of union."[27] (Naipaul would have been familiar with this motto: it was affixed to the British colonial badge for Trinidad during his childhood.) To Salim, the motto's Roman source seem inappropriate for the African context—"Rome was Rome. What was this place?"—and he sees hubris in it, as if the motto were a curse:

To carve the words on a monument beside this African
river was surely to invite the destruction of the town. . . .
And almost as soon as it had been put up the monument
had been destroyed, leaving only bits of bronze and the
mocking words, gibberish to the people who now used the
open space in front as a market and a bivouac[.][28]

A similar irony imbues another Latin motto Salim encounters, this
one associated with the school established by British. The uniform
shirt for the school bears the script *Semper Aliquid Novi*, a shortened
version of *ex Africa semper aliquid novi*—often translated to "Always
something new out of Africa."[29]

Unlike Salim, though, Huismans interprets the monument's motto
sincerely, as "they were words that helped him to see himself in Africa."[30]
He did not mourn "the destruction of the European town, the town that
his countrymen had built" because he saw it as "only a temporary
setback" on the way toward the realization of a grander vision, a more
prosperous mingling of peoples. The town had once been an Arab
colony, then it was European, and now it was African. He clung to an
optimistic view of the town's future despite its setbacks: "Out of simple
events beside the wide muddy river, out of the mingling of the peoples,
great things were to come one day. We were just at the beginning."[31] But
the priest would not live to see beyond that beginning.[32]

During one venture in the jungle to gather cultural artifacts,
Father Huismans is brutally murdered. (For those of you keeping
score at home, that makes this the second consecutive novel in this
book featuring a martyred Christian missionary.) His mutilated,
decapitated corpse is thrown into a boat and floats along the river
until it becomes tangled in water hyacinth, an invasive species that
dominates that waterway. His head is displayed on a spike. Supporters
of the new regime, including a young man close to Salim named

Ferdinand, see what the priest represented as an insult to them and
"going against the god of Africans."[33] But Salim offers a eulogy of sorts:

> The idea Father Huismans had of his civilization had made
> him live his particular kind of dedicated life. It had sent
> him looking, inquiring; it had made him find human rich-
> ness where the rest of us saw bush or had stopped seeing
> anything at all. But his idea of his civilization was also like
> his vanity. It had made him read too much in that mingling
> of peoples by our river; and he had paid for it.[34]

Salim's reference to the monument's Latin motto—"the mingling of
the peoples"—reminds us of Huismans's broad sense of history and
the town's place in it. By Salim's reckoning, the priest had overesti-
mated what the town could be capable of. Yet Huismans's vision of
progress is realistic insofar as it is gradual: improvement comes in
fits and starts, advances followed by, and following, setbacks. In the
case of the uprising in which Father Huismans was killed, the village
developed again afterward.

Although Huismans is the novel's clearest representation of colonial power, Naipaul declines to villainize him. White, Christian, and
European, Huismans is murdered precisely because he represents
the oppressor, and his presence is unacceptable to the rising power.
Yet Salim's presentation of the priest makes clear that this scapegoating
glosses over the priest's much more complex attitude toward the
relationship between Europe and Africa.

The Shadow of the Big Man

Conversely, the nation's president demonstrates the dangers of poor
post-colonial governance. Shortly before Father Huismans's murder,

amid rumors of war and instances of low-scale violence, the new president—known simply as the Big Man and based on Zaire president Mobutu Sese Seko—sends in white soldiers to execute military officers and soldiers. As Salim puts it, the Big Man "had sent terror to our town and region," but also made the locals feel "that for the first time since independence there was some guiding intelligence in the capital, and that the free-for-all of independence had come to an end."[35] Salim himself feels this comfort. Hearing distant gunfire shot by government forces, he thinks of "the promise of order and continuity; and it was oddly comforting, like the sound of rain in the night."[36]

The newfound order and stability that the Big Man brings drive an economic boom. Salim's friend opens a burger franchise, and everyone bragged about "how much [they] had gained with the boom."[37] There are signs of development elsewhere, as the Big Man clears a swath of bush near the rapids to build a small town that becomes known as the Domain. With large buildings and air-conditioned homes, the Domain is part of his attempt to "creat[e] modern Africa . . . a miracle that would astound the rest of the world."[38] But it has no apparent purpose. A proposed model farm was never developed, the swimming pool leaks, and the conference hall stands empty: "The Domain had been built fast, and in the sun and the rain decay also came fast." Eventually, the president determines to develop it into "a university city and research centre."[39] Whatever its purpose, Salim concludes, "the Domain, with its shoddy grandeur, was a hoax," the home of an "Africa of words and ideas . . . (and from which, often, Africans were physically absent)."[40] Salim observes that just as the arrogant colonial motto *miscerique probat populos et foedera jungi* was "a hoax [that] had helped make men of the country in a certain way . . . men would also be made by this new hoax."[41] This new district stands—barely—as a testament to the dangers of central planning as well as the ironic continuity between colonial and post-colonial rule.

The Big Man's rule, a combination of populism and autocracy, presents other dangers. In some towns and villages, a cult based on devotion to the Big Man's mother develops. He controls the use of language, banning certain words to refer to each other—*au revoir monsieur; adieu madame*—and ordering the people to refer to themselves as *citoyens* and *citoyennes*. Where he had once delivered speeches in French, he begins speaking in what Salim calls "the language of the drinking booth and the street brawl, converting himself . . . into the lowest of the low."[42] When political allies fail him, he demonizes them to establish his status "as the friend of the people, the *petit peuple*, as he liked to call them, and he punished their oppressors."[43] He deployed political symbols to convey the message that, as Salim puts it, "we had all become his people . . . we were reminded that we all in various ways depended on him."[44] The Big Man exercises his power in small ways at first, like commandeering commercial aircraft for his own purposes, and then larger ones, like nationalizing private businesses. Salim falls victim to this: when he returns from a trip to London, he finds that his shop has been transferred to a "state trustee."[45] Naturally, this trustee is an incompetent drunk with no experience running a store, yet he still expects Salim "to acknowledge him as the boss."[46] Salim is reduced to more dangerous, illegal, and humiliating business practices and trades, including conducting business with poachers.

Nobody Loves Raymond

"What is sometimes read as Naipaul's contempt for the peoples of the Third World," observes editor and writer Park MacDougald, "is usually a contempt for those in the West whom he sees as enabling their self-destruction."[47] This contempt is conveyed perfectly through a European intellectual named Raymond. A counter-weight to Father Huismans, Raymond is believed to be "the Big Man's white man," an historian who advises the new president and "knows more about the country than anyone on earth."[48] With his glamorous young wife Yvette (more about her later), Raymond lives in a modern house in the Domain, where in a gesture of authenticity they've had the modern furniture "replaced by cushions and bolsters and African mats. Two or three reading lamps had been put on the floor, so that parts of the room were in darkness."[49] Note that Salim's phrasing in that last clause emphasizes the areas without light, drawing attention to the metaphorical meaning of the darkness here: ignorance. Salim enjoys himself at a party there, is amazed by Joan Baez's angelic voice rising from the turntable. But there is something unreal about this superficial mixing of cultures, of Africa and the West; Salim detects that "it was make-believe—I never doubted that."[50]

Raymond's influence on the Big Man dates back to the president's childhood, when the future president's mother brought him to the then-professor for advice. Raymond had been working on a major history of the country, some of which the president is rumored to have read, but he's put that to the side to work on a selection of the Big Man's speeches. As prestigious and powerful as Raymond initially seems, Salim soon learns that he has grown frustrated because his ideas aren't being heard or understood. The country's real power is in the capital, with the president, and Raymond is neutered in the Domain. He'll soon be taking the Big Man's orders. Nonetheless, Raymond remains loyal.

Salim is less concerned with this lack of power than he is with the façade of Raymond's supposed academic credentials. After reading some of his historical scholarship, Salim realizes that Raymond actually knows very little. He bases his findings entirely on the work of other people and never travels to the places he writes about or speaks to the people of Africa. Say what you will about Father Huismans, this was not one of his shortcomings—indeed, he was murdered precisely because he ventured deeply into the nation. Salim concludes that Raymond "had nothing like Father Huismans's instinct for the strangeness and wonder of the place. Yet he had made Africa his subject."[51]

Nonetheless, both Father Huismans and Raymond fetishize or idealize elements of African culture in a way that ultimately dooms them, and Naipaul is not suggesting that the colonial mindset represented by Father Huismans is flawless or uncomplicated. But Salim's account emphasizes the priest's surprising virtues, and particularly his interest in the particulars and specifics of Africa rather than being a detached observer satisfied with abstractions and second-hand accounts, as is the case with Raymond.

Violence and Victimhood

Raymond's wife, Yvette, also plays an important role in the novel as Salim's love interest, and as a catalyst for his worst behavior. She captures his imagination as soon as he meets her at the house party in the Domain, and before long they begin an affair. Salim's sexual encounters had to that point been limited to prostitutes, and his distorted perception of women and relationships consisted of "brothel fantasies of conquest and degradation."[52] For some time his relationship with Yvette is healthier than that low standard: after their first encounter he feels "blessed and remade."[53] They conduct their affair discreetly at first and gradually more openly, even as Salim insists that "adultery was horrible to me. I continued to think of it in the setting of family and community on the coast, and saw it as sly and dishonorable and weak-willed."[54] He's right, of course, but Yvette does not have the same compunctions and invites Salim to spend evenings with her and Raymond after their afternoon trysts. It's a bizarre, domesticized love triangle, a window into a home life he has never experienced. But even he is aware of trouble, noting the "corrupt physical ways our passion had begun to take."[55] Their affair devolves into perhaps the most disturbing moment of violence in the book. After one of their liaisons, Salim is insulted by a joke Yvette makes about his fidelity to her. Outraged, he assaults her, reducing her to the victim of one of his old "brothel fantasies of conquest and degradation."

The always perceptive Algis Valiunas of the Ethics and Public Policy Center quips, "One would be hard pressed to name a more repulsive sexual episode this side of the Marquis de Sade."[56] But it's an important one that makes a key point about victimhood in the novel. Naipaul defended the scene by insisting, "Doesn't it speak of passion . . . of Salim's pain."[57] Similarly, Patrick Marnham interprets it as a powerful evocation of Salim's character, noting that "the speed with which a tender intimacy is transformed into naked hatred turns the scene into one of the most powerful Naipaul ever wrote."[58] And even as Valiunas cringed at the scene's cruelty, he recognized that it signals Salim's naïveté regarding this relationship with Yvette, as well as her callous treatment of him: "the preposterous erotic hopes of dark-skinned men who envision a fairer life with their blonde lovelies collides fatally with the carelessness of white girls out for some Third World sport."[59] This is a plausible reading that is made even more compelling by some important details of Salim's narration.

In his account of the beating, Salim says that Yvette "was hit so hard and so often about the face . . . that she staggered back and allowed herself to fall on the floor."[60] What an odd way to describe his behavior. Quick grammar lesson: the passive voice is the language of evading responsibility. It's what politicians use when they say

"Mistakes were made" instead of "We really screwed up." Using the passive voice here allows Salim to distance himself from the violence he committed. He's denying his own agency.[61] Similarly, when Salim describes the event, he says that Yvette "allowed herself to fall"—more odd phrasing that detaches his brutality from its consequences and implies Yvette's complicity in her own suffering. That same night, recounting his beating of Yvette to a friend, he shirks responsibility by insisting that "she made me spit on her."[62] All of these rhetorical details help Salim dodge responsibility, ignore agency, and suggest he has no control over his situation.

This evasion of responsibility is a remarkable departure for Naipaul's character. In a biographical essay commemorating Naipaul's Nobel Prize, David Pryce-Jones acknowledged that "victimhood might have been his central theme, granted his background. Not at all. . . . Each one of us, his books declare, can choose to be a free individual. It is a matter of will and choice, and above all intellect." According to Pryce-Jones, Naipaul demonstrates "the absolute rejection of victimhood is necessary if we are to meet as we must on an equal footing, and it is no exaggeration to say that he has shifted public opinion towards this understanding as no other writer has done."[63] That is why the scene depicting Salim's abuse of Yvette is so important. It shows Salim falling short of his own expectations for himself, the standard of agency he sets in the novel's first sentence, and plays the victim. Recognizing the evil of how he has treated her, he is for once too weak to accept responsibility and say, "I hit her."

The Low Walls of Civilization

The critic and essayist Joseph Epstein has remarked that "civilization, for Naipaul, is a fragile thing, always in peril."[64] I suggested earlier that Naipaul conveys this point with the image of the garden wall at Salim's family compound on the coast; a similar moment occurs toward the end, when Salim is briefly imprisoned in the makeshift village jail. He recalls that from the market square, the jail's white concrete wall wasn't very high, so it "had never seemed like a real jail. . . . you felt that what went on behind the low wall matched the petty market life in front."[65] Once he's on the other side of those low walls, though, he sees political prisoners tortured. The experience in the jail poisons his memories of times outside of it, yet he also "felt that almost nothing separated me from those men in the courtyard."[66] Building on the imagery of the white wall from earlier in the novel, this passage underscores the tenuous nature of civilization and safety. Author and critic Jeffrey Folks helpfully explains that the prisoners, "separated by the single white wall from the busy, uncomprehending world of the town's marketplace, in which life passes by almost with a sense of normalcy . . . are proof of the terrible fragility of life and of the necessity of a redemptive civilization that offers opportunity, protection, and order."[67]

That terrible fragility recurs in the novel's final scene, which occurs on the river itself. As he had at the novel's start when he left his family's home on the coast, Salim recognizes that he must stand on his own before he is swept away by the tides of history. He boards a steamer to leave the town on the bend in the river. As is typical, a passenger barge is attached to the boat. But there's a difference. Salim explains, "the passenger barge was not towed behind these days—that was now considered a colonial practice. Instead, the barge was lashed to the forward part of the steamer."[68] That night, armed men try to commandeer the steamer. They fail, but the passenger barge becomes detached from the steamer and drifts away. The steamer moves on, its captain too afraid of privateers to rescue the people on the barge, leaving them to drift in the dark on the flow of history. It's a final image of chaos, uncertainty, and terror, caused in part by an arbitrary defiance against a colonial practice.

The essayist and novelist Joan Didion once noted that while crit- ics tended to observe that Naipaul wrote about "the void," what they really meant was that he did not offer "at least token applause in the interests of social progress." Far from a void, she surmised, Naipaul wrote about "a world dense with physical and social phenomena, brutally alive with the complications and contradictions of actual human endeavor."[69] This insight is particularly helpful in understanding the end of *A Bend in the River*. The barge drifts into the darkness; its fate is uncertain. Salim, though, proceeds on the steamer—and, in an ambiguity that recalls the final moment of *Rasselas*, his fate is uncertain, too. We only know he grasped control of it, as the novel's opening sentence anticipates—he recognized the breakdown and left before he could be swept away with it and "become nothing."

At a time when Western values and contributions are consistently condemned, when calls to "de-colonize" ring out on campuses and city streets around the world—and are used to justify barbaric attacks against civilian men, women, and children—*A Bend in the River* helps counter the groupthink that seeks to diminish the achievements of Western culture. Our next novel imagines that culture—and all human life—fading into oblivion.

Chapter Eleven

A Future without Children—P. D. James, *The Children of Men* (1992)

Who doesn't love a good dystopia? From *1984* to *The Walking Dead*, readers and viewers always enjoy seeing a dysfunctional society in action. Part of the allure of these works is that they provide an element of reassurance or gratitude for the fact that as bad as things are, they could always be worse. Paradoxically, we are also drawn to them because they present visions of a society that confirm our worst suspicions about where we're heading. Aldous Huxley's *Brave New World* depicts what Jonah Goldberg calls "a dystopia based on an *American* future" of universal ease and contentment, while George Orwell's vision of *1984* appeals to conservatives because of its warnings about the manipulation of language for political purposes, like when Merriam-Webster quickly updated its definition of *sexual preference* after a Republican Supreme Court nominee used the term.[1] And Margaret Atwood's 1985 novel *The Handmaid's Tale* is nightmare fuel for progressives who think every Republican administration is an aspiring theocratic patriarchy. Dystopias warn us about the logical conclusions of the worst things about our current culture, government, and society. They're great places to visit because we wouldn't want to live there.

P. D. James seems like an unlikely candidate to write a compelling dystopia, having established herself as a successful mystery novelist in the early 1960s. (Her description of that genre is remarkably conservative: "What the detective story is about is not murder but the restoration of order."[2]) She even served as a life peer in the House of Lords, a member of the Conservative Party, beginning in 1991. Around the same time, she read a book review that inspired her to depart from her usual style and create a dystopia. The review, as James described it, dealt with "the dramatic and so far unexplained fall in the fertility rate of western man." Surprised to learn that "young men today are only half as fertile as were their fathers," and shocked by the reviewer's observation that "of the millions of life forms which have inhabited our planet, nearly all have in time died out or were destroyed," James imagined England a generation after "the human race was struck by universal infertility. For twenty-five years no one would have heard a baby cry or heard a child laugh."[3]

She thought things were bad in the early '90s? She hadn't seen anything yet! In England and Wales in 2023, the Total Fertility Rate (TFR) was 1.44 children per woman, "its lowest value since records began in 1938."[4] The situation isn't much better in the United States. In 2024, the National Center for Health Statistics reported that the general fertility rate had dropped to its lowest level on record.[5] And according to the Census Bureau, there were about 4.1 million births in the U.S. in 1990; by 2019, that dropped to 3.7 million.[6] A 2024 Pew Research Center study found that "the share of U.S. adults younger than 50 without children who say they are unlikely to ever have kids rose 10 percentage points between 2018 and 2023 (from 37% to 47%)."[7] Given such numbers, the demographer Nicholas Eberstadt warns that "humans are about to enter a new era of history. Call it 'the age of depopulation' . . . Driven by an unrelenting collapse in fertility, family structures, and living arrangements heretofore imagined only in science fiction novels will become commonplace."[8]

The premise of *The Children of Men* is to follow the logical—and biological—implications of these trends. One reason James's dystopia has aged so well is that, as author and radio host Mark Steyn observes, she bases it "not on some technological gimmick but on some characteristic of our time nudged forward just a wee bit."[9] Or, as journalist John J. Miller puts it, "James did what dystopian novelists have always done: She picked a worrisome trend and extrapolated."[10] As a result, few novels have received as much attention from conservative commentators over the past several decades. *New York Times* columnist Ross Douthat interprets it "as a culturally conservative critique of Western decadence, with Christian themes and motifs cropping up as the possibility of new fertility arises."[11] Author James Bowman observes that it has proven "much more accurate than most eschatological fiction, for it presents an exaggerated version of a problem—namely the gradual depopulation of the developed world through below-replacement fertility rates—that in the years since its publication has begun to seem rather scarily *un*exaggerated."[12] The point is not that James is presenting a vision of our inevitable future; rather, the novel depicts a world where the decline in fertility that we've chosen is no longer a choice but an inevitability—a future in which we are not forced to have children (a progressive fear) but, by nature or God, to not have any—and explores what that would mean for our decisions about how we live our lives, how we choose to be governed, and how we die.

A Nation with No Children in It

James drops us into this world without children *in media res*—not with the start of the fertility crisis, known as the Omega, but a generation into it, in the year 2021, when civilization is well into its decline and humanity seems to have accepted its imminent extinction. Not only have men mysteriously become sterile; even sperm that had been frozen before Omega doesn't reproduce. This detail leaves open the possibility that Omega isn't merely a biological change from within the male body, but a curse or plague from without. The reality of humanity's whimpering end has become especially stark because the youngest person on Earth has just died a pointless and avoidable death at the age of twenty-five. We learn about this event in the novel's opening paragraphs through the perspective of its central character, a middle-aged Oxford history don named Theo Faron. Theo decides to keep a journal the day the youngest man dies, which also happens to be his own fiftieth birthday and the first day of a new year.

Theo is not what you would call a people person. He's not happy about the end of humanity, but you get the impression that he won't miss anyone. He likes living alone. He likes his routine. When an old friend suggests that he move into Theo's large (and largely empty) house, the thought of opening his doors mortifies him. Looking around his drawing room, he describes it as reflective of "a man primarily concerned with the nineteenth century . . . who likes his comfort and who lives alone. There are no family photographs, no board games, no disarray, no dust, no feminine clutter, little evidence, indeed, that the room was ever used." Theo, in short, is a man alone—obsessed with the distant past, but detached from any personal past (as the last detail about his self-sufficiency makes clear) and unconcerned about the future.[13] (That's not to say he doesn't have any family—he has a very important family member, as we'll soon see.) It's easy to read in Theo the self-absorption of Western culture that makes it inhospitable to children, psychologically if not biologically.

There's a distinct irony in Theo's field of study. For one thing, history is history for a doomed species, as Theo himself acknowledges: "History, which interprets the past to understand the present and confront the future, is the least rewarding discipline for a dying species."[14] What's more, the Victorian England of his specialty is particularly remote in time and mind. This irony surfaces during a scene at a library, described as "a secular cathedral to Victorian confidence" and which reflects "Victorian earnestness, the respect for learning, for craftsmanship, for art; the conviction that the whole of man's life could be lived in harmony with the natural world."[15] All of these virtues seem remote from the 2021 of the Omega—nobody builds anything, nobody believes in anything, and human life is out of harmony with the natural world it seems to be departing soon. As Theo wryly observes, when he first visited the museum, there had been a sign telling children to be quiet. There was no need for that now, which hints at another disparity between Theo's chosen historical period and the time in which he lives: the Victorian age is perhaps the period of English history most associated with fertility, fecundity, childhood, and domesticity.

Theo is self-aware enough to recognize his "obsessive self-sufficiency," which he identifies as "one of the reasons for my failed marriage."[16] Elsewhere, he refers to what he calls his "terror of taking responsibility for other people's lives."[17] Perhaps most disturbingly, he feels little remorse for a tragic accident that befell his only child and, in an especially disturbing passage, admits his ex-wife's worst suspicions about his response to their daughter's passing were accurate: "She thought that I cared less, and she was right. She thought that I cared less because I loved less, and she was right about that too. . . . [The daughter] has been dead for almost twenty-seven years and I still think of her with complaint."[18] His lack of concern may be a defense mechanism to protect himself from trauma, or it may signal his ambivalence about the preciousness of human life.

Theo's selfish complacency is troubled when he's approached by a small, unimpressive group of insurrectionists called the Five Fishes. They seek Theo's help in communicating their demands to a man named Xan Lyppiatt, the Warden of England—the most powerful man in the nation, who also happens to be Theo's cousin. The Five Fishes' demands focus on remedying several social injustices that have emerged since the Omega. For one thing, the minister's immigration policy has focused on welcoming what are called Sojourners, who are basically African migrants who do the work the English won't do, but are then sent home once they age out. They also advocate prison reform, and it's easy to see why: the government has transformed the Isle of Man into a violent penal colony. And they want an end to the government's aggressive assisted-suicide program. Theo begrudgingly meets with his cousin to discuss the group's demands, but that's as much as he's willing to do for them—until he discovers that they have a secret that could offer new hope to the world.

The novel is divided into two parts: the first, titled Omega (an unusual name for an opening section), focuses on the basics of the world—and England, in particular—over the past childless generation. In Book II: Alpha, the novel becomes more action-packed and briskly paced, tracing Theo's decision to help the Five Fishes after their mission takes on greater urgency and relevance.

Quasi Mothers and Parodies of Childhood

The first half of the novel reveals the many, and often surprising, ways that the disappearance of children has upended daily life. We hear of economic decline, the "religious and tribal wars of the 1990s," the deadly race riots of 2002.[19] Given the circumstances, it's little wonder that, as Theo describes, people "gave way to the almost universal negativism." He describes it as "a disease, with its soon-familiar symptoms of lassitude, depression, ill-defined malaise, a readiness to give way to minor infections, a perpetual disabling headache."[20] Contributing to this malaise is the mystery behind the infertility: "We are outraged and demoralized less by the impending end of our species, less even by our inability to prevent it, than by our failure to discover the cause. . . . Western science has been our god," and it let them down.[21]

In a novel full of ironies, one of the cruelest is that even though sex has at last been completely liberated from reproductive consequences, it's no fun anymore. Theo's description of a pre-Omega world should sound familiar: "Pornography and sexual violence on film, on television, in books, in life, had increased and became more explicit but less and less in the West we made love and bred children. . . . As a historian, I see it as the beginning of the end."[22] But instead of becoming a paradise of free love, sex became undesirable, unpleasant, and "almost meaninglessly acrobatic. Women complain increasingly of what they describe as painful orgasms: the spasm achieved but not the pleasure."[23] Not surprisingly, the institution of marriage is weak as well: people still marry, but with "less frequency, with less ceremony and often with the same sex." (James wrote this twenty-one years before same-sex marriage was legalized in England and Wales.)

The absence of children has also left gaping social and psychological holes. Theo recalls that early in the crisis, there was a demand for toy dolls among "admiring quasi-mothers" who sought to placate "the frustrated maternal desire."[24] These quasi-mothers even performed "pseudo-births" and buried broken dolls "with ceremony in consecrated ground." In another nod to the increasing silliness of religion, Theo recalls that "one of the minor ecclesiastical disputes of the early 2000s [was] whether churches could legitimately be used for these charades and even whether ordained priests could take part." Though the fad has passed, there are still holdouts. In one of the novel's more haunting moments, Theo sees a woman pushing a stroller with a doll "propped up against the cushions, the two arms, hands mittened, resting on the quilted coverlet, a parody of child-hood, at once pathetic and sinister." Another woman approaches and peers inside as if to admire the doll before seizing it from the stroller and bashing it against a wall. The pseudo-mother is inconsolable.[25] There's a sharp irony to the scene, as the desperate woman, never to have a child, is driven to an act of despair that makes her act like one by caring for a doll and throwing a tantrum when it breaks.

The same instinct that drives women to treat dolls like babies also has them use pets as proxies. Among the weird new rituals of the Omega age is holding birthing parties for pets, which Theo describes as "an obligation, the opportunity to let your friends witness the miracle of emerging life," featuring a celebratory meal and some champagne. For couples, this ritual is a way to "celebrate and consolidate their new life together."[26] Naturally, the government tightly regulates the reproduction of pets, demanding that domestic animals are sterilized after they give birth, restricting how many kittens can be kept, and requiring sterilization of the mother.

The displacement of paternal care with pet-ernal affection is one of the most troubling elements of the novel because it is one of the most familiar. In 2013, the sometime conservative journalist Jonathan V. Last traced the increasing presence of cats and dogs in the lives of Americans, even as these parents are raising (and the pets are playing with) fewer children. "In surveys from 1947 to 1985," Last reported, "fewer than half of Americans reported that they owned a pet. Today American pets outnumber American children by more than four to one."[27] What's more, the average pet owner spends more and more money on medical care, grooming, and even insurance policies for pets. America, Japan, and Italy were experiencing "pet booms"; and "in all three countries, educated, middle-class people have all but stopped having babies. Pets have become fuzzy, low-maintenance replacements for children."[28] The boom has continued since Last published his book more than a decade ago: 66 percent of American households include a pet, and according to the American Pet Products Association, Americans spent an estimated $150.6 billion on pets in 2024, an increase of 60 percent since 2018.[29] This trend has even changed how we refer to our animals. We're no longer cat or dog owners; we're pet parents or dog moms. There's even something called National Pet Parents Day (April 30, for those who celebrate).

The difference between our current condition and what James depicts is important. In the English dystopia of the novel, sterility is not a choice; childlessness is a plague. In the real world, childlessness is a priority. As the journalist and author Timothy P. Carney observes, some time ago "sterility became the central organizing principle of adulthood"[30] Of course, we are not seeing a dystopia on a Jamesian scale because what we're experiencing is neither sudden nor absolute. There are many reasons behind the worldwide demographic decline, from economic pressure to despair to plain old selfishness. It's easy to wonder, though, just how much thought goes into the choice when, according to a 2024 Pew Research study, the most common reason adults ages eighteen to forty-nine gave for being unlikely to have children was "they just don't/didn't want to" (57 percent of respondents).[31] Regardless, the consequences will be serious. Perhaps the despair and sadness of this novel's childless world can remind us of just how invigorating and beautiful (and I know, exhausting, too) new life is.

Death without Children

As James works through the consequences of a world without new human life, she reminds us that it has consequences for human death. This is an interesting twist in the novel's premise: in a world without new life, old life somehow has less value, too. In James's dystopia, the Warden of England uses a program called Quietus to organizes mass suicide rituals for older citizens. The government makes it seem attractive by offering generous payments to the families of the deceased. It also runs sepia-hued propaganda. Theo describes one television commercial with "white-clad elderly being wheeled or helped on to the low barge-like ship, the high, reedy singing voices, the boat slowly pulling away into the twilight, a seductively peaceful scene, cunningly shot and lit."[32]

It becomes clear, though, that the mass suicides aren't quite as voluntary as the government would have them seem. When one of Theo's former colleagues tells him that his aging wife has expressed interest in Quietus, Theo gets the sense that this is more a matter of the husband's desire: "I can imagine what [she] would have thought of such a public exhibition of sacrifice and emotion."[33] Theo's suspicions prove true. On a trip to an abandoned seaside town to witness a Quietus ceremony, he watches a bizarre, pseudo-wedding procession: a group of women in white carry flowers as they walk onto boats, singing hymns. They have clearly been drugged, and they wear weights around their ankles to sink them into the water. Theo is shocked to see among the group his old friend's wife, who struggles to free herself. Underscoring the indignity of the ritual, a wave knocks off her nightdress, exposing her to the small group of onlookers. A guard intervenes, hitting her with a pistol. When Theo tries to intervene, he too is beaten. A guard advises, "Let it be, sir. Let it be."[34]

The Quietus subplot is alarmingly prescient. Consider Canada. (I know, I don't like doing that either, but let's just this once.) In 2016, the Great White North legalized medically assisted suicide and euthanasia through a program with the gruesome acronym of MAID. Six years later (and a year after *The Children of Men* novel is set), a Canadian fashion retailer released what Ross Douthat describes as a "three-minute . . . moody, watery, mystical tribute" to the "holiness of euthanasia," glorifying a thirty-seven-year-old woman's decision to be killed by medical professionals.[35] Columnist David Brooks reports that in 2021, "more than 10,000" Canadians died by physician-assisted suicide, accounting for "one in 30 of all Canadian deaths."[36] That number jumped to 15,343 people in 2023.[37] The program is also remarkably lax. Not only are very few applicants for the program refused (only 915 out of 19,660 requests in 2023, or 4.6 percent), but Alexander Raikin has reported in the *New Atlantis* that authorities rarely investigate possible abuses of the program.[38] Although Canadian law limits the MAID program to patients who have a terminal illness or are experiencing extreme pain, the Associated Press reports instances in which "people were euthanized based on other factors including an 'unmet social need.'"[39] And in James's own England in 2024, the House of Commons paved the way for a law that would allow certain terminally ill adults to get help killing themselves from the state.[40] These programs lack the ritualism of Quietus, but they illustrate how Western nations are walking themselves off the barge and into the ocean.

If there's one thing to be said for the husband (named Jasper) who takes advantage of his wife's declining senses to send her off to a ritual suicide, it's that at least he practices what he preaches by killing himself. His suicide note is in Latin:

> *Quid te exempta iuvat spinis de pluribus una?*
> *Vivere si recte nescis, decde peritis.*

Lusisti satis, edisti satis atque bibisti:
Tempus abire tibi est.

Theo explains that this passage from Horace "says that there's no pleasure in getting rid of one thorn among so many. If you can't live well, get out. He probably found the Latin in the *Oxford Dictionary of Quotations*."[41] Jasper's quotation is indeed included in that reference book, and Theo's gloss corresponds to the one offered there.[42] But it's worth noting that this particular selection of Horace omits some context relevant to the novel. For one thing, the "one thorn" in this passage seems to imply a person, suggesting that Jasper regretted sending his wife off to Quietus, so he decides to join her. But in fact, Horace is referring to the amendment of a vice—that is, he's asking what good it is getting rid of one vice or thorn when there are so many left? What's more, the last lines should read, "*tempus abire tibi est, no potum largius aequo / rideat et pulset lasciva decentius aetas*"—or, as the Loeb Classical Library edition of Horace's *Epistles* translates it, "Tis time to quit the feast, lest, when you have drunk too freely, youth mock and jostle you, playing the wanton with better grace."[43] The irony in the context of James's novel is that there is no youth to force Jasper out of the feast.

"The Carefully Measured Meed of Power"

The Quietus subplot, and the government control that is behind the mass assisted-suicide ceremonies, connects to the novel's broader depiction of the nature and allure of political of power. The dangerous thirst for power is most clearly demonstrated by Theo's cousin Xan, the Warden of England. Xan's initial goals are modest, but he ascends at a time when the people are not jealous of their own power. The country is "sunk in apathy," which annihilates any ambition or enterprise: "with no one wanting to work, services almost at a stop, crime uncontrollable, all hope and ambition lost forever, England had been a ripe plum for [Xan's] picking."[44] Consequently, over the course of the crisis, Xan and his council absorb power for themselves. That means the king has been diminished, falling from "the potent symbol of continuity and tradition" to "an unemployable archaic reminder of what we have lost." Parliament meets only once a year for one month, but it doesn't pass laws or debate bills—it functions only to advise and recommend action to the five-person Council of England.

According to Theo, this system works because it "has the merit of simplicity and gives the illusion of democracy to people who no longer have the energy to care how or by whom they are governed as long as they get what the Warden has promised: freedom from fear, freedom from want, freedom from boredom."[45] Theo explains elsewhere that the people only want "security, comfort, pleasure," a regime that "combines perpetual surveillance with total indulgence," and Xan provides that.[46] James Bowman is on to something when he contends that "the central insight of the novel is that all ideas of social improvement and reform, all justice, hope, and love depend on the existence of future generations for whose sake all the good that we do is ultimately done." If we lose children, "we also lose the ability to care about anything but our own comfort and safety."[47]

Xan expands his power in part because he understands so well what the dispirited and unenterprising people crave. He also knows that they want a show of power. When Theo meets his cousin for the first time in years, he's surprised to see him wearing "the Coronation Ring, the wedding ring of England, the great sapphire surrounded with diamonds and surmounted with a cross of rubies." This seems out of character for Xan, as if he once understood power in a different, more humble way. But Xan explains that "the people need their baubles"—they want regality, some symbol of authority. This is in keeping with his sense of how to marshal his power, which also includes knowing "the wisdom of giving people a choice in matters where choice was unimportant."[48] A population facing its immanent and apparently unavoidable end sees no need to work or to govern itself. The desire for self-governance is supplanted by the desire to be ruled by a figure who displays his power. Xan is happy to oblige.

This thirst for power isn't limited to the heights of government. An inspector who questions Theo has it, too:

> I thought I understood his kind: the petty bureaucrats of tyranny, men who relish the carefully measured meed of power permitted to them, who need to walk in the aura of manufactured fear, to know that the fear precedes them as they enter a room and will linger like a smell after they have left, but who have neither the sadism nor the courage for the ultimate cruelty. But they need their part of the action. It isn't enough for them, as it is for most of us, to stand a little way off to watch the crosses on the hill.[49]

Such tyrants thrive where people have abandoned interest in self-rule. Yet it's also clear that not only the villains are power hungry; even the otherwise virtuous can be tempted to tyranny. In a conversation with a member of the Five Fishes, Theo is struck by how much the rebel sounds like Xan and observes, "So you're proposing to replace one dictatorship with another. Benevolent this time, I suppose. Most tyrants begin that way."[50] Even Theo himself is similarly tempted. After threatening an elderly couple in an effort to help the Five Fishes, he admits that he "enjoyed the excitement, the power, the knowledge that I could do it. It wasn't all horrible. It was for them, but not for me."[51] As we'll see, Theo is tempted further at the novel's conclusion.

Religion at the End of the World

As bleak as this novel's world may be, there is a bright thread of hope running through it. "The novel was not intended to be a Christian fable," James said, "but that, in fact, was what I wrote. . . . [It] has produced more correspondence and more controversy, particularly in theological circles, than any other novel I have written."[52] Christian overtones are clear from the names of the cousins, Theo (enough said) and Xan, which as an abbreviation reminds us of the Christian heritage of the country he governs. Despite their names, however, neither character is particularly religious, and many of the religious figures in the novel deviate from any orthodox Christianity. At the time of the novel, a popular religious movement is sweeping the land, led by an American evangelist named Rosie McClure, "the latest and most successful of the television performers who sell salvation and do very well out of a commodity which is always in demand."[53] According to what Theo calls "her brand of religious hedonism . . . God is love and everything is justified by love." Instead of hymns, she's "resurrected an old pop song of the Beatles, a group of young Liverpool boys in the 1960s, 'All You Need Is Love,' and it is this repetitive jingle, not a hymn, which precedes her rallies." (Theo's belief that he needs to explain who the Beatles were is yet another sign of societal collapse.) It's an empty and immature faith that has no sense of evil or sense of eternity beyond the comforts of the present world.

The impending doom of religion figures prominently in a pair of powerful scenes. In one of the novel's most poignant moments, Theo is in a chapel when a fawn from a nearby meadow makes its way into the sacred building and stands "beside the altar as if it were its natural habitat." The chaplain has to shoo the animal away by "hurling prayer books, thumping its silken sides." To a race not facing its prolonged decline, this moment may have been one of remarkable beauty and even spiritual intensity, an occasion to reflect on God's presence in the natural world, or the natural world's reflection of God's grace and power. It might even recall the words of Saint Francis, as conveyed in the hymn by William Henry Draper: "Let all things their creator bless, / And worship Him in humbleness, / O praise Him! Alleluia!" In the context of Omega, however, its meaning is much more sinister, and the chaplain asks, either in prayer or profanity: "Christ, why can't they wait? Bloody animals. They'll have it all soon enough. Why can't they wait?"[54] This cry of frustration and resignation conveys what Mark Steyn calls "an image of utter civilizational ruin—of faith, knowledge, art and beauty, all lost to the beasts and the jungle."[55]

James excels at creating images with powerful symbolic implications—and another one of these is also set in a church. At the beginning of the novel's second part, Theo describes visiting St. Peter's in Rome and seeing Michelangelo's *Pietà*, the masterpiece sculpture depicting the Virgin Mary holding Christ after the crucifixion. He recalls women looking at it longingly, "the low continual mutter of their prayers as if this ceaseless anguished moan came from a single throat and carried to that unregarding marble the hopeless longing of all the world."[56] It's an especially moving image for the many dooms it represents: of Christianity, of art, of motherhood. The women seem desperate not only for the salvation through Christ that the sculpture anticipates, but also for the incomparable love of motherhood—including even the pain and loss it may entail.

Yet a more orthodox Christianity endures. Two of the Five Fishes are practicing Anglicans: Theo's main contact in the group, Julian, is a convert and another member is an Anglican priest. Luke becomes a Christ figure as the novel develops, and Julian an emblem of the Virgin Mary—but that description oversimplifies the novel's complexities. For all of his many faults, Xan is right when he warns Theo, "Don't romanticize her. She may be the most important woman in the world but she isn't the Virgin Mary."[57] This emerging Christianity corresponds with a conversion of Theo's personality, as he begins to demonstrate compassion and sympathy that had been foreign to him before. When he temporarily severs ties with the Five Fishes, for example, "he felt for the first time an extraordinary loneliness. It wasn't an emotion with which he was familiar. He both distrusted and resented it. Looking down over the empty street, he wished for the first time there was someone, a friend he could trust, in whom he could confide." [58] At the end of the first book, he acknowledges in his journal that "I am fifty years old and have never known what it is to love."[59]

This growth continues in the second half of the novel. Indeed, the novel takes a sharp turn with the development of a new hope: a character becomes pregnant. This inspires Theo to aid the Five Fishes' mission and finally develop a sense of community. In his last journal entry, he confides: "I have never felt so much at ease with other human beings as I have been today with these four strangers to whom I am now, still half-reluctantly, committed and one of whom I am learning to love." In a gesture that signifies his new self, he explains that he hasn't read earlier entries in the journal because of his aversion to his "self-regarding, sardonic and solitary" previous self.[60] The tranquility doesn't last, but Theo's maturation does. The novel's final image is undeniably a hopeful one, alluding to the Holy Family and a new Adam—not a savior, but a rebirth of humanity. Yet the temptation of power which we saw above still lurks. Theo gains possession of the Coronation Ring, slips it on, and begins to imagine how "the world could be fashioned according to his will."[61] The ending reminds us that the survival of humanity also means the endurance of all the virtues and vices of human nature.

James's novel is more than a nightmarish vision of a sterile species facing extinction. It's a consideration of how important children are to how our society functions, how they provide hope and comfort, how they shape what we expect from ourselves and our government. Let's turn now to a novel that is loud with the voices of children.[62]

Chapter Twelve

Miraculous Storytelling and Virtuous Masculinity— Leif Enger, *Peace Like a River* (2001)

I n its review of *Peace Like a River*, the *New York Times* called Leif Enger's debut novel an "unabashed throwback."[1] Although it may have been meant to damn with faint praise, there is truth to the statement, and I suspect this throwback appeal is one reason the book found an audience. Its date of publication was inauspicious: September 11, 2001. The terrorist attacks of that day and the mourning that followed made it difficult to publicize or promote new works of literature and music. But perhaps the tragedy also made readers more open to a book like Enger's. Was the American public especially receptive to religious faith then? Church attendance spiked briefly, suggesting so—as does the success of films like 2002's *Signs* and even 2004's *The Passion of the Christ*. Did our tastes incline toward the nostalgic? Some of the most popular music after the attack was the retro jazz of Norah Jones at a time when "comfort music [was] what record shoppers seem[ed] to be looking for."[2] In early 2002, George F. Will (citing the theater and music critic Terry Teachout) noted that the success of jazz chanteuse Diana Krall, who specialized in recording old standards, suggested a public yearning for traditional forms and familiar arts. "To the lingering 1960s sensibility, formality, decorousness and etiquette seemed authoritarian," wrote Will. "Since Sept. 11 they seem respectful and reassuring."[3]

What makes *Peace Like a River* such a "throwback" is, in large part, its embrace of classic American genres and traditions. As the critic Ron Charles observed in his glowing review of the novel, "Enger has written a novel that's boldly romantic and unabashedly appealing, a collage of legends from sources sacred and profane—from the Old Testament to the Old West, from the Gospels to police dramas."[4] It is the story of a remarkable and tragic year of the Land family from Roofing, Minnesota. The father, Jeremiah, is a janitor at the public school, but he could have been much more. He gave up training for a career in medicine after a life-altering experience: he's picked up by a tornado but somehow escapes unscathed, returned to earth four miles from where he left it. Like Nicholas Farringdon's encounters with evil in Muriel Spark's *The Girls of Slender Means*, Jeremiah's journey in the tornado inspires him to change his life's direction. His previous lofty goals no longer seem to matter. He gives up a career in medicine, "baptized into a life of new ambitions."[5] His wife didn't appreciate his change of careers, which is why he's raising their three children alone when the novel begins. The story is narrated by Jeremiah's second child, an eleven-year-old named Reuben who suffers from terrible asthma but possesses great faith. The two traits are closely related. He believes his very life to be a miracle because he wasn't breathing when he was first born, and it took his father's remarkable intervention to keep him alive. He still experiences frequent asthmatic bouts that require an elaborate and primitive prescription of steam and firm back-slapping. His precocious kid sister, the nine-year-old Swede, is a master storyteller who regales her family with a ballad-in-progress about a cowboy named Sunny Sundown and a charismatic villain named Valdez. Their older brother, Davy, is a rebellious high schooler and, for much of the novel, a fugitive.

The novel begins during a family hunting trip. (That hunting is not presented as the senseless slaughter of innocent animals but good clean fun for the entire family is reason alone to include this novel on a list of books for conservatives.) We learn that Jeremiah recently had an encounter with a couple of local thugs as they attempted to rape a girl—Davy's girlfriend, in fact—in the locker room. The thugs—the memorably named Israel Finch and Tommy Basca—vow revenge, and they get it bit by bit: first by vandalizing the Land home, then by abducting Swede for a joyride, leaving her shaken and bruised, and finally by breaking into the Land residence one night— where Davy shoots them both. Davy stands trial for his crime, but too rebellious to sit around and wait for the jury's verdict, he escapes from prison.

The rest of the Land family leaves Minnesota in search of the fugitive son and makes their way to the Badlands of North Dakota. It becomes a race to see who can find Davy first: the Lands or the feds. Along the way, the family stays at the home of a woman who fills the void created by the departure of Jeremiah's wife. But Davy finds them first and, unbeknownst to the others, brings Reuben to his hideout: the ramshackle home of an off-putting visionary and a young girl he's grooming to be his wife. I won't spoil the ending by saying whether the rest of the family or the law or anyone catches up with Davy. I can say that the quest to bring him home ends in mixed results, including the violent death of one of the Lands.

Do You Believe in Miracles?

If this sounds like a fairly conventional, if action-packed, story so far, that's only because I've withheld a fairly significant detail, which is that Reuben believes that his father can work miracles. His very existence is proof of that: he wouldn't have survived his birth if his father hadn't knocked the doctor out of the way "and said in a normal voice, 'Reuben Land, in the name of the living God I am telling you to breathe.'"[6] Reuben swears that he once saw his father walk on air and is convinced that he also worked a version of the miracle of the loaves, only with a bowl of soup. He mends a cracked saddle with his touch alone and, in an act that also demonstrates his ability to forgive others, heals his boss's pock-marked face right after being fired. Those acts are in addition to Jeremiah surviving that close encounter with the tornado. You've heard the expression *to reap the whirlwind*? Well, the whirlwind reaped Jeremiah—but then it safely placed him back to the earth.

Whenever Reuben relates these miracles, he acknowledges that this isn't how people experience the world, that most readers simply will not believe that a janitor could be capable of suspending the laws of nature, and he leaves it to us to draw our own conclusions. He doesn't badger the reader into his faith; he only testifies to what he has witnessed. His refrain is "Make of it what you will." He understands that most readers will instinctively side with the eighteenth-century philosopher David Hume's contention that "a miracle is a violation of the laws of nature; and as a firm and unalterable experience has established these laws, the proof against a miracle, from the very nature of the fact, is as entire as any argument from experience can possibly be imagined."[7] The literary scholar Harold K. Bush surmises that Reuben "recognizes the general skepticism of most of his audience. In essence, rather than boasting, he is restrained in his selective manner of describing, piece by piece in a post-Enlightenment world, these episodes he is calling miracles." Toward the end of the novel Reuben acknowledges that he has doubts, but Bush rightly surmises that these "strengthen our willingness to trust Reuben, and are fully in keeping with the cross-pressured secular age of our current era."[8]

Reuben distinguishes these remarkable events with the looser definition of a miracle, "things or events that, though pleasant, are entirely normal. Peeping chicks at Easter time, spring generally, a clear sunrise after an overcast week." He's talking about "real miracles," extraordinary events that defy rational or scientific explanations and "bother people, like strange sudden pains unknown in medical literature. It's true: they rebut every rule all we good citizens take comfort in. . . . People fear miracles because they fear being changed—though ignoring them will change you also."[9]

This manner of weaving the miraculous into the everyday connects Enger's novel to the genre known as magical realism. This genre grew out of Latin American literature during the 1960s and 70s, assuming worldwide prestige thanks to the influence of novelists like Gabriel García Márquez (*One Hundred Years of Solitude*) and Isabel Allende (*The House of the Spirits*). Great works of magical realism by Anglophone authors include Toni Morrison's *Beloved* and Salman Rushdie's *Midnight's Children*. What these novels have in common is the fusion of what one scholar calls "two autonomous codes, realism and the fantastic, but, when combined, the presence of magic within realism seems organic."[10] Magical or fantastic events are depicted as if they are part of the everyday, not part of a different reality or science-fictional world of the future or fantasy world of the past.

Magical realism tends to relate to mythology, paganism, local religions, or fantasy. For example, Mark Helprin's *Winter's Tale* features a magical horse, time travel, enormous seafaring vessels, and fantastical landscapes—as well as gritty descriptions of urban life, gang violence, abject poverty, and mortal illness.[11] Enger's application of Christian belief to this tradition, his miraculous realism, is remarkable. Literary scholar Kim Anderson Sasser argues that the novel puts "readers through the perspective of someone whose experiences compare to many Christians across the world in their belief in prayer as communion with God, in God's ability to heal and in the afterlife." It is not "a description of the belief from the outside, as in a work of realism or a religious studies textbook or encyclopædia."[12] In other words, the novel uses magical realism to treat the most radical elements of religious belief seriously.

The book raises fundamental questions for religious believers by asking them to consider, given their belief in the existence of an omnipotent God who can suspend the laws of nature, how they would react if they witnessed what Reuben had—or, more basically, whether they would believe Reuben's testimony themselves. For Jeremiah, there is no doubt. His experience with the tornado secures his faith, and he changes his life accordingly. He maintains that faith as Finch and Basca seek their revenge, telling Reuben why he doesn't fear them: "What these fellows don't realize is, we've already won. The victory is ours."[13] This faith inspires the family to hit the road in search of Davy. As Reuben explains, "Faith brought this about. Faith, as Dad saw it . . . would direct our travels."[14] All of this strikes Reuben as entirely reasonable:

> How could we *not* believe the Lord would guide us? How could we not have faith? For the foundation had been laid in prayer and sorrow. Since that fearful night, Dad had responded with the almost impossible work of belief. He had burned with repentance as though his own hand had fired the gun. He had laid up prayer as if with a trowel. You know this is true, and if you don't it is I the witness who am to blame.[15]

Even apart from miracles, though, Reuben believes in events that are "certainly the work of the Lord—the work of providence, for you timid ones."[16] And at the time of narration, long after the setting of the novel, he "breathe[s] deeply, and certainty enters into me like light, like a piece of science."[17] That's a wonderful image of faith: penetrating and undoubtable, even compared to the scientific knowledge that is often understood as its opposite.

After the family manages to navigate through small towns unnoticed by the many police patrols searching for them, Reuben and Swede struggle to find the right Old Testament analogue for their father. Was he like Moses, forging between a parted sea? Perhaps that was too much, but bigger than Malachi and Obadiah, whose works Reuben can't even remember. The exercise worries Reuben: "But I was troubled. How could we place Dad, or any other living person, among these Old Testament gentlemen? These prophets who'd got up every day and heard from the Lord, regular as setting your table? These who'd struck water from dry rocks?"[18]

For her part, Swede is troubled by the randomness of the miracles. She wonders, if they can somehow manage to escape notice (an especially remarkable feat when you consider that they're driving a car with an Airstream trailer hitched to it), why did they have to worry about filling their tank with gas? Wasn't that something a miracle-worker could sort out? She's not a witness to many of the miracles that her brother sees, but his account of Jeremiah's work on the saddle "was a clincher of sorts for Swede."[19] What's most remarkable about this miracle for most people, Reuben explains, isn't that it was performed, but that Swede had never noticed it, even though she'd sat on the saddle often since her father mended it. Reuben acknowledges, "Odd on the face of it, I know—I know. But we're fearful people, the best of us. We see a newborn moth unwrapping itself and announce, Look, children, a miracle! But let an irreversible wound be knit back to seamlessness? We won't even see it, though we look at it every day."[20] Yet later in the novel, when Jeremiah finds an old, valuable, but unusable guitar at a shop, he works to repair it rather than simply mend it with his touch. What is the logic to his work? Reuben even worries at one point because Jeremiah has gone many days without performing a miracle of any sort.

Davy's an even harder case in this regard—or as Reuben puts it, "Belief is a hard thing to gauge where Davy is concerned."[21] He rebels against his father not only because he believes Jeremiah is too gentle with Finch and Basca, but because he resents the idea of not having control over his destiny. During a conversation with his attorney, Davy bristles at the idea that he wasn't in complete control when he made the conscious decision to shoot the other boys:

> He was not forced, he told Mr. DeCuellar; if he hadn't wanted to shoot those fellows, he wouldn't have done it. To say otherwise suggested that he, Davy, was not in control of his actions. Mr. DeCuellar suggested we are all forced at times; we are none of us wholly our own masters; otherwise, why couldn't Davy simply leave his cell, walk out a free man? And Davy, who could be contrary, replied, Well, maybe I will.[22]

As if to prove his point, Davy indeed escapes from prison—and, to underscore his independence, he does so even as his siblings plan to break him out. We'll return to this aspect of Davy's character soon.

Let Me Tell You a Story

Although there is plenty of death and tragedy in the book, its tone is always warm and inviting. A major factor in this tone is that the book conveys what one early review calls an "old-time joy in storytelling," which is especially evident in Swede's poem-in-progress about Sunny

Sundown and Valdez.[23] "I have noticed that people who love the whole wide parade will just wing off into verse at any chance," Reuben observes. "Swede did it constantly."[24] We encounter passages of her immature but irresistible story through Rueben's transfixed perspective:

> Now Sundown's wound is seeping and he's tilting as he rides;
> His eyes are red and gritty as he scans the canyon's sides.
> He hadn't known the nature of the man whose track he sought,
> And it sickened him to death to see the things Valdez had wrought.[25]

Swede's poetic interludes are light fun in their own right, but as the novel develops, it becomes clear that they are also reflections or retellings of the Land family's experiences.

Swede's poems capture Reuben's attention and imagination; he is her rapt audience. He has also learned from her story-telling skills. Reuben loves addressing the reader directly, as if he's with you at a campfire. "But how could you wake a man knocked cold by love?" he asks us directly.[26] When he tells us that he "waded ashore with measureless relief," he senses our skepticism and adds, "Stay with me now."[27] Approaching a dramatic turn of events, Reuben warns: "Honestly, I hate to even tell you this part. Who wants to hear a story that's nothing but misfortune?"[28] To establish a setting, he asks out of the blue: "Anyway, have you ever been to North Dakota? In good sunlight you can see someone coming eight miles away."[29] It's an informal, friendly approach to storytelling, one that's miles away from the style and tone of Cormac McCarthy (and perhaps more like the work of another favorite of conservatives, Wendell Berry). It could easily slide into corniness, but Enger uses it judiciously enough to avoid that pitfall.

There's another storyteller in the novel: its most sinister villain, Jape Waltzer. A weird visionary, Waltzer looks to the stars and sees constellations that tell what Reuben calls "turned legends," like the one about the boy who murdered his father and became a cannibalistic pirate. When a brave captain slays the terrible savage, he "looked in his polished brass mirror . . . [and] saw not his own face but the pirate's, and the nastiest grin all over it."[30] It's a story about the futility of heroism, the inevitable triumph of evil. Waltzer, like Swede, like anyone, is the stories he tells.

Any parent who's ever read to a child—or, for that matter, anyone who had a parent read to him or her—will appreciate that Enger's use of this storytelling motif probably stems from his own love for reading stories to his children and his memories of his parents reading to him. Before *Peace Like a River*, he had co-written with his brother a series of mystery novels that did not sell particularly well. Enger explains that their failure to reach a wide audience liberated his writing: "I figured since I had given commercial writing my best shot, I was free to just write something that I could read to my wife and kids. When I finished a scene I would gather them around and read it to them, and if it didn't make them laugh or if it didn't provoke some strong reaction, I knew I had to go back to the drawing board." Swede in particular was inspired by Enger's own childhood: "I grew up being read to from [the Canadian poet] Robert Service, who wrote . . . 'The Ballad of Dan McGrew,' 'The Ballad of Blasphemous Bill' and 'The Ballad of the Iceworm Cocktail.' And then there is Robert Louis Stevenson. Mom read us *Treasure Island* every year for many years, starting before I was old enough to understand any of it."[31] The story's very style is the outgrowth of generations sharing stories.

Wanted: Dead or Alive

Closely related to the novel's participation in the tradition of oral storytelling is its connection to the genre of the western. There's something about westerns that makes them especially (though not exclusively) open to expressions of conservatism. The late literary and cultural scholar Paul Cantor explained its appeal nicely:

> In the American imagination, the Western frontier has always been the place to which people go to achieve free-dom and escape the shackles of society. Accordingly, the Western as a genre has traditionally been associated with the American spirit of rugged individualism. The Western hero is typically a loner, standing apart from the crowd, sometimes because of something shady in his past, sometimes because of his peculiar sense of mission, sometimes just because of his heroic virtue itself.[32]

Or as Cantor put it elsewhere, "The Western is the prime example of American popular culture as thought experiment, a test of the nature and value of law and order."[33] One of the most popular modern novelists among conservatives is Cormac McCarthy, himself a master of the literary western in such novels as *Blood Meridian* and *The Border Trilogy* (*All the Pretty Horses*, *The Crossing*, and *Cities of the Plain*), as well as modern adaptations of the form like *No Country for Old Men* and the post-apocalyptic pseudo-zombie book *The Road*. Conservatives are also drawn to these novels in part because McCarthy depicts the fallenness of man and the brutality of human nature. "There is a distinct moral core in McCarthy's best-known fiction," writes author and professor Alexander Riley, "and that core can be identified as conservative and ultimately Christian."[34]

Enger is up to something similar in *Peace Like a River*, but in a manner that is more explicitly Christian and redemptive. There's the likeable outlaw figure of Davy, for one thing, and Waltzer's hideout in the mountains. There are searches for bandits by horseback, shoot-outs, ambushes. There aren't any Indians (or, to use a term John Wayne never did, Native Americans), but there are plenty of ornery and inef-fectual lawmen. It's not just the characters and conventions, though—it's also the issues the novel explores that makes it very much a west-ern. Foremost among those is the question of what it means to be a man. The tension between Jeremiah and Davy, together with the behavior of the villain Waltzer, offer provocative demonstrations of masculine behavior and traits that are especially helpful at a time when masculinity is often viewed with suspicion and derision. The term "toxic masculinity" has become so common over the past decade that the modifier is hardly necessary since any discussion of manliness tends to look at it negatively or, at best, with a tongue firmly in cheek. Manliness is "easy to make fun of," the scholar Harvey Mansfield wrote twenty years ago. "That's particularly true today when the picture of manliness conveyed to us is as direct and unsubtle as the actor Russell Crowe in *Gladiator*, the singer Ted Nugent in *Cat Scratch Fever*, and the wrestler Jesse Ventura in *Governor of Minnesota*."[35] Mansfield's dated references demonstrate that this issue isn't new. Author Christina Hoff Sommers noted in 2000 that one sign it was "a bad time to be a boy in America" was that the definitive image for girls was the celebration of the U.S. Women's National Team winning the World Cup, while for boys it was the Columbine shooting. Sommers argued then that because "it has become fashionable to attribute pathology to millions of healthy male children," we have become blind to the truth that "the energy, competitiveness, and corporal daring of normal, decent males is responsible for much of what is right in the world."[36] More recently, Senator Josh Hawley has noted that men have been told "that to be a man is to be an oppressor; that to display the masculine traits of assertiveness, independence, and risk-taking is to make society unjust; that to work hard at a blue-collar job is a loser's game for those who can't learn to code."[37]

There's no doubt that masculinity can cause harm when misapplied or misunderstood; we saw that play out in the abysmal behavior of certain men in *Evelina*, for example. Mansfield identifies two important traits in manliness: independence and the "ability to command." The former "would keep him from getting involved with other people," while the latter implies an ability to take control of a situation by ordering people around. Mansfield looks to the ultimate western legend to illustrate what these traits entail:

> The typical John Wayne movie shows the conflict between manly independence and manly command, as the question is whether he will be trapped into marriage or some other responsible situation (*Stagecoach*) or remain aloof and wild in his independence (*The Searchers*).[38]

The tensions Mansfield identifies in masculinity are helpful for understanding a several characters in *Peace Like a River*.

The novel shows us the good and the bad of masculine behavior. The good is most clearly represented by Jeremiah, a warm and devoted father who takes seriously his role in his children's lives. In an inversion of stereotypes, it's his wife who abandons the family, leaving her husband to raise the children on his own. So intense is Jeremiah's sense of responsibility for his children that when Davy becomes a fugitive, Jeremiah takes the others with him to track him down; think the Parable of the Good Shepherd, but recast as a family road trip. In these ways, Jeremiah is a great emblem of responsible masculinity, of manly command, but there are independent streaks to him as well.

His initial decision to forsake a medical career shows masculine recklessness, so much so that you could argue that his wife had good reason to be upset at his sudden decision to change careers when they had hungry mouths to feed. (His decision to become a janitor, however, echoes Hawley's point about the dignity of blue-collar work.) There's also something reckless about his search for Davy—picking up and leaving town to find his son before the authorities do. Jeremiah's defining moment of masculinity may be when he rescues a young girl, Dolly, from Finch and Basca. In the girl's account of the episode, Jeremiah's face was "glowing and serene, the way you'd suppose an angel's would be," but he's the angel of vengeance as he beats them with a broom handle, "smiling (Dolly said) though his eyes looked terribly melancholy, whacking Finch and Basca every second or two while the pair of them shrieked in no English you'd recognize."[39] The violence is painful but also funny, even joyful—Dolly herself is laughing throughout—and certainly just, as it protects an innocent victim. Jeremiah wasn't seeking to punish the boys but to save Dolly and (as she believes) to "put the fear of God in 'em."[40]

Davy exhibits a much less disciplined masculinity. He resents the restraint his father exercised, believing "that no mere thrashing was sufficient punishment."[41] He doesn't seek justice and has no sense of mercy; he wants vengeance. When his father goes to the law instead of taking things into his hands, Davy demands, "How many times does a dog have to bite before you put him down?"[42] While his outrage and frustration over Finch and Basca are understandable, the more we (and Reuben) learn about his response, the less justified and more cold-blooded it seems. Like his father, Davy has a sense of duty toward others, but it is unmoored from both the law and basic morality. This is hard for Reuben to recognize because Davy's sense of responsibility applies to his siblings. But ultimately, he becomes the John Wayne of *The Searchers*: exiled, alone, wandering.

Even if Davy's independence is his downfall, he at least demonstrates some masculine virtues, whereas Waltzer has nothing to recommend him. His sense of responsibility is corrupt: where Jeremiah and Davy are inspired to act on their protective impulses by looking out for Dolly, Waltzer cares for a young girl whom he purchased with the intention of making his wife. Waltzer also has visions and prophecies that suggest an extreme form of independence. Consider his reaction when Reuben says grace before eating a meal Waltzer serves:

> "Are you praying over this meal I've provided?"
> "No, Mr. Waltzer." I'd forgotten to pray, though you may believe I felt like doing so now.
> "You are thanking God for the food," he said, "when He did not give it to you. I gave it to you. I gave it to you and did so freely. Thank *me*."[43]

If that doesn't establish Waltzer as the polar opposite of Jeremiah, consider his assertion to Reuben, "you can win the battle . . . but the war is lost long ago," a far cry from the father's assurance (quoted earlier) that "we've already won."[44] Waltzer's evil masculinity—we're talking mercury, asbestos, and hydrochloric acid-levels of toxicity here—is an extreme version of Davy's misplaced nobility. They share an aversion to conventional religious belief, but Waltzer's is more extreme. They share a propensity for armed ambushes against enemies, but Waltzer's is less justified.

There's one more character whose masculinity matters here, and that's Reuben. Reuben understands how different Davy is from himself:

> Davy wanted life to be something you did on your own;
> the whole idea of a protective, fatherly God annoyed him.

I would understand this better in years to come but never subscribe to it, for I was weak and I knew it. I hadn't the strength or the instincts of my immigrant forebears. The weak must bank on mercy—without which, after all, I wouldn't have lasted fifteen minutes.[45]

This passage captures Davy's independence and Reuben's weaknesses. As a physically weak boy with terrible asthma attacks, he simply cannot be as independent as his stronger older brother. Yet he assumes more physical masculinity as the book develops, the result of a combination of independence and reliance on others. He first grows in physical strength by rebuilding a barn in the dead of winter—and in the process becomes his family's breadwinner, his father having been fired—and then through a final intervention by Jeremiah in the novel's climactic scene. As if to confirm this emerging masculinity, Reuben has little luck with the ladies early in the novel, but by the end he's holding hands with his new sweetheart.

White Hat, Black Hat

The Western is also a great vehicle for exploring concepts of good and evil, sometimes in stark shades of black and white, sometimes in complex shades of gray. *Peace Like a River* gives the question of evil interesting treatment through Swede, Reuben's poetic little sister and arguably the best character in the novel. The villain of her epic western, the bandit king Valdez, is charismatic and attractive—he may do bad things, but he does them with style. But Swede's attitude toward this character changes when she has direct contact with evil in her own life, after Finch and Basca abduct her. Reuben explains her conversion:

What Swede knew was that seconds ago she'd been writing down rhymes to describe the bandit king Valdez, . . . growing a soft spot for the bad guy, like every other writer since Milton. Well, no more. The bitter taste of Israel Finch's palm, his unwashed smell, her own terror at the proximate unknown—all this took the sheen off villainy.[46]

As she continues to write the poem, Swede suffers a distinct brand of writer's block, becoming unable to give the central villain the send-off he deserves. She explains to Reuben that she struggled to imagine her hero defeating the villain, and makes him think "Valdez was no invention. That he was real and coming toward us on solid earth. A preposterous idea, wouldn't you say? Yet it blazed up, so scary in its brightness that I made a wall against it in my heart, in the deepest place I owned."[47] What Swede and Reuben fear is the enduring presence of an undefeatable evil. It is an entirely reasonable fear.

The manifestation of that fear is Waltzer. Though not as charming as Valdez, he is every bit as elusive. The novel's final pages make the parallel between Swede's character and Waltzer clear when Davy listens to her recitation of her ballad: "He was particularly attentive to her treatment of the bandit king Valdez, who he said was exactly right: savage, random, wolflike—and also probably uncatchable, right down through time."[48] Moments later, Waltzer emerges from hiding and attacks the family, killing one of them. Swede? Davy? Jeremiah? Jeremiah's new wife? Does Reuben tell his story from the grave? I'll never tell.

The Grateful Conservative

I want to end this chapter with a very brief discussion of a passing reference to an important conservative concept. Despite all of the tragedy and loss the characters experience, one of the last scenes is a moment of enormous gratitude. An appropriate image in the epilogue occurs at a Thanksgiving table—the first Thanksgiving after the aforementioned death of the family member I'm not naming—when the family "held hands round the table for a prayer of gratitude."[49] This is another American tradition, of course—something that most families do every year, right before they fall asleep watching the Lions game or head to the mall to join a stampede. The Land family has suffered extraordinary loss and tragedy, yet they still gather to give thanks for their gifts.

It is a very conservative moment. Author (and, full disclosure, my boss) Yuval Levin has said, "To my mind, conservatism is gratitude. Conservatives tend to begin from gratitude for what is good and what works in our society and then strive to build on it, while liberals tend to begin from outrage at what is bad and broken and seek to uproot it."[50] Similarly, Patrick M. Garry calls gratitude "the central pillar of conservative philosophy. . . . Prior to formulating any policy position or political message, the conservative must first recognize a deep gratitude for the fruits of the past. Those fruits are what present conservatives seek to protect and nourish."[51] Reuben's gratitude for his past and what it has given him is perhaps why Reuben is so ready to continue holding the hand of the person sitting beside him, a character I've only mentioned in passing but with whom he goes on to have his own family. Grateful for the miraculous fruits of his remarkable pasts, he builds.

Our next novel also revolves around a remarkable family, albeit one whose father is unable to perform miracles to help them through their many crises.

Chapter Thirteen

What Doesn't Show Up in the Box Score— Christopher Beha, *The Index of Self-Destructive Acts* (2020)

ne of the most quoted first sentences of a novel belongs to Leo Tolstoy's *Anna Karenina*: "All happy families are alike; each unhappy family is unhappy in its own way."[1] What makes this statement so compelling isn't that it's necessarily true— the Land family from *Peace Like a River* seems like a very happy family, but I can't imagine another like it—but that it gets to the heart of something about family dysfunction, which is that it's very entertaining, provided you're not actually involved in it.

In *The Index of Self-Destructive Acts*, Christopher Beha immerses readers in the unhappy ways of New York City's Doyle family circa 2009. Beha's third novel, and his most ambitious one to date, presents a broad view of the family's downfall, as well as the decline of the people around them. This novel grapples with some of the most consequential events of our century so far: the terror attacks of 9/11, the ensuing wars in Afghanistan and Iraq, and the financial collapse of 2008. Like many American families, the Doyle family was affected by all of these events; unlike most American families, the Doyle family played a role in them, too.

As is the case with the other novels we're exploring, *The Index of Self-Destructive Acts* addresses issues and concerns that may be of particular interest to conservative readers, and does so in a manner that demonstrates sympathy for, or understanding of, conservative principles and traditions. As the most recent of the novels, though, the world it depicts is the most like our own. The events it narrates and that shape the lives of its characters will still resonate for many readers, in large part because the Republican party and the conservative movement in the United States have been formed by them. The novel includes manifestations of what we now call cancel culture, considers the various sources of meaning and humanity in a turbulent world, and illustrates the temptations and opportunities offered by great wealth in a capitalist economy. At the same time, Beha's novel hints at the fissures that have developed in the conservative movement over the past fifteen years.

$$HB + WP + BK + E / (IP/9)$$

The novel's strange title refers to a tool created by the innovative baseball statistician Bill James to track a pitcher's capacity to be his own worst enemy. James defined the Index of Self-Destructive Acts as "the total number of hit batsmen, wild pitches, balks, and errors by a pitcher, per nine innings."[2] Beha uses the concept as a conceit for the poor decisions that characters make, often against their better judgment, undoing their lives and hurting the people they love. Or, as novelist Joshua Hren puts it, "this statistic becomes a guiding metaphor for a vast catalogue of characters who commit sins, decided aberrations that sink their self-interests."[3]

The family at the center of the novel is the Doyles, the four of whom are grappling with the consequences of their own—and each other's—self-destructive behavior. The father, Frank, had been a columnist for the nation's most important newspaper, the *New York Herald*, before a racist joke destroyed his career the autumn before the novel begins. He's also a die-hard Mets fan who wrote two books about baseball, the titles of which (*The Crack of the Bat* and *The Smell of the Grass*) hint at his romantic attitude about the sport. His old-fashioned love of baseball may call to mind Charles Krauthammer or George F. Will; his late-career support for the Iraq War and exile from the left, as well as his drinking, have shades of Christopher Hitchens.

Frank worked his way up from a hard-scrabble childhood; his wife, Kit, took over her father's successful investment firm and navigated it through different challenges before selling it. But the financial crisis of 2008 has imperiled her savings, and with Frank unemployed, her desperation to support her family leads her to commit insider trading. Meanwhile, her daughter Margo is taking time away from her graduate work in poetry at Yale after ending a romantic affair with her much older adviser. Margo's own index of self-destructive acts includes the kind of reply-all/staff-wide gaffe that terrifies anyone who's ever used email. Her brother, Eddie, is a recently discharged veteran of the Iraq War who, floundering without a sense of purpose in civilian life, is bamboozled by a street preacher who prophecies that the world will end on November 1, 2009. (Spoiler alert: it does not.)

Although the plot revolves around the Doyles, the first character we meet is Sam Waxworth, a twentysomething numbers wiz and blogger from Wisconsin who first gained attention by developing an algorithm that predicted baseball statistics, and then developed another algorithm that predicted, with stunning accuracy, the 2008 election. (Politicos and stat-heads will recognize the similarity between Waxworth and the real-life Nate Silver, who rose to prominence based on his success predicting the 2008 presidential elections.) Waxworth's pristine prognostications drew the attention of prominent editors, so he ventured from America's Dairyland to the City that Doesn't Sleep to start a data-driven blog for a prestigious journal. His first assignment: to write a profile about Frank Doyle, whom he intends "to bury . . . once and for all."[4] There are two more important non-Doyles: Sam's wife, Lucy, who eventually makes the trip from Madison to Manhattan, but only after Sam has started a fling with Margo Doyle; and Justin Price, a wealthy hedge-fund investor who received a scholarship funded by the Doyles for disadvantaged students and eventually became a close friend of Eddie's and a colleague of Kit's.

The novel's beautiful structure helps Beha, like a great center fielder, cover a lot of ground gracefully. "He knots everything and everyone together artfully and with increasing intensity," says novelist Randy Boyagoda.[5] Each of the novel's four sections spans two months between April and November 2009—roughly corresponding to the duration of the Major League Baseball season, and ending on the day that Eddie's prophet predicts the world will end. The narrator is third-person omniscient throughout, but the chapters alternate in perspective between its central characters. Like a super-sized version of *The Girls of Slender Means*, there are many chronological leaps back and forth, as well as a handful of poetic excerpts.

Beha bristles when reviewers and interviewers compare him to Tom Wolfe—"Wolfe has not influenced me at all," he once said.[6] But admirers of Wolfe's marvelous *The Bonfire of the Vanities* are likely to appreciate *The Index of Self-Destructive Acts*. Like Wolfe, Beha has a keen eye for contemporary mores and manners and isn't afraid to poke fun at his characters' follies. Both novels also feature breathtaking conclusions that bring together a disparate series of plotlines. One significant difference is that Beha's voice is more restrained and his pen is less poisonous—there's a touch of medicine at its tip, or at least he offers a spoonful of sugar as he applies it.

Numbers Don't Lie (but They Don't Tell the Whole Truth)

The novelist Adam O'Fallon Price rightly calls *The Index of Self-Destructive Acts* "a big, rich, complex novel of ideas" that showcases "a serious intellect working through not only a story but through the philosophical problems of our moment."[7] One of the most compelling ideas its characters keep coming back to is the question of the best intellectual framework for making sense of the world as it is, was, and will be. Some of the novel's best scenes revolve around conversations that Sam has with either Margo or Frank, high-minded and compelling discussions about human understanding.

The first such scene occurs when Sam goes to Opening Day at the new Mets ballpark with Frank to interview him for his profile. Despite their competing perspectives, the two men get along better than either had expected, and during a conversation about their different perspectives of the game (the kind of conversation that baseball fans have all the time), Frank complains that Sam's over-emphasis on obscure statistics "tak[es] all the beauty out of the game," while Sam complains that Frank's love of lore is irrelevant. He asks, "Why do we need to tell lies about the world in order to make it beautiful? What an impoverishing idea. The sky is beautiful as the sky. We don't need to pretend there's a God in His heaven up there."[8] Sam represents what Frank calls "the numerarchy," whose pernicious influence was destroying everything close to him:

It had long ago taken over his wife's world, the world of finance, convincing everyone that computer modeling could eliminate risk, an idea that had led to some of the most irrational behavior in human history and taken the whole economy down. It had half ruined the first love of his life—baseball—and now it had set its sights on the second—politics. These people were the enemy.[9]

Sam believes that everything can be quantified, boiled down to a numerical score, and evaluated objectively and rationally. His lack of patriotism doesn't help Frank's impression of him, either: as an American flag is unfurled and fighter jets roar overhead, Frank admires the celebration of honor and sacrifice while Sam asks, "What does it say about a great democracy that it has to insist upon itself this way? It's more appropriate for some tiny totalitarian outpost that spends its take from the state-owned mineral mine on parades and uniforms while the public starves."[10]

Sam again expresses his algorithmic, un-romantic way of thinking when he visits an art museum with Margo. I admit that one reason I love this scene is that the characters are admiring the work of one of my favorite artists (the Romantic-era landscape painter J.M.W. Turner) while discussing one of my favorite poems ("Lines Written a Few Miles above Tintern Abbey") by one of my favorite poets (William Wordsworth). After Margo recites a line from the poem, Sam insists that the world is "a lot more intelligible than people let on. Occasionally we don't like what it's saying to us, so we pretend that the messages are indecipherable." Margo, he assumes, "would have to insist on the mystery at the heart of everything."[11] She is, after all, more Wordsworth than Waxworth.

Later, Margo tells Sam about how her father taught her to read poetry, which influenced her own desire to become a poet. "I want my own words banging around in someone's head like that."[12] It's a powerful evocation of a writer's desire for immortality—to which

Sam, ever the downer, replies, "Committing stuff to memory seems sort of outdated. . . . Now you can just call it up on your phone any time you want." Poor Sam doesn't realize that recall and reference are different. One resides in the self, and the other is stored in the cloud. Nor, as Margo puts it, does he acknowledge that "innovations have costs. Nothing is got for nothing."[13]

Margo and Sam also spar over the concept of greatness—"there is no abstract quality called 'greatness,'" he insists—and consider the meaning of the search for meaning via baseball. Sam tells her:

> I love the game. . . . But what does baseball mean? The answer is: nothing. It's a game, a fun way to pass the time. To your father that isn't enough. Baseball can't just be enjoyable; it has to be *significant*. If baseball—or poetry, or whatever—gives you pleasure, that's great. It doesn't need to mean something on top of that.[14]

Notice how similar Sam's language here is to what he said to her father about the existence of God ("The sky is beautiful as the sky. We don't need to pretend there's a God in his Heaven up there"). Sam again emphasizes the primacy of "material conditions" and rejects the notion of "the world behind the world" that gives life meaning. "We are in a golden era of quantification," he tells Margo. "I'm sure there's plenty of stuff we're still not counting correctly, but the point is that everything that really exists *could* be counted. That's what it means for something to exist. Either it's there or it's not." He reduces love to "a practical decision to pair ourselves off in mutually beneficial ways, to reproduce our genes."[15] Swoon!

The critic and omnivorous reader John Wilson points out that although "there's monumental arrogance in [Sam's] outlook . . . there's also a genuine desire to know, to understand."[16] That desire is central to many other characters: to Margo and Frank, as we've seen. For Eddie Doyle, the false prophet offers a coherent view of the world, or at least its destruction. For Sam's wife, desperate to understand the mysterious illness she suffers, a psychic offers answers. Nonetheless, Sam's is an especially cold and reductive way of looking at the world. Clearly data is an important element in improving life—policy-makers, for example, must take empirical evidence into account when making decisions or considering legislation—but Sam reduces everything to quantification. *It can be counted, therefore it is.* As Margo tries to explain to him, this attitude fails to take love and other emotions into account, not to mention ethics and morality. But one of the first things we learn about Sam is that he focuses on "the factic-ity of things. The world, in Waxworth's view, was a knowable place, once you stripped away the dead tradition and wishful thinking built up over millennia of misunderstanding."[17] Here he's singing the same song as Miles Coverdale in *The Blithedale Romance*—though Sam would have no time for Miles's poetic sensibility. And not even Miles would agree with Sam's belief that ethics "was mostly a matter of reason. There was something irrational about evil, the very word slightly silly in its grandiosity."[18]

Algorithm Is Gonna Get You .

The conversations between Sam and the Doyles, in all of their rep-etitions and variations, are about more than just interesting ideas; in them, the characters explain their motives and express their per-sonalities. "Beha is excellent at establishing his characters as rep-resentatives of particular intellectual worldviews," writes one reviewer; "he doesn't have to pin them down because they keep trying to do it to one another."[19] This is a major reason that this book, despite its heftiness, moves so quickly. What Sam observes about Frank's daughter is true of many characters, including himself: "For Margo, ideas *were* personal."[20] And through these conversations, we understand that Sam believes that everything can be quantified, boiled down to a numerical score and evaluated objectively and rationally.[21]

But Sam's aspirations fall short; despite his faith in numbers, his systems are far from infallible. The first year of his baseball algorithm, Sam lost a competition to a competitor who had no system at all and simply guessed all of his predictions. Similarly, when Sam develops an algorithm to find the best possible apartment in New York, calculating distances, square feet per dollar, proximity to public transportation, quality of view, and hipness, he finds an apartment located above what he thought was a restaurant—only to discover that it is "a warehouse full of live, caged birds" that stinks to high heaven.[22] But his relationship with Margo is the most difficult test of his faith in the power of human rationality, as "none of it made any sense."[23] After some self-examination, flipping through his own personal index of self-destructive acts, Sam concludes that running up against his desire to quantify the world was the reality that irrationality is unavoidable, no matter how you counted the numbers, because "something in us *wanted* to be irrational. Something wanted, perhaps, to be wrong. We hated nothing more than indisputable evidence, because we wanted to dispute. . . . We had more and more information, which ought to make our decisions better, but all we did with this information was to find new ways to fuck up."[24] To put it terms of a sports cliché, there are some things that don't show up in the box score, things that cannot be precisely measured, yet still matter.

Beha has explained that one of the ideas he was trying to explore in the novel was "the extent to which we can even live according to a worldview in the first place. Sam has this idea that you can manage the risk of life by using cost-benefit analyses and game theory to work out all life's choices. Part of the point of the novel is that you can't actually outsource living your life to some algorithm." Frank's perspective, what Beha calls "the view of poetry, tragedy, and memory—does win. But maybe that's just me wanting it to." [25] Elsewhere, though, Beha has warned against overstating the superiority of Margo and Frank's perspective:

> If I'd thought that one of these characters was absolutely right and the other wrong, I would not have been interested in writing a novel about them. . . . There is something both appealing and repulsing in both views, which is what makes them novel material.[26]

Fair enough. Flip back to the chapter about *Waverley* to recall the dangers of excessively poetic visions. Margo and Frank won't be donning tartan and heading to the Highlands, but their own self-destructive acts demonstrate the shortcomings of their perspective. To name one: before his disgrace, Frank's last column had been a takedown of Sam's methods and why "those projections would be proven wrong." They were too remote, Frank believed: the "political statheads" could never know as much as people with actual contact with everyday Americans, who (Frank believed) would prefer stability over risk-taking and vote for John McCain, no matter what the polls said. But Sam was right and Frank was wrong.[27]

In the same interview quoted above, Beha offers a mild defense of what he calls the "mania for quantification" by suggesting that "its opposite is on its way down the road to the dismissal of experts."[28] Outright dismissal of experts is foolish; but this remark came in the summer of 2020, a time when many Americans were growing more skeptical of them. Sam's algorithmic approach to life has more adamant proponents in the real world. You can see it in progressive aspirations for a technocracy, a form of government run by experts and removed from democratic will. As columnist Megan McArdle puts it, the "danger in the technocratic class" is that, "funneled through an ever-expanding system in which they are paid to sit around and think about things, observe things, and write things, but never actually do things, our information mandarins are frequently totally disconnected from the people and processes they are supposed to rule."[29] Indeed, even his wife recognizes that Sam "seemed to distrust democracy itself, which treated every opinion, even the most uninformed, as equal." Experts, Sam believes, were better capable of "organizing a society" and discerning "right and wrong answers. . . . A sensible nation would put those people in charge and go about its business."[30] In addition to this un-democratic attitude, Waxworth's scorn for "the dead tradition and wishful thinking built up over millennia of misunderstanding" can also lead to an excessive detachment from the past and tradition, a belief that previous ways of knowing have nothing to teach us.[31] In a word, presentism.

There are absurd versions of this argument presented by convicted crypto-fraudster Sam Bankman-Fried (another quantitative Sam!) who posited that, based on simple numbers and Bayesian principles of probability (to which Sam Waxworth refers multiple times), it's impossible to believe that William Shakespeare is actually the greatest writer to have lived. "About half the people born since 1600 have been born in the past 100 years," he speculated, "but it gets much worse than that. When Shakespeare wrote almost all Europeans were busy farming, and very few people attended university; few people were even literate. By contrast there are now upwards of a billion literate people in the United States."[32] But Bankman-Fried commits the same fallacy as Waxworth, believing in the infallibility of numbers and odds and failing to consider the humanity, form, and substance of great art, reducing its production—and the combination of talent and culture required to create it—to game theory.

This is not suggest that contributions from stat-heads like Waxworth have not yielded remarkable benefits. They have. But as Artificial Intelligence continues to advance, it becomes more important to consider what distinguishes distinctively human thought from advanced computer models and formulas. We will need to articulate what it is precisely that elevates human thought and wisdom above the outputs of our marvelous technological feats. These debates will feature a conflict between Sam's hard-headed empiricism and the more humanistic counterweight provided by Frank and Margo Doyle. There's a helpful reminder of the dangers of Sam Waxworth's mindset—and of scientific hubris more generally—embedded in his last name: in Greek myth, Icarus's wax wings melted when the boy flew too close to the sun.

Self-Destruction and Cancel Culture

Like many great characters we've encountered, Frank Doyle is deeply flawed yet likable. A long-time liberal columnist, his support for the Iraq War even during its bleakest years made him a pariah and earned him a reputation as a *neocon*. A New Deal Democrat, he had always considered himself simply "a liberal" and senses that while he's been standing still, the ground beneath him has shifted: "Frank hadn't given up on his party. His party had given up on liberalism. They didn't even use the word anymore. They said instead that they were 'progressives,' as if any movement into the future was necessarily better than the status quo."[33]

Frank's support for the Iraq War damaged his reputation; a baseball game destroyed it. Frank's downfall occurs several months before the novel begins. After a few drinks at a Mets game, he's invited to join the broadcast booth for an impromptu interview. (Baseball fans will enjoy Beha's skillful mimicry of commentators Tim McCarver and Joe Buck.) When he's asked a question about presidential candidate Barack Obama, Frank cracks a couple of offensive jokes about Obama's background and race. Within minutes, his remarks have become the stuff of scandal and cancellation.[34]

Beha has said that this plotline was inspired by an episode that occurred in 2007, when political talk-show host (and former shock jock) Don Imus made a racist joke about a women's college basketball team.[35] Imus apologized for the remarks and was initially suspended by his networks. But after some of his show's most prominent advertisers withdrew their sponsorship and high-profile figures like Al Sharpton, Jesse Jackson, and then-Senator (and presidential candidate) Barack Obama spoke out, both shows were canceled. But Imus's career was far from over: he was back on the radio with a different network before the end of that year and back on cable television by late 2009. He remained on the air until his retirement in 2018.

Frank doesn't enjoy the same happy ending. What makes him vulnerable to cancelation is that his reputation had already taken a hit because of the Iraq War; whereas many of his colleagues had walked back their support of the invasion, Frank stood firm. The paper's new management, looking for an excuse to let him go, seized the opportunity by suspending him and qualifying his return on apologizing for his comments (to which he grudgingly agrees) and a second condition they know he'll refuse: giving up drinking. For Frank, that is a step too far.[36]

It's easy to imagine a version of this plotline that puts Frank in a more sympathetic light, perhaps by having him say something obviously inoffensive, or putting him in conflict with a superior who willfully misconstrues his remarks. What makes this plotline so compelling is that it is morally complex. Frank's jokes were racist and merited an apology. His drunkenness is hardly an excuse. At the same time, it's also easy to see why Frank would expect better treatment from the *Herald*, and why he'd hope for forgiveness all these months later (even if he doesn't ask for it).

Here again, Sam's plotline runs parallel to Frank's. While his blog and profile of Frank go over well, Sam soon faces charges of plagiarism and is unceremoniously fired. Desperate to salvage his fledgling career, he lands another book contract, this time for a memoir recounting his rapid rise and sudden fall in journalism. The proposal includes a remarkable insight: "The things that can't be proven are the only things worth talking about in the first place."[37] Alas for poor Sam, the sentiment isn't as original as Sam thought, and his plans collapse once again.

There are differences between Sam's disgrace and Frank's cancelation. The most obvious one is that Sam, being much younger, is more likely to have an opportunity for redemption. Another is that Frank's remarks were obviously more offensive than Sam's plagiarism. On the other hand, Sam committed his misconduct as part of his work; Frank was enjoying a baseball game when he made his racist remarks. Does that make them more excusable? Are either of these characters treated justly, or are they both subject to mere vengeance? If Frank were younger and progressive, would the *Herald* have been more forgiving?

Another disgraced character deserves our attention: Justin Price, the recipient of a Doyle scholarship, friend of Eddie's, and Kit's protégé. His actions probably have the most serious consequences to the most people, and he suffers greatly as a result. What's interesting about him, though, is that he seems the most prepared for his fall. Although he faces significant jail time, the congregation of the church to which he donated generously—not because he believed in God, but because his mother was a devout

Christian—treats him warmly the day before he is to be arrested, with the pastor thanking him publicly for his generosity and the "whole church [singing] to Justin."[38] The scene's power is complicated by the pastor ignoring Justin's desire to, simply put, not make too much mention of God during the event, but it is nonetheless a warm and remarkable display of public encouragement and forgiveness that Frank and Sam do not enjoy.

The contrast between this scene and the treatment Sam and Frank experience underscores what many Americans have observed over the past several years: cancel culture leaves no room for forgiveness. That grace is withheld, replaced by shame and exile. Unfortunately, whether shame and exile will be meted out or forgiveness afforded often depends on the transgressor's political leanings. Frank didn't have a prayer.

The Wealth of a Nation

For all of the ways that *The Index of Self-Destructive Acts* is sympathetic to conservative perspectives, it does not present a stirring defense of the market capitalism that has been central to the conservative movement in America for the past forty-five years—nor is it entirely critical of it. This nuanced economic vision is appropriate for a novel set in the wake of a major financial crisis. The novel does not suggest the crisis was the inevitable result of flaws inherent in a capitalist system; as I quoted above, Frank lays the blame on the hubris of experts who think they can eliminate risk from the market, and Justin similarly sees it as the result of "complex financial engineering [used] to outsmart supposedly sophisticated institutional investors."[39] Along the way, Beha connects this subplot with Sam's and Frank's by emphasizing the irrationality of the market, including the beliefs that it was possible to eliminate risk or outsmart the market.

We've seen the novels by Cather and Naipaul convey a sense of the importance of hard work, self-reliance, and property generally emphasized by conservatives. In this novel, by the time we encounter Beha's characters, they have already made their wealth. Justin has done so in, shall we say, extra-legal manners, but only after he leaves the mentorship of Kit Doyle. For her part, Kit seems to have spent the entirety of her career as an investment banker on the up-and-up, navigating difficult regulatory and competitive environments before selling her firm to an entity with the ominous name of UniBank, which proceeded to collapse and leave her without out a revenue stream. Especially with Frank out of work, their old lifestyle was suddenly unsustainable. Her criminality is an aberration, and for most of her life she had generally put her wealth to good use, particularly through a scholarship program for disadvantaged minority youth called the Bootstrappers (a name that perhaps pokes fun at conservative visions of upward mobility), which is how Justin came into their circle. Justin wonders about the motives behind the Doyles' kindness to him, why they ended up taking him under their wings and roof, but he ultimately concludes that what mattered was that they gave at all: "The family's ideal of noblesse oblige was easy to mock, but the alternative wasn't a world without great wealth; it was a world where the wealthy felt no obligations."[40] Whatever the motivation for it, the Doyle's charitable giving is an act of their free will that expands the opportunities of others.

The novel features a much more predatory character in the form of a crooked equity broker named Dan Eisen, who hires Justin and pressures him into using his old connections for illegal ends. The money comes quickly, and "the usual multigenerational cycle of wealth . . . was more and more frequently playing out over a single life span, but Justin had managed to squeeze it into a matter of years."[41] Justin gives generously to his mother's church, in large part out of guilt for how the money was earned, and we have seen the gratitude the congregation feels for that. What complicates this philanthropy, though, is that it was the fruit of illegal activity, and his donation is money laundering, albeit with holy garments. "I've been trying to do some good with that money," Justin explains, "But no amount of good will change where it came from."[42]

Although it seems as if the characters fleecing the market will serve their punishment, there is a level of injustice in it all since the forces behind the actual financial crisis will be unpunished. This sense of injustice, this lack of accountability, is another reason *The Index of Self-Destructive Acts* will be so interesting to conservatives in the 2020s: it hints at some of the forces and concerns that have brought the fissures and divisions that have developed in the Republican Party over the past decade, and which led to the rise of an intra-GOP populist faction. The national conservative movement is in large part a response to the power of multi-national corporations. What's more, the post-traumatic stress disorder among conservatives over the Iraq War is evident within the Doyle family, as Eddie resents his father for urging the war on while Frank himself remains a firm supporter of the efforts to bring democracy to Iraq.

Where There's a Will

The Index of Self-Destructive Acts begins with a question: "What makes a life, Sam Waxworth sometimes wondered—self or circumstance?"[43] The answer eventually becomes clear: self. Why is that it? As Margo explains, it's because (contrary to Sam's fatalism) "humans have free will. . . . that's what introduces all the uncertainty into the system: humans can *swerve*."[44] Beha underscores that emphasis on human agency by making nearly all of the novel's characters agents—with the possible exception of Lucy (Sam's wife). None of them is a victim. They are harmed by other people, but they suffer the most because of their own actions. Even Sam realizes "that he'd brought everything on himself. . . . He'd acted irrationally, he'd fucked up his life in the process."[45] Though it's possible to say that he and Frank are punished too harshly, it is clear that their own serious lapses in judgment led to their suffering. Actions have knock-on effects that harm others and put them in difficult situations, and too often those characters react in the wrong way. They all have free will and exercise it poorly.

Throughout the novel, there are reminders that nothing endures. A scam-artist prophet warns the people of New York City that the world will end later that year (and right in the middle of a Yankees' World Series title!). In Kit's lifetime, the Twin Towers rise and fall, and even though for many New Yorkers, "those buildings had been forces of nature, the very definition of permanence, but after all they'd been there for only a generation."[46] And Frank, poor Frank, seeks to collect his wisdom into a final book project whose completion seems less and less likely. If comedy is the genre of beginnings, especially of marriages, drama is the genre of endings. *The Index of Self-Destructive Acts* sees many endings—it's not too much to say that it's a novel about endings: marriages, careers, freedom, lives. George F. Will has claimed that "the foundational conservative insight can be expressed in two words: nothing lasts."[47] Margo sees the truth of this insight late in the novel, when she concludes that the false prophet's "great mistake was not to believe that the world would come to an end, but to think that it wasn't ending every day. Every thing was always ending, and nothing simply ended outright."[48] There is a poignant tragedy to this truth, but Margo's insight also hints at an invigorating continuity within change—a subtly optimistic, and very conservative, way of looking at the world.

Conclusion

A cheap trick that novelists like to use for character development is having the character express his or her opinion about books, and especially fiction. If the character likes reading, and especially reading novels, then of course the reader—who happens to be enjoying a novel—will like that character. That's why readers of George Eliot's *Middlemarch* may be drawn to the ambitious physician Tertius Lydgate when they learn that as a young man, "It had already occurred to him that books were stuff, and that life was stupid."[1] Conversely, the Anglo-Irish novelist Maria Edgeworth shapes our skepticism of the wonderfully named Harriet Freke in her novel *Belinda* when that character declares, like a nineteenth-century Sam Bankman-Fried, "Books only spoil the originality of genius: very well for those who can't think for themselves—but when one has made up one's opinion, there is no use in reading."[2] Ditto the pompous William Collins in *Pride and Prejudice* when he "protest[s] that he never read novels."[3] And don't tell me to read another book when I mention that a reason children know to loathe Harry Potter's cousin Dudley is the corpulent brat's room has "shelves . . . full of books. They were the only things in the room that looked as though they'd never been touched."[4]

This technique is not just pandering. It gets at a shared understanding between author and reader (not to mention the character, or at least the good ones) that books shape minds in important and lasting ways. Maybe it's a bit snobby, but it's effective, and it has the virtue of also being true.

The great literary critic Lionel Trilling gets at this truth well when he calls the novel "the most effective agent of the moral imagination":

> [I]ts greatness and its practical usefulness lay in its unremitting work of involving the reader himself in the moral life, inviting him to put his own motives under examination, suggesting that reality is not as his conventional education has led him to see it. It taught us . . . the extent of human variety and the value of this variety.[5]

Trilling here is describing the act of sympathetic engagement I discussed in the introduction, and which our old friend Evelina exercised so well herself. "Reading deepens," writes columnist Peggy Noonan. "Reading makes your mind do work. You have to follow the plot, imagine what the ballroom looked like, figure the motivations of the characters—*I understand what Gatsby wants!* All this makes your brain and soul develop the habit of generous and imaginative thinking." This is in sharp contrast to so many of the media that take our attention away from reading fiction. "Social media is passive," continues Noonan. "The pictures, reels and comments demand nothing, develop nothing. They give you sensations, but the sensations never get deeper. Social media gets you stuck in you."[6] That much is obvious from a simple act of juxtaposition. A person reading a book and a person watching TikTok are both looking down, but the person with the book will be looking intensely at the pages, perhaps with furrowed eyebrows as she moves her eyes along the pages, spellbound. The person on TikTok looks passive by comparison, her eyes fixed on the small screen, her mouth open, hypnotized. They both may be in different worlds, but only one world seems inviting to the outsider.

Of course, you already know this. That's why you're reading the conclusion of this book instead of scrolling through Instagram. I'm reminding you because it's important to remember that reading is different and that it matters, if we also care about the ideas and principles of conservatism itself.

It's a common and accurate intra-conservative complaint that we're not good at telling stories. We think there's something unfair about using stories to persuade people because arguments are to be won with logic and empirical data. Storytelling is too much about emotion, and that's for liberals. That's foolish. "Argument has its place," argues author Rod Dreher, "but story is what truly moves the hearts and minds of men. The power of myth—which is to say, of storytelling—is the power to form and enlighten the moral imagination, which is how we learn right from wrong, the proper ordering of our souls, and what it means to be human."[7] Nobody reads a novel to be persuaded. They read a novel to meet memorable characters, to be told compelling stories, to imagine powerful scenes and images, to encounter lives unlike their own, and to delight in the language. But those elements can persuade and convince—or at a minimum they can introduce people to ways of thinking and knowing they had not considered or crystalize what they had merely intuited. The novels I've written about in this book are just a few of the countless great works that present conservative ideas thoughtfully and artfully.

Because a few of the novels I discussed in the preceding pages feature prominent water imagery, I might as well include some in this conclusion. Twenty years ago, novelist Mark Helprin warned conservatives that any inroads they make politically "can easily be washed away—in a generation, in a decade, year, month, or minute—by culture, the great Conservative terra incognita."[8] With this metaphor, he was anticipating the expression made famous by journalist Andrew Breitbart: "Politics is downstream from culture." Yes, of course political events and decisions—the laws that govern a nation, the actions and institutions that are funded or taxed—can affect the culture. But the reverse relationship gets less attention, especially from conservatives. Works of art, high and low, help shape how we understand everyday life and what we want for ourselves and our families.

In light of that relationship between culture and politics, Helprin considered the success the Left has had in taking control of America's most important institutions and expressed skepticism over the Right's ability to either reassert control of them or rid them of destructive influences. Instead, the more promising pathway to shape the culture was for conservatives to "make and keep alive the works and principles to which these institutions can turn in the crisis of their bankruptcy."[9]

Much has changed in the two decades since Helprin offered that advice. I write these paragraphs the day after Donald Trump's second presidential inauguration. He won re-election in part because Americans have seen for themselves just how much damage progressivism has inflicted on our most important institutions, including our educational system. We have seen encouraging changes in higher education, in particular, as Diversity, Equity, and Inclusion programs have been pared back or shut down and some schools have established centers for civil discourse and civic education. Even progressive English professors are turning to more conservative approaches to teaching and studying literature out of the recognition that fewer students are interested in politicized pedagogy and scholarship.[10]

Nonetheless, Helprin's point remains relevant: to shape our politics, to influence the direction of our country, conservatives must reinvigorate our culture; and to do that, they must "make and keep alive" valuable works and principles. This book is a modest contribution to the effort in the keeping alive, and perhaps in the process inspiring others to make such work of their own. You can keep them alive, too, by sharing these works yourself. Suggest one or two or, what the hell, thirteen of these books to your book club. Assign a couple to your students. Give them as presents. Talk about them at parties. Design big red hats that say Make America Read Again. (Okay, maybe not that last one.)

A conservativism that is at once thoughtful and energetic, that is both committed to ideas and what Calvin Coolidge called "anxious for the fray," must know and perpetuate great works of art, including fiction.[11] I hope this book has given you a fuller sense of some of those remarkable works, deepened your understanding of conservative ideas, and inspired you to read more great fiction.

Acknowledgments

T he cast of characters who helped this book along could fill a Victorian novel, though there isn't a Grandcourt to be seen. Harry Crocker of Regnery Publishing got things started with an email, and his colleagues Tom Spence and Elizabeth Kantor provided indispensable early ideas and guidance. At Skyhorse, I'm grateful to Tony Lyons for rescuing me from the orphanage, and to Kathryn Riggs for her editorial attention and extraordinary patience (and to her newborn daughter for being a good sleeper).

I could not have written this book without the support and resources of the American Enterprise Institute. President Robert Doar has been a valuable sounding board, and Yuval Levin, the director of AEI's department of Social, Cultural, and Constitutional Studies, has been a model of serious intellectual work who also lets me borrow his Burke and Kirk. Thanks to them, I can write while the sun's up. Several of my colleagues helped with drafts of my earliest chapters: Tim Carney, Matthew Continetti, Benjamin Storey, Adam White, Gary Schmitt, and Jeffrey A. Rosen. I also benefitted from conversations with Karlyn Bowman, Ross Douthat, Andrew Ferguson, Joshua Katz, Kevin Kosar, Katja Liebmann, Tony Mills, Brent Orrell, Nicole Penn, Christine Rosen, Jenna Silber Storey, and Thomas Chatterton Williams. Ten years ago, if you had written a novel that had those people as my colleagues, I would have told you to revise it into something more plausible. Of course, I also benefited enormously from the help of the three resourceful, intelligent, and well-read research associates who labored under my yoke at various times over the past couple of years: Luis Parrales, Noah Rosenfield, and Lauren Collins. Tori Tinsley provided timely pinch-hitting.

Many other people have shared ideas over the course of casual conversations, email exchanges, phone calls, or encounters at those DC cocktail parties that are supposed to turn people into progressives. Thanks especially to Gerard Alexander, Mark Bauerlein, Joseph Bottum, Joseph Capizzi, Steven Dunkirk, Dana Gioia, Eliana Johnson, Andrew Klavan, Micah Mattix, Daniel McCarthy, John J. Miller, Taryn Okuma, Karen Swallow Prior, Peter Robinson, William Hillman Rogers, Barton Swaim, and John Wilson.

I'm glad I'm not delivering these thanks at a podium because I'd start getting weepy here. My parents taught me and my siblings to love reading, whether it was by buying us a good book every birthday and Christmas (and doing the same for their dozens of grandchildren) or reading passages aloud from the newspaper over breakfast. I probably inherited my love of writing, and my fondness for arguing about it, from my late father, Antonin Scalia, who also introduced me to some of the conservative thinkers who feature prominently in these pages. My mother, Maureen McCarthy Scalia, gave me her love for and taste in literature, and that has made all the difference. My parents also blessed me with seven great brothers and sisters, plus another who's okay, I guess, and over the years they've recommended books, given me books, and read some of this book. If they buy copies for all of their children and grandchildren, I'll be able to retire soon.

My own children—Dominic, Julian, Philippa, and Georgina—helped with a few citations and, by barging into my home office and being too noisy in the basement, sharpened my skills of concentration. I'm excited for them to love a few of the novels, and think about some of the ideas, in this book.

Most of all, my wife. Adele is smart and good enough to be an Eliot character, beautiful and quotable enough for Spark, and Trini enough (*steups*) for Naipaul. She guided me to the place where I could write this book, and gave me the good sense and strength to see it through.

Discussion Questions

Samuel Johnson, *The History of Rasselas, Prince of Abissinia*

1. One of the work's most famous remarks is Imlac's proclamation that "Human life is every where a state in which much is to be endured, and little to be enjoyed."[1] It's a memorable line—but is it *true*? Do you think the book accurately depicts human nature, particularly concerning ambition and satisfaction?

2. What did you make of the ending of the book? Were you frustrated by its ambiguity? Did you interpret it as a hopeful resolution or a despairing finish?

3. Is Imlac a reliable mentor? Were there moments in the book when you believe his insights were undermined or contradicted? How does he compare to other guides featured in these novels, such as Arthur Villars from *Evelina* or Mordecai Cohen from *Daniel Deronda*?

Frances Burney, *Evelina*

1. What is your opinion of the novel's use of the epistolary form? Does organizing the narrative around a series of letters help Burney develop her characters, create suspense, or explore themes in interesting or surprising ways?

2. The novel features many different versions of Evelina's name, a mysterious poetic depiction of her, people using her name without permission, and a forged letter written to her. What do details like these suggest about the security of identity in the novel? How does that concern relate to other themes that interested you?

3. Of course, the character who matures the most in the novel is Evelina, but Orville, does, too. How is that maturation manifest, and what causes it?

Walter Scott, *Waverley*

1. What do you make of the novel's resolution? For example, what is the significance of what happens to the Baron of Bradwardine's estate? What is represented by the marriage of Edward with the woman he marries?

2. Over the course of the novel, to what degree do you find yourself sympathizing with the Jacobite cause? The Highlanders? Why? What events or insights spark this reaction?

3. Imagine you are in charge of educating Edward. What books (fiction or non-fiction!—but not including *Waverley*, because that would be cheating) would you assign to help him prepare for his military duties, overcome his disappointments regarding his father's political career, and resist the allure of Bonnie Prince Charlie's cause?

Nathaniel Hawthorne, *The Blithedale Romance*

1. Do you think the commune is doomed by its very nature as a proto-socialist enterprise, or is it a combination of personal conflict and rivalries that dooms it?

2. Consider the novel's subplot of the Veiled Lady. Do that storyline's pseudo-spiritual elements relate to the novel's broader depiction of human nature?

3. How reliable a narrator is Miles Coverdale? What reasons are there to be skeptical of his judgments and conclusions, even as he relates the events years after they occurred? Does his final revelation in particular undermine his assessments of any particular characters?

George Eliot, *Daniel Deronda*

1. What is it about Daniel's desire to establish a Jewish state that makes it seem less utopian or foolish than what Hawthorne's characters expect from Blithedale? Notwithstanding our knowledge that such a state would eventually be established (albeit long after Daniel's life), is there something in what Daniel says or does that makes his bold ambitions more practical?

2. Imagine you're writing a sequel to the novel that focuses (as the literary critic F. R. Leavis wished Eliot had) on Gwendolen's fate. What life would you imagine her living—still a single and childless widow caring for her parents and siblings? A single woman and successful singer? Happily remarried—and if so, to whom?

3. What is your reaction to the concept of communication with separateness advocated by Daniel's grandfather and embraced by Daniel? From a national perspective, what might that entail for a pluralistic democracy such as the United States in the twenty-first century?

Willa Cather, *My Ántonia*

1. How do Jim Burden's childhood relationship with Ántonia and the state of his present marriage bolster or diminish your trust in him as a narrator? What lessons from Ántonia's life do you think Jim could apply to his own?

2. The backstory of Peter and Pavel, who fled Europe after abandoning the members of a wedding party to ravenous wolves, has the quality of a parable. Accepting that premise, what are some possible lessons of their tale?

3. Imagine you are a presidential candidate at a time when massive numbers of illegal immigrants are crossing America's borders. There is a general sense that the situation is unsustainable, but this is balanced by the popular belief that "we are a nation of immigrants." How would you use *My Ántonia* to illustrate the importance of your preferred policy?

Zora Neale Hurston, *Their Eyes Were Watching God*

1. What does Janie learn through her relationships with different men? Does she ever approach the idealized sense of blossoming that she sees as a young woman beneath the pear tree?

2. The scholar Carla Kaplan has said that in this novel, Hurston was not interested in depicting a uniform black culture but in "depicting black difference."[2] Where is that most apparent? How does that challenge our present-day understandings of race and identity?

3. Does Janie's journey remind you of what other young men and women experience in the novels explored in this book, such as Edward Waverley, Evelina, and Rasselas and his companions?

Evelyn Waugh, *Scoop*

1. In the introduction to this book, I mentioned that a common claim for the value of fiction is that it helps readers develop their sense of empathy, making them better people. Do you think that's true of a satire like *Scoop*? If not empathy, are there other traits, skills, or virtues Waugh's novel might help hone?

2. Does Waugh recognize any advantages or admirable elements of journalism? Are there advantages of the profession that Waugh's novel overlooks? If there were a twenty-first century version of this novel, what episodes or indictments would you want to see included?

3. Despite the sharp contrasts between Ishmaelia and England, are there important or surprising similarities between them? If so, what might have been Waugh's purpose in hinting at these commonalities?

Muriel Spark, *The Girls of Slender Means*

1. Nicholas is obviously attracted to the beautiful Selina, but he also seems drawn to Joanna. Why do you think that is? Do you get the sense that, in some way, she prepared him for his martyrdom?

2. What do you make of Spark's narrative techniques? For example, how does the omniscient but detached voice of the narrator affect your understanding of the novel's events? What about the novel's asynchronous structure? And are there moments when the narrator's irony reminds you at all of Waugh's?

3. What exactly is it about what Nicholas sees in the May of Teck Club and at the victory party that leads him to conversion?

Are you convinced, as he seems to be, that a vision of evil can be as effective a source of grace as a vision of good?

V. S. Naipaul, *A Bend in the River*

1. How would you characterize Salim's opinion of Africa's colonial history? Does he resent the colonists? Does he see them as oppressors and Africans as the oppressed?

2. What is the symbolic significance of the river—does it play a role similar to the water and river imagery of *Rasselas*? What do you make of the references to the water hyacinth, the invasive species in which Father Huismans's body was found?

3. Do you recognize any overlap between Waugh's admittedly humorous or satirical depictions of European imperial designs on Africa with Naipaul's visions? To what extent are the two novels in conversation about this topic? Consider also how Naipaul's novel relates to Eliot's occasional references to British colonialism in *Daniel Deronda*.

P. D. James, *The Children of Men*

1. Of the consequences of the infertility crisis the novel depicts, which strike you as the most chilling and relevant to our time? Is it the exploitative immigration policy? The inhumane prisons? The Quietus program? Something else?

2. Grab some popcorn and watch the 2006 adaptation of the novel, directed by Alfonso Cuarón and starring Clive Owen. Is it faithful to the original? What major differences do you notice, and how did those changes undermine or advance your understanding of James's source material?

3. How does this novel's representation of governmental power compare to what we've seen in other novels in this book? For example, in what ways is the Warden comparable to the Big Man from Naipaul's *A Bend in the River*?

Leif Enger, *Peace Like a River*

1. The novel's title is from a nineteenth-century hymn titled "It Is Well with My Soul." The full hymn is easy to find through a basic internet search. Here's the first verse:

> When peace like a river attendeth my way,
> When sorrows like sea billows roll;
> Whatever my lot, thou hast taught me to say,
> 'It is well, it is well with my soul.'

With that reference in mind, how appropriate is the novel's title? How do the novel's contents play off the hymn's message?

2. Is justice finally realized in the novel? That is, are the villains appropriately punished under the law? Does Davy in particular endure appropriate punishment for his crimes? Are there different ways of understanding what justice entails in the context of Enger's novel?

3. What do you think the novel suggests about the human instinct for storytelling? Who are the novel's primary storytellers and what obstacles do they face when they tell their tales? Are they able to overcome them to share their stories?

Christopher Beha, *The Index of Self-Destructive Acts*

1. In the novel's conflict between rational, predictable behavior and impulsive, unpredictable acts, where do you find yourself standing—are you more of a Waxworthian or a Doyleite?

2. Is there a particular character you think is treated unfairly or unjustly—or someone who deserves more severe punishment or comeuppance than he or she receives? Who and why?

3. Place the novel's depiction of human ambition and happiness in conversation with *Rasselas* and *Daniel Deronda*. Are Johnson, Eliot, and Beha making similar points—or at least asking similar questions—about the nature of human desire or the need for an underlying ambition or purpose to realize happiness?

Appendix II

If You Liked . . . Try . . .

Readers looking for even more works of high literary merit that present conservative ideas in thoughtful ways, or that explore themes of particular interest to conservatives, will find more great material in the following list. Again, I have restricted to these suggestions to Anglophone fiction.

Samuel Johnson, *Rasselas*

- **Tobias Smollett, *The Expedition of Humphry Clinker* (1771)**—like *Rasselas*, a novel about what one learns during travel—but more optimistic, and with a lot of bawdy humor. Themes of social order and the changes brought by economic growth are at the fore.
- **Samuel Johnson, *A Journey to the Western Islands of Scotland* (1775) and James Boswell, *The Journal of a Tour of the Hebrides with Samuel Johnson, LL.D.* (1785)**—I'm cheating again because neither of these is a novel, but accounts of a trip that Johnson took with his young friend (and future biographer) James Boswell in 1773. If you enjoyed the psychological insights and moral considerations of *Rasselas*, you'll love these, which you can usually find collected in a single volume.

Frances Burney, *Evelina*

- **Samuel Richardson, *Clarissa: or the History of a Young Lady*** (1748)—One of the first great English novels tells the story of a virtuous but mistreated young woman who is the victim of the relentless pursuit and machinations of a sinister villain named Lovelace. Warning: this very, very long novel does not end as happily as *Evelina*.
- **Maria Edgeworth, *Belinda* (1801)**—Another young woman learning about her place in the world, with complex discussions of virtue, education, and marriage. More overt in its political and philosophical references than *Evelina*, it includes references to thinkers like Edmund Burke and Jean-Jacques Rousseau.
- **Jane Austen, *Pride and Prejudice* (1813)**—I didn't write about any Austen novels in this collection because I assume you don't need another person telling you to read her novels. But just in case you have yet to heed that sound advice, *Pride and Prejudice* is a good place to start if you enjoyed the relationship between Evelina and Orville.

Walter Scott, *Waverley*

- **James Fenimore Cooper, *The Last of the Mohicans* (1826)**— Deeply informed by Scott's fiction, Cooper's best-known novel is set during the French and Indian Wars and features the conflicts between British colonists, their French enemies, and warring Native American tribes. It also features one of American literature's first great characters, Natty Bumppo (a.k.a. Hawkeye, a.k.a. Leatherstocking, a.k.a. Pathfinder).
- **Mark Twain, *Personal Recollections of Joan of Arc* (1896)**—I mentioned that Twain liked to complain about Scott, but he did try his hand at historical fiction with this surprisingly

sympathetic depiction of the French patriot and Catholic saint, told from the perspective of her personal secretary. Twain called this his favorite of his works.

- **Lewis Grassic Gibbon,** *Sunset Song* **(1932)**—Gin it's changing Scots life you seek, read this underrated classic. Although it's an unabashedly socialist work, Gibbon's novel (the first in a trilogy) is also a touching depiction of a fading agricultural life and the connections between tenant farmers and those who lived on the land before them.

Nathaniel Hawthorne, *The Blithedale Romance*

- **Joseph Conrad,** *Under Western Eyes* **(1911)**—Conrad's main character, a Russian student named Razumov, is a more extreme revolutionary than Hawthorne's aspiring farmers, but like *Blithedale,* this is a fascinating and tense exploration of political ideas, human passions, and conflicting loyalties.
- **Saul Bellow,** *Mr. Sammler's Planet* **(1970)**—The novel's title character struggles with the social and cultural changes in the New York City (and United States) of the late 1960s. If, as Irving Kristol quipped, a neo-conservative is a liberal who was mugged by reality, this is the ultimate neo-conservative novel. Other Bellow novels I considered for this book are *The Dean's December* (1982) and *Ravelstein* (2000).

George Eliot, *Daniel Deronda*

- **Walter Scott,** *Ivanhoe* **(1819)**—Set in twelfth-century England, Scott's best-known novel follows the adventures of a knight returning from the crusades and seeking to restore justice and order. Like Eliot's final novel (which refers to it several times), the status of Jews in England is also a central theme.

- **Anthony Trollope, *Phineas Finn* (1869)**—The euphonically named title character is a young Irishman striving for success and influence after surprisingly winning a seat in Parliament. A fast-moving and compelling account of political ambition and moral integrity.
- **Edith Wharton, *The House of Mirth* (1905)**—Wharton's second novel is set across the Atlantic a couple of decades after Eliot's novel, but its strong-willed and beautiful heroine, Lily Bart, faces many of the same challenges and choices as Gwendolen Harleth. Her fate is less ambiguous.

Willa Cather, *My Ántonia*

- **Lee Smith, *Oral History* (1983)**—This family saga set in Appalachia tracks the continuity between generations despite social and cultural change. I could have easily recommended it under *Peace Like a River* for its magical realist elements or *The Blithedale Romance* for its comically delusional intellectual.
- **Wendell Berry, *Hannah Coulter* (2004)**—As Cather did with her Prairie Trilogy, Wendell Berry has created a series of novels set in the rural United States. In Berry's case, the region is the fictional Port William, Kentucky, the home of Hannah Coulter and her kin. In this novel, Coulter tells the story of her marriages, family, and way of life over the twentieth century.

Zora Neale Hurston, *Their Eyes Were Watching God*

- **Ralph Ellison, *Invisible Man* (1952)**—The second half of this classic American novel features plot points and ideas about race and socialism that will be especially interesting to conservatives. (However, the first half offers a much harsher critique of Booker T. Washington than Mrs. Turner did.)

- **Percival Everett,** *Erasure* **(2001)**—The basis for the award-winning film *American Fiction* (2023), Everett's novel depicts the frustrations of a black writer whose work is not considered "black enough" until he writes parody that is praised for its authentic depiction of underclass black culture. (Unlike the film, the novel includes a subplot about the murder of an abortion doctor.)

Evelyn Waugh, *Scoop*

- **P. G. Wodehouse,** *Code of the Woosters* **(1938)**—There's nothing inherently conservative about Wodehouse's hilarious novels, though conservatives do tend to love them. Light subject matter but superb prose, complex plots, and memorable characters.
- **Kingsley Amis,** *Lucky Jim* **(1954)**—A lot has changed in academia since Amis wrote this classic, but it remains one of the best send-ups of academic life and among the funniest novels ever written.
- **Christopher Buckley,** *Thank You for Smoking* **(1994)**—Buckley's novel hilariously satirizes both the cynicism of the tobacco lobby and the neo-puritanism of its worst critics, not to mention the unseriousness and duplicity of the news media.

Muriel Spark, *The Girls of Slender Means*

- **James Hogg,** *The Private Memoirs and Confessions of a Justified Sinner* **(1824)**—This wonderfully weird gothic novel, set in eighteenth-century Scotland, explores themes that would later obsess Spark, particularly the dangerous belief that some people are above the standard moral code.
- **Graham Greene,** *The End of the Affair* **(1951)**—A powerful story of jealousy, lust, and religious conversion set in London

during World War II, written by another Catholic convert (and an early supporter of Spark's).

- **Muriel Spark,** *A Far Cry from Kensington* **(1988)**—This book is set around the same time as *The Girls of Slender Means* and explores some of the same themes of evil, religious belief, and literary culture in a more straightforward, first-person narrative style.

V. S. Naipaul, *A Bend in the River*

- **Robert Penn Warren,** *All the King's Men* **(1946)**—Naipaul keeps his charismatic politician in the background, but Warren brings him front and center in this Pulitzer Prize–winning novel about a Louisiana populist based on Huey Long.
- **Joan Didion,** *A Book of Common Prayer* **(1977)**—After her Marxist daughter commits an act of political radicalism and becomes a fugitive, a wealthy and naïve American woman flees to Central America and gets caught up in the tumult of third-world politics.
- **Philip Roth,** *American Pastoral* **(1997)**—In what is widely considered the greatest novel of Roth's long career, a successful man's life unravels after his daughter falls prey to the political radicalism of the 1960s.

P. D. James, *The Children of Men*

- **Walter M. Miller Jr.,** *A Canticle for Leibowitz* **(1959)**—Set thousands of years after the world is ravaged by nuclear war, this dystopian novel traces the attempts of a Catholic religious order known as the Leibowitzians to preserve knowledge and salvage civilization.
- **Walker Percy,** *Love in the Ruins* **(1971)**—Percy's third novel, narrated by an institutionalized psychiatrist and set (as the full

title indicates) "at a time near the end of the world," is a strange, prescient satire about a United States troubled by spiritual emptiness, social fragmentation, and political and religious extremists.

- **Lionel Shriver, *The Mandibles: A Family, 2029–2047* (2016)**—Using as its triggering premise a global economic collapse in 2029, this speculative novel traces the struggles of a once-wealthy American family amid social and financial chaos. Like James, Shriver bases her dystopia (where the IRS is renamed the Bureau for Social Contribution Assistance, but is known as SCAB) on the worst possible outcome of current trends.

Leif Enger, *Peace Like a River*

- **Charles Portis, *True Grit* (1968)**—Portis's classic western is about a young girl's devotion to her father and her quest for revenge. Like Enger's novel, it explores questions about mercy, justice, and redemption.
- **Marilynne Robinson, *Gilead* (2004)**—Robinson's Pulitzer Prize–winning second novel is a quiet and deep (like a river!) reflection on faith, forgiveness, and family, told from the perspective of an aging Congregationalist pastor in Iowa.
- **Cormac McCarthy, *The Road* (2006)**—Another Pulitzer Prize winner, McCarthy's novel follows a father and son trying to survive in a post-apocalyptic America with more cannibals than plants and animals. A zombie novel without zombies.

Christopher Beha, *The Index of Self-Destructive Acts*

- **Mark Helprin, *Winter's Tale* (1983)**—A richly written fantasy about love, sacrifice, and New York City. In 2006, it was included on the *New York Times* list of the best works of American fiction of the last twenty-five years.

- **Tom Wolfe, *Bonfire of the Vanities* (1987)**—What I said about Jane Austen I could also say about this novel: I didn't devote a chapter to it because I assume you don't need another person telling you to read it. But in case you do need that one more recommendation, here it is. Wolfe's masterpiece is both hilarious and exciting.
- **Alice McDermott, *Charming Billy* (1998)**—Another New York City novel (Queens, to be precise), McDermott's National Book Award–winner is much quieter and concise than the others in this category, but no less powerful. After the death of a charismatic but troubled man, his family examines the tragedy of his alcoholism and the heartbreak that may have caused it.

Notes

Introduction

1   If you'd like help visualizing this anecdote, rewatch the 1986 Rodney Dangerfield film *Back to School*, which was filmed at the University of Wisconsin and includes a scene set in the same bookstore. Though in that movie, Dangerfield's character discourages students from buying used books.

2   Good news: many members of the Resistance did read another book! Bad news: it was *The Handmaid's Tale*.

3   National Endowment for the Arts, "Reading at Risk: A Survey of Literary Reading in America," June 2004, https://www.arts.gov/impact/research /publications/reading-risk-survey-literary-reading-america. The percentage of eighteen-to-twenty-four-year-olds who reported reading literature in 1982 was 59.8 percent. That plummeted to 42.8 percent in 2002, while the oldest demographic was at 36.7 percent.

4   National Endowment for the Arts, "Reading on the Rise: A New Chapter in American Literacy," January 2009, 4, 7, https://www.arts.gov/sites /default/files/ReadingonRise.pdf.

5   National Endowment for the Arts, "U.S. Trends in Arts Attendance and Literary Reading: 2002–2017," September 2018, 9, www.arts.gov/sites/default /files/2017-sppapreviewREV-sept2018.pdf.

6   National Endowment for the Arts, *Arts Participation Patterns in 2022*, October 2023, 11, www.arts.gov/sites/default/files/2022-SPPA-final.pdf.

7   Risa Gelles-Watnick and Andrew Perrin, "Who Doesn't Read Books in America?," Pew Research Center, September 21, 2021, https://www.pewre search.org/fact-tank/2021/09/21/who-doesnt-read-books-in-america/.

8   Jeffrey M. Jones, "Americans Reading Fewer Books Than in Past," Gallup, January 10, 2002, https://news.gallup.com/poll/388541/americans-reading -fewer-books-past.aspx.

9   Dana Gioia, "Preface" in "Reading at Risk," National Endowment for the Arts, 2004, vii, https://www.arts.gov/impact/research/publications/reading -risk-survey-literary-reading-america.

10   Nathan Heller, "The End of the English Major," *New Yorker*, February 27, 2023, https://www.newyorker.com/magazine/2023/03/06/the-end-of -the-english-major.

11   Joseph Bottum, *The Decline of the Novel* (Chicago: St. Augustine's Press, 2019), 42–3.

12   Russell Kirk, "The Moral Imagination," in *Literature and Belief*, vol. 1 (Provo: Brigham Young University Press, 1981), 40.

13   John Agresto, *The Death of Learning: How American Education Has Failed Our Students and What to Do about It* (New York: Encounter Books, 2022), 8.

14   Kirk, "The Moral Imagination," 40.

15   Ralph Ellison, "Introduction" in *Invisible Man* (New York: Vintage International, 1982), xx.

16   Amy A. Kass, Leon R. Kass, and Diana Schaub, eds., *What So Proudly We Hail: The American Soul in Story, Speech, and Song* (Wilmington: ISI Books, 2011), xix.

17   "President Obama & Marilynne Robinson: A Conversation—II" *New York Review of Books*, November 19, 2015, https://archive.is/ZSY1S.

18   Christine Seifert, "The Case for Reading Fiction," *Harvard Business Review*, March 6, 2020, https://hbr.org/2020/03/the-case-for-reading-fiction.

19   Megan Schmidt, "How Reading Fiction Increases Empathy and Encourages Understanding," *Discover*, September 2, 2020, https://www.discover magazine.com/mind/how-reading-fiction-increases-empathy-and-encourages -understanding.

20   This doesn't mean all avid readers are brimming with sympathy. As Gary Saul Morson points out, "Stalin himself was a voracious reader." Gary Saul Morson, *Wonder Confronts Uncertainty: Russian Writers on the Timeless Questions and Why Their Answers Matter* (Cambridge, MA: The Belknap Press of Harvard University Press, 2023), 43.

21   Flannery O'Connor, "Some Aspects of the Grotesque in Southern Fiction," from *Mystery & Manners*, ed. Sally and Robert Fitzgerald (New York: Farrar, Straus & Giroux), 43.

22   C. S. Lewis, "Preface" [1944], in St. Athanasius the Great of Alexandria, *On the Incarnation*, trans. John Behr (Yonkers: St. Vladimir's Seminary Press, 2011), 11.

23   Among the most significant differences between genre fiction (not that there's anything wrong with that!) and literary fiction is that works in the latter category are more likely to emphasize character-driven conflict;

include a higher quality of writing and a deeper attention to language; and have fewer predictable plot conventions and narrative formulas.

24   The Modern Library, "100 Best Novels," https://sites.prh.com/modern -library-top-100.

25   Roger Scruton, *Beauty: A Very Short Introduction* (Oxford: Oxford University Press, 2011), 110.

26   Micah Mattix, "The Integrity of Poetry," *First Things* (330: February 2023), 30–31, https://www.firstthings.com/article/2023/02/the-integrity-of-poetry.

Chapter One

1   Samuel Johnson, *The Rambler* No. 4, *Samuel Johnson: Selected Poetry and Prose*, ed. Frank Brady and W. K. Wimsatt (Berkeley: University of California Press, 1977), 155.

2   Ibid., 156.

3   Ibid.

4   Ibid., 157.

5   Ibid. This passage is a remarkable articulation of what Russell Kirk identifies as the moral imagination, quoted in my introduction.

6   *Caveat lector*: by including *Rasselas* in this book, I'm cheating a bit because it qualifies as a novel only insofar as it's a relatively long fictional narrative. "The proper term for *Rasselas*'s genre is sometimes disputed," explains the great eighteenth-century British literature scholar Jack Lynch. He continues, "it's probably most often called an Oriental tale, but some prefer to see it as a Menippean or Varronian satire. In any case, avoid calling it a novel." My sincere apologies to Professor Lynch! I simply couldn't resist recommending Johnson's Oriental tale to conservative readers, even if it meant being liberal with my definitions. Jack Lynch, "*Rasselas*," 1998, https: //jacklynch.net/Johnson/Guide/rasselas.html.

7   Quoted in James Boswell, *Life of Samuel Johnson* [1791] (New York: Oxford World's Classics, 2008), 731. Boswell follows this observation with a fact-check: "Numerous instances to refute this will occur to all who are versed in the history of literature" (ibid.).

8   As you may have noticed, there are two spellings for this place: Abissinia and Abyssinia. When referring to and quoting Johnson's work, I will use the former spelling because that is the one used in the Penguin edition I cite. Otherwise, I will use the modern spelling of Abyssinia.

9   Samuel Johnson, *The History of Rasselas, Prince of Abissinia* (London: Penguin Classics, 2007), 8. College football fans and Penn State grads may

be more familiar with the name Happy Valley as the home of the Nittany Lions. *Rasselas* is not the only great eighteenth-century work of literature to feature a place name that doubles as the site of a storied college football program. Oliver Goldsmith, a friend of Johnson, wrote a poem called "The Deserted Village," whose first line is: "Sweet Auburn, loveliest village of the plain. . . ."

10   Ibid., 9.

11   Ibid., 33.

12   Ibid., 36.

13   Johnson, *Rasselas*, 43.

14   Samuel Johnson, *The Idler* No. 51 "Domestic Greatness Unattainable," *Samuel Johnson: Selected Poetry and Prose*, ed. Frank Brady and W. K. Wimsatt (Berkeley: University of California Press, 1977), 251.

15   Samuel Johnson, "The Vanity of Human Wishes," *Samuel Johnson: Selected Poetry and Prose*, ed. Frank Brady and W. K. Wimsatt (CA: University of California Press, 1977), ll. 1–4, 11–14.

16   Johnson, *Rasselas*, 29.

17   This absence of individual characterization distinguishes *Rasselas* from the other works I discuss in this book. See the *caveat lector* in note 6 above.

18   Johnson, *Rasselas*, 30.

19   Ibid.

20   Ibid., 32.

21   Howard Trivers, "Universalism in the Thought of the Founding Fathers," *Virginia Quarterly Review*, Summer 1976, https://www.vqronline.org/essay/universalism-thought-founding-fathers#:~:text=The%20Enlightenment%20was%20characterized%20by,origin%20as%20a%20national%20state.

22   Samuel Johnson, "Taxation No Tyranny," in *Political Writings*, ed. Donald Greene (New Haven: Yale University Press, 1977), 454.

23   George W. Bush, "Address to the United Nations General Assembly," September 21, 2004, https://2009–2017.state.gov/p/io/potusunga/207564.htm.

24   Joseph R. Biden, "Remarks by President Biden on the United Efforts of the Free World to Support the People of Ukraine," March 26, 2022, https://www.whitehouse.gov/briefing-room/speeches-remarks/2022/03/26/remarks-by-president-biden-on-the-united-efforts-of-the-free-world-to-support-the-people-of-ukraine/.

25   Steven Pinker, *The Blank Slate: The Modern Denial of Human Nature* (London: Penguin Group, 2002), 169.

26 George F. Will, "The Consciousness Project," *National Review*, December 2023, 45.
27 Johnson, *Rasselas*, 23.
28 James Madison, *Federalist*, no. 51, in *The Federalist Papers*, by Alexander Hamilton, James Madison, and John Jay (New York: Signet Classics, 1961), 319.
29 Samuel Johnson, *A Dictionary of the English Language*, vol. 2 (London: J.F. and C. Rivington, L. Davis, T. Payne and Son, 1785). A reliable online edition of Johnson's dictionary is available at johnsonsdictionary.com. One of the quotations Johnson provides to illustrate this meaning of the word, attributed to the Anglican bishop Francis Atterbury, sounds like something that Imlac himself may have told Rasselas: "We find our souls disordered and restless, tossed and disquieted by passions, ever seeking happiness in the enjoyments of this world, and ever missing what they seek."
30 Johnson, *Rasselas*, 11.
31 Ibid., 12.
32 Ibid., 13.
33 Ibid., 14.
34 Ibid., 22.
35 Ibid., 80.
36 Ibid., 36.
37 Ibid., 106.
38 Ibid., 96.
39 Thomas Sowell, *The Vision of the Anointed: Self-Congratulations as a Basis for Social Policy* (New York: Basic Books, 1995), 142.
40 Johnson, *Rasselas*, 106.
41 Ibid., 111.
42 Ibid., 112.
43 Benjamin Storey and Jenna Silber Storey, *Why We Are Restless* (Princeton: Princeton University Press, 2021), 176.
44 Ibid., 177.
45 Ibid., 182.
46 Ibid., 181.
47 Samuel Johnson, *The Rambler*, no. 5 (Tuesday, April 3, 1750), in *The Yale Edition of the Works of Samuel Johnson Vol III: The Rambler*, ed. W. J. Bate and Albrecht B. Strauss (New Haven: Yale University Press, 1969), 25.
48 Ibid., 29–30.

Chapter Two

1   Alexis de Tocqueville, *Democracy in America*, trans. Harvey C. Mansfield and Delba Winthrop (Chicago: University of Chicago Press, 2000), 541–42.

2   Senator Rick Scott, et. al., "Letter to Majority Leader Chuck Schumer," September 19, 2023, https://www.rickscott.senate.gov/services/files/2A7E C7D9–0152-414F-A08C-A8A203ED3CE9.

3   Peggy Noonan, "The Senator's Shorts and America's Decline," *Wall Street Journal*, September 21, 2023, https://www.wsj.com/articles/the-senators -shorts-and-americas-decline-fetterman-dress-code-boebert-79b8f2aa ?mod=article_inline.

4   Editorial Board, "A Casual New Dress Code Doesn't Suit the U.S. Senate," *Washington Post*, September 19, 2023, https://www.washingtonpost.com /opinions/2023/09/19/senate-dress-code-john-fetterman/.

5   During the eighteenth and nineteenth centuries, manners could mean (as Johnson defined it) "ceremonious behaviour, studied civility" or "general way of life, morals; habits." In this chapter, I will use it according to the former definition. Samuel Johnson, *A Dictionary of the English Language*, vol. 2 (London: J. F. and C. Rivington, L. Davis, T. Payne and Son, 1785).

6   Frances Burney, "42. From *Journal* March 1778," *Journals and Letters*, ed. Peter Sabor and Lars E. Troide (London: Penguin Classics, 2001), 86.

7   Ibid., 98.

8   Frances Burney, *Evelina, or the History of a Young Lady's Entrance into the World* (Oxford: Oxford World's Classics, 2008), 17.

9   Ibid., 20.

10   Ibid., 21.

11   Ibid., 162.

12   Ibid., 9.

13   Abrams and Geoffrey Galt Harpham, *A Glossary of Literary Terms*, 10th ed. (Independence: Wadsworth Cengage Learning, 2012), 254.

14   Burney, *Evelina*, 10.

15   Ibid., 35.

16   Mrs. Selwyn may remind *Pride and Prejudice* readers of Mr. Bennet, whose excessive irony was a constant source of entertainment but also an impediment to the health of his personal relationships, particularly with the most frequent subject of that irony, his wife.

17   Ibid., 269.

18   Ibid., 378.

19 Ibid., 386.

20 Ibid., 69–70.

21 Ibid., 85.

22 Ibid., 183–84.

23 Ibid., 186.

24 Ibid., 186–87.

25 Ibid., 149. I suspect there's an ironic pun at work in the ditch, too. During a visit to the opera, Duval had wished to have been seated "in the pit," the section where the orchestra performs. The captain grants her wish.

26 Ibid., 150.

27 Margaret Anne Doody, *Frances Burney: The Life in the Works* (New Brunswick: Rutgers University Press, 1988), 53. Alas, Doody may stretch her claim to the breaking point by adding, "the ditch itself seems an image of the female sexual organ, and Madame Duval's name indicates the value of femaleness, the humility of the female estate, in contrast to the proud erection of mountain in the name of the father Bel*mont*."

28 Burney, *Evelina*, 292.

29 Ibid.

30 Ibid., 311.

31 Ibid., 312.

32 Ibid., 295.

33 Edmund Burke, *Reflections on the Revolution in France* [1790] (New York: Oxford World's Classics, 1993), 76.

34 Margaret Anne Doody hints at this interpretation when she notes of the race scene, "women have no defender—so much for chivalry." Doody, *Frances Burney*, 56.

35 Burney, *Evelina*, 401.

36 Ibid., 287.

37 Ibid., 262.

38 Ibid., 30–31.

39 Ibid., 401.

40 Ibid., 296.

41 Ibid., 124.

42 Ibid., 355.

43 Tocqueville, *Democracy in America*, 581.

44 Andy Ackerman, dir. "The Finale," *Seinfeld*, Season 9, Episode 23, NBC, 1998.

45   David Mandel, dir. "The Ida Funkhouser Roadside Memorial," *Curb Your Enthusiasm*, Season 6, Episode 3, HBO, 2007.

46   Roger Scruton, "Real Men Have Manners," *City Journal*, Winter 2000, https://www.city-journal.org/article/real-men-have-manners.

Chapter Three

1   The success of the Waverley novels didn't stop Scott from writing anonymously—he continued to use pseudonyms for all of his novels, even after he revealed his identity as the author of *Waverley* in 1825. One reason Scott is so enjoyable is that he really has fun with some of these fake identities.

2   Russell Kirk, *The Sword of Imagination: Memoirs of a Half-Century of Literary Conflict* (Grand Rapids: William B. Eerdmans Publishing Co., 1995), 434.

3   Russell Kirk, *The Conservative Mind: From Burke to Eliot* (Washington: Regnery, 2001), 119. Scott himself declared his admiration for Burke, proclaiming of the *Reflections* that "no political prophet ever viewed futurity with a surer ken" (*Life of Napoleon Buonaparte, Emperor of the French*, 1827).

4   John Henry Newman, "The Very Rev. Dr. Newman to J.R. Hope-Scott, Esq. Q.C.," in Robert Ornsby, *Memoirs of James Robert Hope-Scott*, vol. II, 2nd ed. (John Murray, 1884), 253. This future saint of the Catholic church anticipated one of my complaints in this chapter when he wrote, "It has been a trouble to me that [Scott's] works seemed to be so forgotten now" (ibid.).

5   John Henry Newman, "Prospects of the Anglican Church," in *Essays Critical and Historical*, vol. I, ed. Andrew Nash (Leominster: Gracewing, 2019), 270.

6   If you've ever wondered about the source of the term "trickle-down economics," often used by Democratic critics of supply-side economics, an early inspiration may occur when one of Scott's characters describes the contributions of a rash spender, recently deceased: "Bethink thee, how this poor man's vanity gave at least bread to the laborer, peasant, and citizen; and his profuse expenditure, like water spilt on the ground, refreshed the lowly herbs and plants where it fell." Walter Scott, *Chronicles of the Canongate* (London: Penguin Classics, 2003), 34.

7   Other great Romantic novels explore the importance of good reading and proper educational guidance: See, for example, Mary Shelley's *Frankenstein*

(1818), Jane Austen's *Northanger Abbey* (1817), and Maria Edgeworth's less famous, but still excellent, *Belinda* (1801). Going back further in time and to the continent, the plot of Miguel Cervantes's *Don Quixote* (1605 and 1615) revolves around the title character's delusional response to chivalric romance.

8 Walter Scott, *Waverley* (London, England: Penguin Classics, 2012), 12.

9 Most of the OED's illustrations for the first sense of "desultory" relate to the act of reading, including the first four, which range from 1740–1838.

10 Scott, *Waverley*, 15.

11 Ibid., 14.

12 Ibid., 12.

13 Ibid., 14.

14 Ibid., 13.

15 Ibid., 15.

16 Ibid., 16.

17 Alan Jacobs, *The Pleasures of Reading in an Age of Distraction* (Oxford: Oxford University Press, 2011), 33.

18 Scott, *Waverley*, 24.

19 Ibid., 33–34.

20 Ibid., 33.

21 One of the people Edward visits in the Highlands, the Baron of Bradwardine, is the first iteration of the pedantic comic figure characters who populate most of Scott's novels. He is in some regards the polar opposite of Edward: serious, unromantic, and rigorous in his study. But with pedants like Bradwardine, Scott indicates that there are dangers in being *too* focused in or absorbed by one's reading interest.

22 Scott, *Waverley*, 77.

23 Ibid., 84.

24 Ibid., 112–13, 115, 122.

25 Ibid., 133.

26 Ibid.

27 Ibid., 132.

28 Ibid., 206.

29 John Henry Newman, *The Idea of a University* (Worcester: Assumption Press, 2014), 374–76.

30 Scott, *Waverley*, 233. There's a note of irony in the tone of this lament, which echoes the kind of melodrama Edward might have encountered in one of his silly romances.

31   Ibid., 301.
32   Ibid., 149.
33   Douglas Mack and Suzanne Gilbert, "Scottish History in the Waverley Novels," in *Approaches to Teaching Scott's Waverley Novels*, ed. Evan Gottlieb and Ian Duncan (New York: Modern Language Association, 2009), 32.
34   Oakeshott, "On Being Conservative," *The Portable Conservative Reader*, ed. Russell Kirk (London: Penguin Books, 1982), 573. I can't resist quoting a definition of what conservatism should *not* be, from George Eliot: a character in *Middlemarch* holds a type of conservatism that held "that whatever is, is bad, and any change is likely to be worse." George Eliot, *Middlemarch* (New York: 2019), 370.
35   There are readers who interpret Waverley as a pro-Jacobite novel. For example: Julian Meldon D'Arcy, *Subversive Scott: The Waverley Novels and Scottish Nationalism* (Reykjavík: Iceland University Press, 2005).
36   Barton Swaim, "With the Election behind Us, Read This Novel," *Washington Post*, December 29, 2016, https://www.washingtonpost.com/blogs/post-partisan/wp/2016/12/29/with-the-election-behind-us-read-this-novel/. Swaim also wrote a very good essay about Scott for the *Weekly Standard*: "Scot on the Rocks," October 24, 2011: 33–37.
37   Scott, *Waverley*, 342.
38   Ibid., 348.
39   Arthur Herman, *How the Scots Invented the Modern World* (New York: Three Rivers Press, 2001), 310.
40   Scott, *Waverley*, 348.
41   Oakeshott, "On Being Conservative," *The Portable Conservative Reader*, ed. Russell Kirk (London: Penguin Books, 1982), 571.
42   Matthew Continetti, *The Right: The Hundred-Year War for American Conservatism* (New York: Basic Books, 2022), 415.
43   Scott, *Waverley*, 363, 364.
44   Samuel Johnson, *A Dictionary of the English Language*, vol. 2 (London: J. F. and C. Rivington, L. Davis, T. Payne and Son, 1785).
45   Edmund Burke, "Letters on a Regicide Peace," vol. 3 of *Selected Works of Edmund Burke* (Indianapolis: Liberty Fund, 1999), https://oll.libertyfund.org/titles/canavan-select-works-of-edmund-burke-vol-3.
46   Scott, *Waverley*, 363.
47   Ibid.

48   Ibid., 236. Even after this experience, Edward still considers himself "partial to the Highlanders." He just realizes he isn't one (ibid., 307).

49   Joseph Bottum, *The Decline of the Novel* (South Bend: St. Augustine's Press, 2019), 69.

50   *The Roots of Romanticism*, ed. Henry Hardy, 2nd ed. (Princeton: Princeton University Press, 2013), 158.

51   Hazlitt, "The Pleasure of Hating," *The Spirit of Controversy and Other Essays*, ed. Jon Mee and James Grande (Oxford: Oxford World's Classics, 2021), 299–300.

52   Scott, *Waverley*, 317.

53   G. K. Chesterton, *Charles Dickens: A Critical Study* (New York: Dodd Mead and Company, 1906), 248. Not quite the dignity of *all* men, though: in a darkly comic passage, an unsavory character has his head bashed in during battle, which "satisfied the world that the unfortunate gentleman had actually brains, the end of his life thus giving proof of a fact greatly doubted during its progress. His death was lamented by few" (Scott, *Waverley*, 242).

Chapter Four

1   I'd like to quote more of the song, but Lennon believed in copyright laws, which means that quoting more verses would be unaffordable. Imagine no possessions, indeed!

2   Frank Meyer, "The Recrudescent American Conservatism," in *American Conservativism: Reclaiming an Intellectual Tradition*, ed. Andrew Bacevich (New York: Library of America, 2020), 33.

3   Jonah Goldberg, "Immanent Corrections," *National Review*, January 16, 2002, https://www.nationalreview.com/2002/01/immanent-corrections-jonah -goldberg/.

4   Edmund Burke, *Reflections on the Revolution in France*, ed. L. G. Mitchell, Oxford World's Classics, reissue edition (Oxford: Oxford University Press, 2009), 21.

5   Thomas Sowell, *A Conflict of Visions: Ideological Origins of Political Struggles* (New York: William & Morrow, 1987), 32–33.

6   Henry James, *Hawthorne* (London: Macmillan and Co., 1879), 82.

7   Brenda Wineapple, *Hawthorne: A Life* (New York: Random House Trade Paperbacks, 2003), 154. After Hawthorne's departure, the community began adapting the more radical socialist principles of Charles Fourier, and it dissolved in 1847.

8   Nathaniel Hawthorne, *The Blithedale Romance* (London: Penguin Classics, 1983), 1.
9   James, *Hawthorne*, 77.
10   Hawthorne, *The Blithdale Romance*, 6.
11   Ibid., 12.
12   Ibid., 19.
13   Ibid., 140.
14   Ibid., 63.
15   Ibid., 44.
16   Ibid., 72.
17   Ibid., 1.
18   Ibid., 25.
19   Ibid., 9, 65–66.
20   Ibid., 66.
21   Ibid., 40–41.
22   Ibid., 66.
23   Ibid., 66.
24   Ibid., 81–82.
25   Ibid., 82.
26   Ibid., 128.
27   Ibid., 129.
28   Ibid., 130.
29   Ibid., 130–31.
30   Ibid., 68.
31   Fans of Flannery O'Connor will recognize this technique, as she uses it with the Misfit at the end of her short story "A Good Man Is Hard to Find." Although O'Connor did not necessarily borrow this method from Hawthorne, she did admire him and compared his desire "to keep for fiction some of its freedom from social determinisms, and to steer it in the direction of poetry" to her own approach. Flannery O'Connor, "The Grotesque in Southern Fiction," in *Mystery and Manners: Occasional Prose*, ed. Sally and Robert Fitzgerald, (New York: Farrar, Straus, & Giroux, 1970), 45–46. She also felt what biographer Brad Gooch called "a sense of kinship" with Hawthorne's daughter Rose, a Catholic convert who founded a Dominican order of nuns. Gooch, *Flannery: A Life of Flannery O'Connor* (New York: Little, Brown and Company, 2009), 328.
32   Hawthorne, *The Blithedale Romance*, 132.
33   Ibid., 131.

34   Ibid., 134.

35   Ibid., 124.

36   Roger Scruton, *The Meaning of Conservatism*, 3rd ed. (South Bend: St. Augustine's Press, 2002), 13.

37   Michael Oakeshott, "The Wisdom of Our Ancestors," in *The Portable Conservative Reader*, ed. Russell Kirk (New York: Penguin, 1982), 578. Aristotle had a similar view: "Now those who love each other for their utility do not love each other for themselves but in virtue of some good which they get from each other. . . . and thus these friendships are only incidental; for it is not as being the man he is that the loved person is loved, but as providing some good or pleasure. Such friendships, then, are easily dissolved, if the parties do not remain like themselves[.]" Aristotle, *Ethics*, trans. David Ross (Oxford: Oxford University Press, 1986), 195, VIII.3.

38   Hawthorne, *The Blithedale Romance*, 57.

39   Ibid., 43.

40   Ibid., 55.

41   Ibid., 56.

42   Herman Melville, *Moby Dick* (New York: Macmillan, 1964), 246.

43   Hawthorne, *The Blithedale Romance*, 70.

44   Ibid., 71.

45   Ibid., 28–29.

46   Ibid., 120.

47   Ibid., 122–23.

48   Ibid., 123–24.

49   Ibid., 224.

50   Ibid., 227.

51   Ibid., 44.

52   Nathaniel Hawthorne, "Earth's Holocaust," *Nathaniel Hawthorne's Tales*, ed. James McIntosh (New York: W. W. Norton & Company, 1987), 144.

53   Ibid., 145, 156.

54   Ibid., 146.

55   Ibid., 158.

56   Ibid., 159.

57   Russell Kirk, *The Conservative Mind* 7th ed. (Washington: Regnery, 2001), 259. Kirk also included "Earth's Holocaust" in his anthology *The Portable Conservative Reader* (New York: Penguin Books, 1982).

58   See, for example: Kamala Harris, "Remarks by Vice President Harris at a Reception in Celebration of Hispanic Heritage Month," October 18,

2023, https://www.whitehouse.gov/briefing-room/speeches-remarks/2023/10/18/remarks-by-vice-president-harris-at-a-reception-in-celebration-of-hispanic-heritage-month/.

Chapter Five

1   Gertrude Himmelfarb, *The Jewish Odyssey of George Eliot* (New York: Encounter Books, 2009), 68.

2   Clare Carlisle, *The Marriage Question: George Eliot's Double Life* (New York: Farrar, Straus and Giroux, 2023), 219.

3   Himmelfarb, *The Jewish Odyssey of George Eliot*, 4, 6.

4   Quoted in Carlisle, *The Marriage Question*, 220.

5   Himmelfarb, *The Jewish Odyssey of George Eliot*, 117, 6.

6   George Eliot, *Daniel Deronda* [1876], ed. Graham Handley (New York: Oxford University Press, 1999), 305.

7   Ibid., 275.

8   Roger Scruton, *How to Be a Conservative* (London: Bloomsbury, 2014), viii. I'm indebted to Michael Q. McShane for drawing my attention to this insight, about which he writes in the introduction for a collection we co-edited: *Conservative Persuasions: An Introduction for College Students* (Washington: American Enterprise Institute, 2023).

9   Carlisle, *The Marriage Question*, 213.

10   Christopher Hitchens, "In Defense of *Daniel Deronda*," *The Threepenny Review*, no. 39 (Autumn 1989), 9.

11   Eliot, *Daniel Deronda*, 3.

12   Ibid., 7.

13   Ibid., 224.

14   Ibid., 13.

15   Ibid., 243.

16   Ibid., 117.

17   Ibid.

18   Ibid., 118.

19   In his defense, Mr. Gascoigne's first appeal to a sense of duty is well-placed. His son Rex, spurned by Gwendolen, is disconsolate and determined to emigrate to Canada. Mr. Gascoigne forbids it and scolds Rex for "suppos[ing] that because you have fallen into a very common trouble, such as most men have to go through, you are loosened from all bonds of duty—just as if your brain had softened and you were no longer a responsible being" (Eliot, *Daniel Deronda*, 73). Here at least his appeal

to duty is sensible and may have unexpected long-term benefits: in the novel's final pages, there is a hint that Rex may finally marry Gwendolen after all.

20 Ibid., 377.
21 Ibid., 371.
22 Ibid., 647.
23 Ibid., 149.
24 Ibid., 304–5.
25 Ibid., 305.
26 Ibid., 397.
27 Ibid., 557.
28 Ibid., 207.
29 Ibid., 249.
30 Ibid., 262.
31 Ibid., 279.
32 Ibid., 126.
33 Ibid., 130.
34 Ibid., 267.
35 Ibid., 253.
36 Ibid., 266.
37 Ibid., 500.
38 Ibid., 492.
39 Ibid., 500.
40 Ibid., 563.
41 Ibid., 253.
42 Ibid., 677.
43 Ibid., 449.
44 Ibid., 450.
45 Ibid., 608.
46 Ibid., 609.
47 George Eliot, "The Modern Hep! Hep! Hep!," in *Impressions of Theophrastus Such* (New York: Harper & Brothers, 1879), 203.
48 Ibid., 220.
49 Jonah Goldberg, "Nations, Nation-States, and Nationalism," *The Dispatch*, February 23, 2024, www.thedispatch.com/newsletter/gfile/nations-nation -states-and-nationalism. Elsewhere, Goldberg warns that "nationalism shorn of negating qualifiers has no internal checks, no limiting principles that mitigate against giving in to collective passion." See Jonah Goldberg, *Suicide of the West* (New York: Crown Forum, 2017), 313.

50 Roger Scruton, "The Need for Nations," RogerScruton.com, https://www
.roger-scruton.com/articles/276-the-need-for-nations.

51 Rich Lowry and Ramesh Ponnuru, "For Love of Country," *National Review*, February 6, 2017, https://www.nationalreview.com/2017/02/nationalism-conservatism-are-compatible-trump-imperfect-vessel/.

52 Irving Kristol, "The Coming 'Conservative Century'," in *Neoconservatism: The Autobiography of an Idea* (New York: The Free Press, 1995), 365.

53 Scruton, "The Need for Nations."

54 Roger Scruton, "The Case for Nations," *Wall Street Journal*, June 2, 2017, https://www.wsj.com/articles/the-need-for-nations-1496421583.

55 Eliot, "The Modern Hep! Hep! Hep!," 202–3.

56 Ibid., 230.

57 Eliot, *Daniel Deronda*, 609.

58 "Zionism from the Standpoint of Its Victims" [1979], in *The Edward Said Reader*, ed. Moustafa Bayoumi and Andrew Rubin (New York: Vintage Books, 2000), 123.

59 Susan Meyer, "'Safely to Their Own Borders': Proto-Zionism, Feminism, and Nationalism in *Daniel Deronda*," *ELH* 60 (1993): 736.

60 Adam Kirsch, *On Settler Colonialism: Ideology, Violence, and Justice* (New York: W. W. Norton & Company, 2024), 106.

61 Ruth Wisse, "The Political Vision of Daniel Deronda: Separateness with Communication," *Daniel Deronda: George Eliot's Novel of Jewish Nationalism*, 2017, https://tikvahfund.org/course/daniel-deronda.

62 Eliot, *Daniel Deronda*, 4.

63 Marc E. Wohlfarth, "*Daniel Deronda* and the Politics of Nationalism," *Nineteenth-Century Literature* 53.2 (September 1998), 205–6.

64 Aleksandar Stević, "Convenient Cosmopolitanism: *Daniel Deronda*, Nationalism, and the Critics," *Victorian Literature and Culture* 45.3 (August 2017), 598.

65 Wisse, "The Political Vision of Daniel Deronda: Separateness with Communication." Wisse's eight-part lecture series is an invaluable resource for anyone interested in this novel and is available at Tikvah.org.

66 Eliot, *Daniel Deronda*, 453.

Chapter Six

1 Joan Acocella, "Cather and the Academy," *New Yorker*, November 27, 1995, 60.

2   James Woodress, *Willa Cather: A Literary Life* (Lincoln: University of Nebraska Press, 1987), 293.

3   Indeed, Acocella herself occasionally leans toward this affirmativist note, like when she observes that even as "Cather is describing life's terrors she never stops asserting its beauties: the fingers of light, the orchard shot with gold." Acocella, "Cather and the Academy," 63.

4   Woodress, *Willa Cather*, 293.

5   Katherine Anne Porter, "Reflections on Willa Cather," in *Collected Stories and Other Writings*, ed. Darlene Harbour Unrue (New York: Library of America, 2008), 541.

6   Tom Perrotta, "Entirely Personal," Review of *The Selected Letters of Willa Cather*, *New York Times Book Review*, April 28, 2013, https://www.nytimes.com/2013/04/28/books/review/selected-letters-of-willa-cather.html.

7   Porter, *Collected Stories and Other Writings*, 549.

8   Woodress, *Willa Cather*, 290.

9   Ibid., 285.

10   Ibid., 289.

11   Willa Cather, *My Ántonia* (Boston: Houghton Mifflin Company, 1954), 2.

12   Ibid., 173.

13   Ibid., 146.

14   Ibid., 5.

15   Ibid., 8.

16   Ibid., 12.

17   Ibid., 28.

18   Matthew 17:2 (KJV).

19   Woodress, *Willa Cather*, 298.

20   Curtis Dahl, "An American Georgic: Willa Cather's *My Ántonia*," *Comparative Literature* 7, no. 1 (1955), 43–51.

21   Cather, *My Ántonia*, 156.

22   Ben Sasse, *The Vanishing American Adult: Our Coming-of-Age Crisis and How to Rebuild a Culture of Self-Reliance*, (New York: St. Martin's Press, 2017), 239.

23   Lionel Trilling, "Willa Cather," *New Republic* (February 9, 1937), https://newrepublic.com/article/76896/willa-cather.

24   Cather, *My Ántonia*, 31–33.

25   This paradox challenges Samuel Johnson's aversion to specificity, which we encountered in *Rasselas*.

26   Porter, *Collected Stories and Other Writings*, 550.

27   H. L. Mencken, *H. L. Mencken's Smart Set Criticism*, ed. and comp. William H. Nolte (Washington: Gateway Editions, 2000), 266.

28   The Pretenders, "My City Was Gone," B-side to "Back on the Chain Gang," Sire Records, 1982.

29   Rush Limbaugh, "Origins of the EIB Theme Song," *The Rush Limbaugh Show*, May 13, 2011, https://www.rushlimbaugh.com/daily/2011/05/13/origins_of_the_eib_theme_song/.

30   John J. Miller, "Rockin' the Right," *National Review*, June 5, 2006, https://www.nationalreview.com/2006/06/rockin-right-john-j-miller/.

31   Cather, *My Ántonia*, 197.

32   Ibid.

33   Ibid., 2.

34   Trilling, "Willa Cather."

35   Joseph Epstein, "Willa Cather: Listing Toward Lesbos," *The New Criterion* 2.4 (December 1983), https://newcriterion.com/issues/1983/12/willa-cather-listing-toward-lesbos.

36   Ronald Reagan, "Remarks at the Presentation Ceremony for the Presidential Medal of Freedom," Ronald Reagan Presidential Library & Museum, January 19, 1989, https://www.reaganlibrary.gov/archives/speech/remarks-presentation-ceremony-presidential-medal-freedom-5.

37   Ronald Reagan, "Statement on Signing the Immigration Reform and Control Act of 1986," Ronald Reagan Presidential Library & Museum, November 6, 1986, https://www.reaganlibrary.gov/archives/speech/statement-signing-immigration-reform-and-control-act-1986.

38   Joseph Epstein, *The Novel: Who Needs It?* (New York: Encounter Books, 2023), 13.

39   Cather, *My Ántonia*, 65.

40   Ibid., 70. Catholic readers may also read Anton's story as also a powerful account of devotion to the Eucharist.

41   Ibid., 58.

42   Ibid., 73.

43   Ibid., 114. (And no, that's not a typo–the character says "Americy.")

44   Ibid., 84.

45   Ibid., 129.

46   Ibid.

47   Ibid., 128.

48   Porter, *Collected Stories and Other Writings*, 541.

49   Cather, *My Ántonia*, 226.

50   Ibid., 215.

51   Ibid., 229.

52   Ibid., 235.

53   Ibid., 226–27.

54   Ibid., 1–2.

55   Janis P. Stout, *Willa Cather: The Writer and Her World* (Charlottesville: University of Virginia Press, 2000), 148.

56   Ibid., 146.

57   Woodress, *Willa Cather*, 293.

58   Cather, *My Ántonia*, 227.

59   Bradley J. Birzer, "*My Ántonia at 100*," The Imaginative Conservative, August 29, 2018, https://www.theamericanconservative.com/my-antonia-at-100/.

Chapter Seven

1   Ralph Ellison, "Recent Negro Fiction," *New Masses*, August 5, 1941, 22, 24.

2   Alain Locke, "Jingo, Counter-Jingo and Us," *Opportunity: Journal of Negro Life*, January, 1938 (XVI.1), 10.

3   Richard Wright, "Two Negro Novels," *New Masses*, October 5, 1937, 25.

4   "Alice Walker Shines Light on Zora Neale Hurston," *PBS: American Masters*, https://www.pbs.org/wnet/americanmasters/alice-walker-film-excerpt-walker-puts-zora-neale-hurston-back-in-spotlight/2869/.

5   "Edwidge Danticat: By the Book," *New York Times*, August 8, 2013, https://www.nytimes.com/2013/08/11/books/review/edwidge-danticat-by-the-book.html.

6   Henry Louis Gates Jr., "Introduction," *You Don't Know Us Negroes and Other Essays*, ed. Genevieve West and Henry Louis Gates Jr. (New York: Harper Collins, 2022),13.

7   John H. McWhorter, "Thus Spake Zora," *City Journal*, Summer 2009, https://www.city-journal.org/article/thus-spake-zora.

8   John McWhorter, "Why The [sic] National Review Would Have Loved Zora Neale Hurston," *New Republic*, August 17, 2009, https://newrepublic.com/article/68564/why-the-national-review-would-have-loved-zora-neale-hurston.

9   Roger Clegg, "Wrapped in Zora," *National Review*, April 13, 2004, https://www.nationalreview.com/2004/04/wrapped-zora-roger-clegg/. John J. Miller devoted an episode of his indispensable *National Review* podcast *The Great Books* to *Their Eyes Were Watching God*, featuring Dedra Birzer of Hillsdale College: Episode 96, August 13, 2019,

https://www.nationalreview.com/podcasts/the-great-books/episode-96
-their-eyes-were-watching-god-by-zora-neale-hurston/.

10   Dwight Garner, "In Zora Neale Hurston's Essays, the Nonfiction of a
Nonconformist," *New York Times*, January 10, 2002, https://www.nytimes
.com/2022/01/10/books/review-zora-neale-hurston-you-dont-know-us
-negroes-essays.html?searchResultPosition=8.

11   "Mourner's Bench: Why the Negro Won't Buy Communism," in *You Don't
Know Us Negroes*, 283.

12   Zora Neale Hurston, "How It Feels to Be Colored Me," in *You Don't Know
Us Negroes and Other Essays*, 187.

13   Ibid., 189.

14   McWhorter, "Thus Spake Zora."

15   Alice Walker, "Saving the Life That Is Your Own: The Importance of Models
in the Artist's Life," in *In Search of Our Mothers' Gardens: Womanist Prose*
(San Diego: Harcourt, 1993), 6.

16   Zora Neale Hurston, *Their Eyes Were Watching God* (New York: Amistad,
2006), 11.

17   Ibid., 1.

18   Ibid., 14–15.

19   Ibid., 21.

20   Ibid., 24–25.

21   Ibid., 31.

22   Ibid., 29.

23   Ibid., 43.

24   Ibid., 71.

25   Ibid., 117.

26   Ibid., 124.

27   Ibid., 133.

28   Ibid., 148.

29   Ibid., 106, 128.

30   Ibid., 128.

31   Shawn E. Miller, "'Some Other Way to Try': From Defiance to Creative
Submission in *Their Eyes Were Watching God*," in *Bloom's Modern Critical
Interpretation: Zora Neale Hurston's* Their Eyes Were Watching God, ed.
Harold Bloom (New Haven: Bloom's Literary Criticism, 2008), 187.

32   Valerie Boyd, *Wrapped in Rainbows: The Life of Zora Neale Hurston* (New
York: Scribner, 2004), 22. Boyd quotes from Washington's *The Negro in
Business* (1907).

33   Hurston, *Their Eyes Were Watching God*, 34–35.
34   Ibid., 45.
35   Ibid., 47.
36   Ibid., 47.
37   Ibid., 49.
38   Ibid., 50.
39   Ibid., 88.
40   Zora Neale Hurston, "Negroes Without Self Pity," in *You Don't Know Us Negroes and Other Essays*, 244.
41   Hurston, *Their Eyes Were Watching God.*, 14.
42   Ibid., 171.
43   Ibid., 39.
44   Ibid., 189.
45   Ibid., 140.
46   Ibid., 141.
47   Ibid., 142.
48   Ibid., 145.
49   Rosemary V. Hathaway, "The Unbearable Weight of Authenticity: Zora Neale Hurston's *Their Eyes Were Watching God* and a Theory of 'Touristic Reading'," *Journal of American Folklore* 117 (464): 181.
50   Hurston, *Their Eyes Were Watching God*, 142. A similar image of Washington appears in Tom Wolfe's novel *A Man in Full*. A black character named Roger White II—called Roger Too White by his peers—reflects that in his college years, "If you were a proponent of Booker T. Washington, then you were worse than out of it. The way people acted, you might as well have been waving a placard for Lester Maddox of George Wallace or Eugene Talmadge. But damn it all, Booker T. was no Uncle Tom! He never kowtowed to no white man!" Tom Wolfe, *A Man in Full* (New York: Farrar, Straus Giroux, 1998), 22.
51   Hathaway, "The Unbearable Weight of Authenticity," 181–82.
52   "Booker T. Washington, "Delivers the 1895 Atlanta Compromise Speech," History Matters: The U.S. Survey Course on the Web, https://historymatters.gmu.edu/d/39/.
53   Robert J. Norrell, *Up from History: The Life of Booker T. Washington* (Cambridge, MA: Belknap, 2011), 124, 220.
54   Washington, *Up From Slavery* [1901] (New York: Penguin Classics, 1986), 208.

55   John McWhorter, "The Resurrection of Booker T. Washington, *Forbes*, February 6, 2009, https://www.forbes.com/2009/02/06/booker-washington -dubois-opinions-bookreviews_0206_john_mcwhorter.html?sh =3d3ddc8f413c. Among the schools bearing Washington's name is the high school where the character Steve Hightower taught in *The Steve Harvey Show*. In a more recent television series, Washington is represented negatively in *Self Made*, a Netflix drama about C. J. Walker, the first American black woman to become a millionaire.

56   Glenn C. Loury, "Two Paths to Black Power," *First Things*, October 1992, https://www.firstthings.com/article/1992/10/two-paths-to-black-power. Thomas Sowell has suggested that the divide between Du Bois and Washington has been greatly exaggerated. Though the two men had their disagreements, they were not as severe as is they are often perceived and are more a matter of emphasis. See Thomas Sowell, *Black Rednecks and White Liberals* (New York: Encounter Books, 2006), 231–35.

57   W. E. B. Du Bois, *The Souls of Black Folk*, in *Writings* (New York: Library of America, 1986), 398, 403.

58   W. E. B. Du Bois, "The Talented Tenth," in *Writings* (New York: Library of America, 1986), 184.

59   Boyd, *Wrapped in Rainbows*, 151.

60   Zora Neale Hurston, "The Emperor Effaces Himself," in *You Don't Know Us Negroes and Other* Essays, ed. Genevieve West and Henry Louis Gates Jr. (New York: Harper Collins, 2022), 178. Interestingly, in this brief work Hurston also casts Du Bois in a favorable light, eliding the distinctions between him and Washington in opposition to what she viewed as the clear and present danger presented by Garvey.

61   Zora Neale Hurston, *Jonah's Gourd Vine* [1934] (New York: Harper Perennial, 1990), 148.

62   Zora Neale Hurston, "Which Way the NAACP?," in *You Don't Know Us Negroes and Other* Essays, ed. Genevieve West and Henry Louis Gates Jr. (New York: Harper Collins, 2022), 303.

63   Boyd, *Wrapped in Rainbows*, 118.

64   Jason Riley, "Black Politics," *Forbes*, October 15, 2014, https://www.forbes .com/sites/realspin/2014/10/15/black-politics-an-excerpt-from-please -stop-helping-us-by-jason-l-riley/. This article is based on Riley's *Please Stop Trying to Help Us: How Liberals Make It Harder for Blacks to Succeed* (New York: Encounter Books, 2014).

65 "Booker T & W. E. B.: The Debate between W.E.B. Du Bois and Booker T. Washington," *PBS Frontline*, date unknown, https://www.pbs.org/wgbh/frontline/wgbh/pages/frontline/shows/race/etc/road.html.

66 Walker, "Saving the Life," 12.

Chapter Eight

1 "American Views 2022: Part 2 Trust, Media and Democracy," *Knight Foundation*, February 15, 2023, https://knightfoundation.org/reports/american-views-2023-part-2/.

2 Ross Douthat, "Trump's Lesson for the Media and Ron DeSantis," *New York Times*, May 13, 2023, https://www.nytimes.com/2023/05/13/opinion/trump-desantis-town-hall.html.

3 William F. Buckley Jr., "Evelyn Waugh, R.I.P.," *National Review*, June 30, 2004, https://www.nationalreview.com/2004/06/evelyn-waugh-rip-william-f-buckley-jr/.

4 Richard Brookhiser, "Waugh and Me," *National Review*, October 10, 2017, https://www.nationalreview.com/corner/waugh-and-me-richard-brookhiser/.

5 Robert Hutton, "Putting the Boot in . . ." *The Critic*, July 2021, https://thecritic.co.uk/issues/july-2021/putting-the-boot-in/.

6 Steerpike, "The Books Which MPs Recommend This Summer," *The Spectator*, July 23, 2021, https://www.spectator.co.uk/article/the-books-that-mps-recommend-this-summer/.

7 Evelyn Waugh, *Scoop* (New York: Back Bay Books, 2012), ix.

8 Evelyn Waugh, *Scoop* (London: Penguin Books, 2000), 16. Unless otherwise noted, subsequent quotations will be from this edition of the novel.

9 Ibid., 74–75.

10 Ibid., 75.

11 Ibid., 76.

12 Evelyn Waugh, *Scoop* (New York: Back Bay Books, 2012), ix.

13 Waugh, *Scoop*, 77.

14 Ibid., 78.

15 Christopher Hitchens, "Introduction," in *Scoop* (London: Penguin Books, 2000), ix.

16 Waugh, *Scoop*, 78.

17 Ibid., 50.

18 Ibid., 51.

19 Ibid., 42.

20   Ibid., 140.
21   Ibid., 138.
22   Ibid., 64.
23   Ibid., 66.
24   Ibid., 67.
25   Ibid., 170.
26   Ibid., 97.
27   George Orwell, "Looking Back on the Spanish War," in *A Collection of Essays* (New York: Harcourt, Inc., 1981), 197.
28   Waugh, *Scoop*, 101.
29   Ibid., 115.
30   Ibid., 118.
31   Ibid., 145–46.
32   Ibid., 188.
33   Ibid., 166.
34   Paris Review, "The Art of Fiction No. 30," Summer-Fall 1963, https://www.theparisreview.org/interviews/4537/the-art-of-fiction-no-30-evelyn-waugh.
35   Waugh, *Scoop*, 16.
36   Ibid., 179.
37   "Politics and the English Language" in *George Orwell: A Collection of Essays*, Harcourt: 157.
38   Orwell, "Looking Back on the Spanish War," 159.
39   Waugh, *Scoop*, 139.
40   David Lebedoff, *The Same Man: George Orwell and Evelyn Waugh in Love and War* (New York: Random House, 2008), 204–5.
41   Waugh, *Scoop*, 26–27.
42   Ibid., 196–197.
43   Ibid., 210.
44   Ibid., 23–24.
45   Ibid., 76–77.
46   Ibid., 172.
47   Ibid., 177.
48   Waugh, *Scoop* (New York: Back Bay Books, 2012), ix.
49   Some elements of this chapter first appeared in Christopher J. Scalia, "Dystopian Fiction Is Big Now. But Here's a Book for People Worried about Fake News," *Washington Post*, March 21, 2017, https://www.washingtonpost.com/posteverything/wp/2017/03/21/dystopian-fiction-is-big-now-but-heres-a-book-for-people-worried-about-fake-news/.

Chapter Nine

1   William F. Buckley Jr., "Toward an Empirical Definition," in *American Conservatism: Reclaiming an Intellectual Tradition* (New York: Library of America, 2020), 23.

2   Russell Kirk, "Introduction," in *The Portable Conservative Reader*, ed. Russell Kirk (New York: Penguin Books, 1982), xv.

3   Muriel Spark, *The Prime of Miss Jean Brodie* [1961] (New York: Harper Perennial Modern Classics, 2009), 117.

4   "Writing with Intent: The Artistry of Muriel Spark," *Commonweal*, 21 April 1989: 234.

5   Rosemary Goring, "Introduction," *The Girls of Slender Means* (Edinburgh: Polygon, 2018), xiv.

6   Muriel Spark, "How I Became a Novelist," in *The Informed Air: Essays*, ed. Penelope Jardine (New York: New Directions, 2014), 46.

7   Muriel Spark, *The Girls of Slender Means* (New York: New Directions, 1963), 9. All subsequent quotations from the novel itself will be from this edition, though I will quote paratext from other editions.

8   Ibid., 8.

9   Ibid., 17.

10 Ibid., 19.

11 Ibid., 95.

12 Ibid., 10.

13 Ibid., 42.

14 Ibid., 140.

15 *Commonweal*, 236.

16 "Unrivalled Deftness: The Novels of Muriel Spark," in *Hidden Possibilities: Essays in Honor of Muriel Spark*, ed. Robert E. Hosmer, Jr., 114.

17 Spark, *The Girls of Slender Means*, 64.

18 The repetition of poetic lines, the bouncing around in time: these elements make the novel spellbinding—but also, *caveat lector*, occasionally challenging.

19 Goring, "Introduction," *The Girls of Slender Means*, xi.

20 Spark, *The Girls of Slender Means*, 12.

21 Ibid., 50.

22 Ibid., 26.

23 Ibid., 30.

24 Ibid., 77.

25 Ibid., 104.

26   Ibid., 57.

27   *Catechism of the Catholic Church*, 483; section 1996, https://www.usccb
      .org/sites/default/files/flipbooks/catechism/484/.

28   Newman, "The Calls of Grace." https://www.newmanreader.org/works
      /ninesermons/sermon3.html.

29   Ibid.

30   Spark, *The Girls of Slender Means*, 57.

31   Ibid., 57–8.

32   Ibid., 58.

33   Ibid., 65.

34   Ibid., 92.

35   Ibid., 7.

36   Ibid., 71.

37   Ibid., 84–85.

38   Ibid., 85.

39   Ibid., 142.

40   Goring, "Introduction," *The Girls of Slender Means*, xii–xiii.

41   George F. Will, "Crises and the Collectivist Temptation," *Washington
      Post*, April 3, 2020, https://www.washingtonpost.com/opinions/crises
      -and-the-collectivist-temptation/2020/04/02/751241b8–74fa-11ea-87da
      -77a8136c1a6d_story.html.

42   Martin Stannard, *Muriel Spark: The Biography* (New York: W. W. Norton 7
      Company, 2010), 59.

43   Spark, *Curriculum Vitae*, 140–41.

44   Goring, "Introduction," *The Girls of Slender Means*, xiv.

45   Spark, *The Girls of Slender Means*, 9.

46   Ibid., 72.

47   Ibid., 52.

48   Anthony Burgess, *Ninety-Nine Novels: The Best in English Since 1939: a
      Personal Choice* (London: Allison & Busy, 1984), 88.

49   Introduction to the 2013 Folio edition of *The Girls of Slender Means*, xiii.

50   "Fascinated by Suspense," in *Hidden Possibilities*, 246.

51   "The Large Testimony of Muriel Spark," in *Hidden Possibilities*, 33.

52   Muriel Spark, *Curriculum Vitae* (New York: New Directions, 1992), 98.

53   Spark, *The Girls of Slender Means*, 127.

54   *Commonweal*, 237.

55   Graham Foster and Alan Taylor, "Two Novels by Muriel Spark," *Ninety-
      Nine Novels: The Podcast*, October 12, 2022, https://www.anthonyburgess
      .org/blog-posts/ninety-nine-novels-two-novels-by-muriel-spark/.

Chapter Ten

1   V. S. Naipaul, "Our Universal Culture," *City Journal*, Summer 1991, https: //www.city-journal.org/article/our-universal-civilization.

2   One quibble about his praise here: what we've encountered in other novels should alert us to the dangers of the "perfectibility" to which Naipaul referred—perhaps "more perfect" is the more appropriate (if grammatically imperfect) phrase.

3   As biographer Patrick French explains of Naipaul's disappointing academic performance, "it was a slight consolation to learn that J.R.R. Tolkien had said his Anglo-Saxon paper was the best in the university." Patrick French, *The World Is What It Is: The Authorized Biography of V. S. Naipaul* (New York: Vintage, 2008), 115. I would be failing in my duties as a husband if I did not take this opportunity to boast that in 2004, my wife won the same Trinidadian national scholarship.

4   French, *The World Is What It* Is, 253.

5   Patrick Marnham, "Introduction," in V. S. Naipaul, *A Bend in the River* (New York: Everyman's Library, 2019), viii.

6   Frantz Fanon, *The Wretched of the Earth*, trans. Constance Farrington (New York: Grove Press, 1963), 94.

7   Marnham, "Introduction," *A Bend in the River*, xxi.

8   David Pryce-Jones, "V. S. Naipaul, 1932–2018," *New Criterion*, October 2018, https://newcriterion.com/issues/2018/10/v-s-naipaul-19322018.

9   French, *The World Is What It Is*, 386.

10   Ibid., 387.

11   Edward Said, "Intellectuals in the Post-Colonial World," *Salmagundi* 70/71 (Spring/Summer 1986), 53.

12   Conor Cruise O'Brien, Edward Said, and John Lukacs, "The Intellectual in the Post-Colonial World: Response and Discussion," *Salmagundi* 70/71 (Spring/Summer 1986), 79. Conor Cruise O'Brien's response to Said's claim during this conversation is spot on: "That's not true. He's talking about human beings living in very confused and desperate situations. There is no trace of a racialist bias in Naipaul, and I don't see why when you disapprove of his views it's necessary to bring in the question of race or innate characteristics" (Ibid., 79–80).

13   "Transcript: President Obama on What Books Mean to Him," *New York Times*, January 16, 2017, https://www.nytimes.com/2017/01/16/books /transcript-president-obama-on-what-books-mean-to-him.html.

14   Geoffrey Wheatcroft, "A Terrifying Honesty," *The Atlantic*, February 2002, https://www.theatlantic.com/magazine/archive/2002/02/a-terrifying-honesty/302426/.

15   V. S. Naipaul, *A Bend in the River* (New York: Everyman's Library, 2019), 9.

16   Jeremy Carl, "A Man of Universal Letters," *Claremont Review of Books* (digital exclusive), October 25, 2018, https://claremontreviewofbooks.com/digital/a-man-of-universal-letters/.

17   Naipaul, *A Bend in the River*, 24.

18   Ibid., 26.

19   Ibid., 28.

20   This happens to be the same setting for Joseph Conrad's novella *Heart of Darkness*, to which *A Bend in the River* is often compared, and which Naipaul admired.

21   Naipaul, *A Bend in the River*, 28.

22   Ibid., 68.

23   Ibid., 31.

24   Ibid., 63.

25   Ibid., 65.

26   Ibid., 64.

27   Ibid., 63.

28   Ibid., 64.

29   Ibid., 39. The phrase is a variation of *Semper aliquid novi Africam adferre*, from Pliny the Elder's first-century AD work *Historia Naturalis*. *The Oxford Dictionary of Quotations*, ed. Elizabeth Knowles, 5th ed. (New York: Oxford University Press, 1999), 578. The common English translation provides the title of Karen Blixen's famous memoir, *Out of Africa*, which was adapted to an Oscar-winning film starring Robert Redford and Meryl Streep.

30   Naipaul, *A Bend in the River*, 64.

31   Ibid., 65.

32   The novel includes another motto of sorts that might trouble conservatives, but which I think ultimately reinforces a conservative reading of the novel. Salim has an ambitious friend from the African coast, Indar, who frequently offers some version of this insight: "We have to learn to trample on the past, Salim" (Ibid., 138). This attitude allows Indar to establish solid ground on which to build his own destiny in New York City and then London. He fails in finding this footing, however, and eventually decides to return home. He wants to trample the past, but it keeps regrowing under his feet.

33   Naipaul, *A Bend in the River*, 82.

34   Ibid.

35   Ibid., 77.

36   Ibid., 79.

37   Ibid., 100.

38   Ibid., 101.

39   Ibid., 102.

40   Ibid., 103, 123.

41   Ibid., 103.

42   Ibid., 202.

43   Ibid., 205.

44   Ibid., 165.

45   Ibid., 250.

46   Ibid., 257.

47   Park MacDougald, "The World as He Saw It," *The Point Magazine*, August 13 2018, https://thepointmag.com/criticism/world-as-he-saw-it-v-s-naipaul-1932–2018/.

48   Naipaul, *A Bend in the River*, 124.

49   Ibid., 127.

50   Ibid.

51   Ibid., 177.

52   Ibid., 170.

53   Ibid., 172.

54   Ibid., 188–89.

55   Ibid., 182.

56   Algis Valiunas, "Bleak House: The World of V. S. Naipaul," *The Weekly Standard*, August 5, 2002, https://www.washingtonexaminer.com/weekly-standard/the-bleak-house-of-vs-naipaul.

57   French, *The World Is What It Is*, 379.

58   Marnham, "Introduction," in Naipaul, *A Bend in the River*, xix.

59   Valiunas, "Bleak House."

60   Naipaul, *A Bend in the River*, 215.

61   When Naipaul discussed the scene with his wife, he too pointed out the importance of the passive voice: "He said that he had worked carefully—using the passive voice—'she was hit'—'I hit her' would be to make Salim just a tough man." French, *The World Is What It Is*, 380.

62   Naipaul, *A Bend in the River*, 216..

63 David Pryce-Jones, "Naipaul Is Truly a Nobel Man in a Free State," *The Nobel Prize in Literature 2001: Biographical*, https://www.nobelprize.org /prizes/literature/2001/naipaul/biographical/.

64 Joseph Epstein, "A Cottage for Mr. Naipaul," *The New Criterion*, October 1987, https://newcriterion.com/issues/1987/10/a-cottage-for-mr-naipaul.

65 Naipaul, *A Bend in the River*, 261–62.

66 Ibid., 264.

67 Jeffrey Folks, "V. S. Naipaul's *A Bend in the River*: A Tragic Vision of Evil," *Modern Age* Winter 2016, 32. Importantly, when Naipaul represents the West in *A Bend in the River*, he does not glorify it or suggest that it is innately superior to Africa. Salim's acquaintances who seek education and prosperity in the United States and England are disappointed. When Salim himself visits London, he encounters "something shrunken and mean and forbidding" (Naipaul, *A Bend in the River*, 225).

68 Naipaul, *A Bend in the River*, 270.

69 Joan Didion, "Without Regret or Hope," *New York Review of Books*, June 12, 1980, https://archive.is/fD2Xh.

Chapter Eleven

1 Jonah Goldberg, *Liberal Fascism: The Secret History of the American Left, from Mussolini to the Politics of Change* (New York: Broadway Books, 2007), 349. Regarding Merriam-Webster, Snopes.com explains: "Following the Oct. 13, 2020, confirmation hearing of Judge Amy Coney Barrett, U.S. President Donald Trump's pick for the Supreme Court, dictionary publisher Merriam-Webster updated its definition and usage guidelines its entry of 'sexual preference' to include a statement to the effect that use of the term is 'offensive.'" (Madison Dapcevich, "Did Merriam-Webster Update Its Entry on 'Sexual Preference' after Barrett Hearing?," Snopes, October 20, 2020, https://www.snopes.com/fact-check/merriam-webster-barrett-sexual/.)

2 *Oxford Dictionary of Quotations* (New York: Oxford University Press, 2009), 430.

3 P. D. James, *Time to Be in Earnest: A Fragment of Autobiography* (New York: Alfred A. Knopf, 2000), 199.

4 "Births in England and Wales: 2023," Office for National Statistics, October 28, 2024, https://www.ons.gov.uk/peoplepopulationandcommunity/births deathsandmarriages/livebirths/bulletins/birthsummarytablesenglandand wales/2023. Britain's Office for National Statistics defines the Total Fertility Rate as "the average number of live children that a group of women would

have if they experienced the age-specific fertility rates for the calendar year in question throughout their childbearing lifespan." These numbers do not refer to male fertility explicitly, which was the specific topic that so shocked James, but nonetheless reinforces the general concern for the failure of humans to reproduce.

5   National Center for Health Statistics, "U.S. Fertility Rate Drops to Another Historic Low," news release, April 25, 2024, https://www.cdc.gov/nchs/pressroom/nchs_press_releases/2024/20240525.htm.

6   Anne Morse, "Stable Fertility Rates 1990–2019 Mask Distinct Variations by Age," Census.gov, August 14, 2023, https://www.census.gov/library/stories/2022/04/fertility-rates-declined-for-younger-women-increased-for-older-women.html.

7   Rachel Minkin, Juliana Menasce Horowitz, and Carolina Aragão, "The Experiences of U.S. Adults Who Don't Have Children," Pew Research Center, July 25, 2024, https://www.pewresearch.org/social-trends/2024/07/25/the-experiences-of-u-s-adults-who-dont-have-children/.

8   Nicholas Eberstadt, "The Age of Depopulation: Surviving a World Gone Gray," *Foreign Affairs*, November/December 2024, https://www.foreignaffairs.com/world/age-depopulation-surviving-world-gone-gray-nicholas-eberstadt.

9   Mark Steyn, "A Baroness on Barrenness," *Steyn Online*, August 3, 2020, https://www.steynonline.com/10509/a-baroness-on-barrenness.

10 John J. Miller, "P. D. James's Still-Haunting Vision in *Children of Men*," *National Review*, November 1, 2021, https://www.nationalreview.com/magazine/2021/11/01/p-d-jamess-still-haunting-vision-in-children-of-men/.

11 Ross Douthat, *The Decadent Society: How We Became the Victims of Our Own Success* (New York: Avid Reader Press, 2020), 48.

12 James Bowman, "Our Childless Dystopia," *New Atlantis*, Winter 2007, https://www.thenewatlantis.com/publications/our-childless-dystopia.

13 P. D. James, *The Children of Men* (New York: Alfred A. Knopf, 1993), 31.

14 Ibid., 11.

15 Ibid., 106.

16 Ibid., 16.

17 Ibid., 24–25.

18 Ibid., 29.

19 Ibid., 98.

20 Ibid., 9.

21   Ibid., 5.

22   Ibid., 7–8.

23   Ibid., 116.

24   Ibid., 34

25   Ibid., 34–35.

26   Ibid., 114.

27   Jonathan V. Last, *What to Expect When No One's Expecting: America's Coming Demographic Disaster* (New York: Encounter Books, 2013), 2.

28   Ibid., 3.

29   Michelle Megna, "Pet Ownership Statistics 2024," *Forbes*, October 29, 2024, https://www.forbes.com/advisor/pet-insurance/pet-ownership; "Manufacturers & Pet Product Brands Industry Trends and Stats," American Pet Products Association, accessed December 17, 2024, https://www.americanpetproducts.org/press_industrytrends.asp.

30   Timothy P. Carney, *Family Unfriendly: How Our Culture Made Raising Kids Much Harder Than It Needs to Be* (New York: Harper Collins, 2024), 275.

31   Pew Research Center, "The Experiences of U.S. Adults Who Don't Have Children," July 25, 2024, https://www.pewresearch.org/social-trends/2024/07/25/the-experiences-of-u-s-adults-who-dont-have-children/.

32   James, *The Children of Men*, 47.

33   Ibid.

34   As we'll see, this is not the only time the novel uses lyrics from a Beatles song.

35   Ross Douthat, "What Euthanasia Has Done to Canada," *New York Times*, December 3, 2022, https://www.nytimes.com/2022/12/03/opinion/canada-euthanasia.html. The video (which you can view at https://www.adforum.com/creative-work/ad/player/34674540/all-is-beauty/simons) fails to mention that the woman was unable to secure palliative care from Canada's government health system.

36   David Brooks, "The Outer Limits of Liberalism," *The Atlantic*, May 4, 2023, https://www.theatlantic.com/magazine/archive/2023/06/canada-legalized-medical-assisted-suicide-euthanasia-death-maid/673790/.

37   "Fifth Annual Report on Medical Assistance in Dying in Canada, 2023," Government of Canada, December 11, 2024, https://www.canada.ca/en/health-canada/services/publications/health-system-services/annual-report-medical-assistance-dying-2023.html.

38 Ibid.; Alexander Raikin, "A Pattern of Noncompliance," *New Atlantis*, November 11, 2024, https://www.thenewatlantis.com/publications /compliance-problems-maid-canada-leaked-documents.

39 Maria Cheng, "Committee Reviewing Euthanasia in Canada Finds Some Deaths Driven by Homelessness Fears, Isolation," Associated Press, October 18, 2024, https://apnews.com/article/canada-euthanasia-deaths -doctors-nonterminal-nonfatal-cases-cd7ff24c57c15a404347df289788e f6d.

40 Becky Morton, "MPs Back Proposals to Legalise Assisted Dying," BBC, November 29, 2024, https://www.bbc.com/news/articles/ckgzkp79npgo.

41 James, *Children of Men*, 162. James appreciated that resource herself, writing in her autobiography that it was "always a useful source when in trouble" for titles (*Time to Be in Earnest*, 98). James is herself quoted in similar reference books, with remarks that will delight conservatives, including one I quoted above and this: "I believe that political correctness can be a form of linguistic fascism, and it sends shivers down the spine of my generation who went to war against fascism." *The Oxford Dictionary of Literary Quotations*, ed. Peter Kemp (Oxford: Oxford University Press, 1997), 36.

42 *Oxford Dictionary of Quotations* (New York: Oxford University Press, 2009), 411. I have not been able to find an edition published before James's novel to confirm my suspicion that she found the quotation there, rather than the editors including it after 1992.

43 Horace, *Satires. Epistles. The Art of Poetry*, trans. H. Rushton Fairclough, Loeb Classical Library 194 (Cambridge, MA: Harvard University Press, 1926), 215–16.

44 James, *Children of Men*, 59.

45 Ibid., 89.

46 Ibid., 11, 58.

47 Bowman, "Our Childless Utopia."

48 James, *Children of Men*, 33.

49 Ibid., 127. In *The Bonfire of the Vanities*, Tom Wolfe conveys this sense through the point of view of an assistant district attorney who feels "in every cell and every neural fiber . . . nothing less than the Power. . . . It was the power of the government over the freedom of its subjects." He thrills "to see *the looks on their faces*—as they stare back at you, courier and conduit of the Power . . . and now to see *that little swallow of fright* in a

perfect neck worth millions—well, the poet has never sung of that ecstasy or even dreamed of it[.]"

50   James, *Children of Men*, 166.
51   Ibid., 218.
52   James, *Time to Be in Earnest*, 199.
53   James, *Children of Men*, 48–49.
54   Ibid., 36.
55   Steyn, "A Baroness on Barrenness," https://www.steynonline.com/10509/a-baroness-on-barrenness.
56   James, *Children of Men*, 138.
57   Ibid., 238.
58   Ibid., 130.
59   Ibid., 133.
60   Ibid., 176–77.
61   Ibid., 241. The moment calls to mind the power of the one true ring in J. R. R. Tolkien's *The Lord of the Rings* trilogy, with its constant temptation to the wearer to descend into selfishness and power.
62   Some elements of this chapter first appeared in Christopher J. Scalia, "England's Real-Life Quietus," *RealClearBooks*, December 11, 2024, https://www.realclearbooks.com/2024/12/11/englands_real-life_quietus_1077832.html.

Chapter Twelve

1   Katherine Dieckmann, "Miracle Worker," *New York Times*, September 9, 2001, https://www.nytimes.com/2001/09/09/books/miracle-worker.html.
2   Neil Straus, "Pop Life: The Sound of Silence?," *New York Times*, March 20, 2003, https://www.nytimes.com/2003/03/20/arts/the-pop-life-the-sound-of-silence.html. Jones won eight Grammys in 2003, including Album of the Year for the previous year's *Come Away with Me* and Record of the Year for the single "Don't Know Why."
3   George F. Will, "Onward and Upward," *Washington Post*, March 12, 2002, A21, http://ontology.buffalo.edu/smith/courses01/rrtw/Will4.htm. Of course, this wasn't true of every successful novel or album from the era. Jonathan Franzen's novel *The Corrections*, published just a week before Enger's work, is, one of the best of the best American novels of the twenty-first century so far, but it's far from comfort food. Other cultural works that were either produced or released shortly before 9/11 gained special meaning because of their timing. The band Wilco released the album *Yankee Hotel Foxtrot* on its

website a week after the terror attacks, but its lyrical references to burning buildings, American flags, and a "war on war" assumed significance the band couldn't have imagined when recording it. The same is true of its cover, which is an image of two towers.

4 Ron Charles, "Cowboys and Wonders," *Christian Science Monitor*, September 6, 2001, www.csmonitor.com/2001/0906/p14s1-bogn.html.

5 Leif Enger, *Peace Like a River* (New York: Grove Press, 2001), 55.

6 Ibid., 3.

7 David Hume, *An Enquiry Concerning Human Understanding*, ed. L.A. Selby-Bigge (Oxford: Clarendon Press, 1990), X.1.114.

8 Harold K. Bush, "Miracles and the Postsecular: Some 'Unscientific' Thoughts on *Peace Like a River* and *Mariette in Ecstasy*," *Christianity & Literature* 69: 116–117.

9 Enger, *Peace Like a River*, 3.

10 Kim Anderson Sasser, "From the Inside of Belief: Magic and Religion," in *Magical Realism and Literature*, ed. Christopher Warnes and Kim Anderson Sasser (Cambridge: Cambridge University Press, 2020), 252–53.

11 *Winter's Tale* is a particular favorite among conservatives in part because Helprin is a foreign policy expert who worked in the Reagan administration and writes a regular column for the *Claremont Review of Books*. See Appendix II.

12 Sasser, "From the Inside of Belief," 258, 260.

13 Enger, *Peace Like a River*, 25.

14 Ibid., 130.

15 Ibid., 131.

16 Ibid., 187.

17 Ibid., 311.

18 Ibid., 168.

19 Ibid., 173.

20 Ibid., 173–74.

21 Ibid., 310.

22 Ibid., 65–66.

23 Alden Mudge, "Riding the Wave of Leif Enger's Dazzling Debut," *Book Page*, September 2001, https://www.bookpage.com/interviews/8109-leif-enger-fiction/.

24 Enger, *Peace Like a River*, 151.

25 Ibid., 35.

26 Ibid., 33.

27   Ibid., 300.
28   Ibid., 75.
29   Ibid., 151.
30   Ibid., 268.
31   Mudge, "Riding the Wave of Leif Enger's Dazzling Debut."
32   Paul Cantor, *The Invisible Hand in Popular Culture: Liberty vs. Authority in American Film and TV* (Lexington: University Press of Kentucky, 2012), 25.
33   Paul Cantor, *Pop Culture and the Dark Side of the American Dream: Con Men, Gangsters, Drug Lords, and Zombies* (Lexington: University Press of Kentucky, 2019), 10.
34   Alexander Riley, "Cormac McCarthy: Conservative Novelist," *Academic Questions* 2022 (35.2), 95–96.
35   Harvey Mansfield, *Manliness* (New Haven: Yale University Press, 2006), 21.
36   Christina Hoff Sommers, *The War against Boys: How Misguided Feminism Is Harming Our Young Men* (New York: Simon & Schuster, 2000), 13–14.
37   Josh Hawley, *Manhood: The Masculine Virtues America Needs* (Washington: Regnery, 2023), 9.
38   Mansfield, *Manliness*, 17.
39   Enger, *Peace Like a River*, 24.
40   Ibid., 25.
41   Ibid.
42   Ibid., 36.
43   Ibid., 233.
44   Ibid., 268, 25.
45   Ibid., 56.
46   Ibid., 35.
47   Ibid., 101.
48   Ibid., 298.
49   Ibid., 309.
50   Yuval Levin, "Conservatism Is Gratitude," Bradley Prize Remarks, June 12, 2013, https://eppc.org/publication/conservatism-is-gratitude/.
51   Patrick M. Garry, "Conservatism's Central Meaning: Gratitude," *The Imaginative Conservative*, November 22, 2022, https://theimaginativeconservative.org/2022/11/conservatism-central-meaning-gratitude-patrick-garry.html.

Chapter Thirteen

1   Leo Tolstoy, *Anna Karenina* (1877), trans. Richard Pevar and Larissa Volokhonsky (New York: Penguin, 2000), 1.

2   Bill James, *The New Bill James Historical Abstract* (New York: The Free Press, 2001), 904. James conceded, "The Index of Self-Destructive Acts is kind of a garbage stat, because it puts together separate and unrelated acts into a single category. I like it, nonetheless, because it makes useful information out of four statistical categories which are, by themselves, too small to sustain any conclusions." Baseball geeks may be interested to know that some very good pitchers have had historically high ISDAs, including Orel Hershiser, Randy Johnson, Nolan Ryan, and David Cone.

3   Joshua Hren, "Cracks of Faith in the Secular Self," *Catholic World Report*, October 2020, https://www.catholicworldreport.com/2020/10/14/cracks -of-faith-in-the-secular-self/.

4   Christopher Beha, *The Index of Self-Destructive Acts* (Portland: Tin House, 2020), 22.

5   Randy Boyagoda, "*The Index of Self-Destructive Acts*—the best-laid plans," *Financial Times*, 16 July 2020, https://www.ft.com/content/98f5e5c4–32f0 –4467-91ac-c5ffbbce0f3a.

6   Rand Richards Cooper, "Baseball, Journalism, and the Big New York City Novel: An interview with Christopher Beha," *Commonweal*, July 26, 2020, https://www.commonwealmagazine.org/baseball-journalism-and-big -new-york-city-novel.

7   Adam O'Fallon Price, "Craft Corner: *The Millions* Interviews Christopher Beha," *The Millions*, July 23, 2020, https://themillions.com /2020/07/craft-corner-the-millions-interviews-christopher-beha.html.

8   Beha, *The Index of Self-Destructive Acts*, 58.

9   Ibid., 53.

10   Ibid., 55.

11   Ibid., 104.

12   In one of the novel's many subtle ironies, while Margo's poetic ambitions are unrealized, her more practically minded brother manages to sneak a phrase "into the consciousness of the age" through his work on a successful beer advertisement: "flavor-sealed for freshness." Ibid., 31.

13   Ibid., 104–5.

14   Ibid., 195.

15   Ibid., 109–10.

16   John Wilson, "Why Humans Self Destruct," *National Review*, June 4, 2020, https://www.nationalreview.com/magazine/2020/06/22/why-humans-self-destruct/.

17   Beha, *The Index of Self-Destructive Acts*, Ibid., 6.

18   Ibid., 301.

19   Benjamin Markovits, "A Numbers-Cruncher Confronts Emotion and Other Unquantifiable Matters," *New York Times*, May 5, 2020, https://www.nytimes.com/2020/05/05/books/review/christopher-beha-index-self-destructive-acts.html.

20   Beha, *The Index of Self-Destructive Acts*, 305.

21   Another recent novel, Julius Taranto's *How I Won a Nobel Prize*, makes a similar point about the limits of quantitative thinking. The main character, who is trying to determine whether to stay with her husband, creates a 377-row spreadsheet of "potential outcomes from breaking up, each of which had a positive or negative cardinal value, e.g., +1 or -2. Each outcome also had a likelihood between 0 and 1, representing the percentage chance that this particular outcome would in fact occur." But she eventually realized that his knowledge of her "decimated any chance of quantifying what he meant in my life." Julius Taranto, *How I Won a Nobel Prize* (New York: Little, Brown and Company, 2023), 172; 190–91.

22   Beha, *The Index of Self-Destructive Acts*, 13.

23   Ibid., 302.

24   Ibid., 497. Sam reminds me of a character from Evelyn Waugh's *Brideshead Revisited* (1945), a military officer named Hooper. To the novel's narrator, Charles Ryder, Hooper represents an impoverished way of thinking that is representative of the modern world. Ryder contrasts his upbringing, which elevated martial heroism, with Hooper's childhood: "Hooper was no romantic. . . . [A]t the age when my eyes were dry to all save poetry . . . Hooper had wept often, but never for Henry's speech on St. Crispin's Day, nor for the epitaph at Thermopylæ. The history they taught him had had few battles in it but, instead, a profusion of detail about humane legislation and recent industrial change." Evelyn Waugh, *Brideshead Revisited* (New York: Penguin Books, 1962), 17–18.

25   Cooper, "Baseball, Journalism, and the Big New York City Novel."

26   Price, "Craft Corner."

27   Beha, *The Index of Self-Destructive Acts.*, 52.

28   Price, "Craft Corner."

29   Megan McArdle, "The Technocratic Dilemma: What Experts Don't Know Can Kill a Program," *Daily Beast*, July 12, 2017, https://www.thedailybeast.com/the-technocratic-dilemma.

30   Beha, *The Index of Self-Destructive Acts*, 142.

31   Ibid., 6.

32   Michael Lewis, *Going Infinite: The Rise and Fall of a New Tycoon* (New York: W. W. Norton & Company, 2023), 29. As if it couldn't get any worse, Lewis also says of Bankman-Fried's education: "All of the humanities was like this for him: dopey stuff he wanted mainly to escape but that somehow always lurked just around every corner. In choosing a college to attend, Sam sought to ensure he'd never again be made to write an essay about Jane Austen." Ibid., 30.

33   Beha, *The Index of Self-Destructive Acts*, 226.

34   For the purposes of clarity, I concur with Ross Douthat's helpful definition of cancelation: "an attack on someone's employment and reputation by a determined collective of critics, based on an opinion or an action that is alleged to be disgraceful and disqualifying." Ross Douthat, "10 Theses about Cancel Culture," *New York Times*, July 14, 2020, https://www.nytimes.com/2020/07/14/opinion/cancel-culture-.html.

35   *Commonweal*. The speed with which the news carries also recalls the notorious cancelation of Justine Sacco, who made a racist joke before boarding a plane bound for Africa and was oblivious to the uproar her remarks caused until her flight landed eleven hours later. See Jon Ronson, "How One Stupid Tweet Blew Up Justine Sacco's Life," *New York Times Magazine*, February 12 2015, https://www.nytimes.com/2015/02/15/magazine/how-one-stupid-tweet-ruined-justine-saccos-life.html.

36   Another exceptional novel that explores race and what we now call cancel culture is Philip Roth's *The Human Stain* (2001), in which a college professor is fired for using the word *spook*, which some of his students interpret as a racist slur. More recently, a character from Lionel Shriver's *The Motion of the Body through Space* (2020) is fired over unjust accusations of racial bias.

37   Beha, *The Index of Self-Destructive Acts*, 507.

38   Ibid., 463.

39   Ibid., 351.

40   Ibid., 190.

41   Ibid., 89.

42   Ibid., 367.

43   Ibid., 5.

44   Ibid., 305.

45   Ibid., 500.

46   Ibid., 292.

47   George F. Will, "The Consciousness Project," *National Review*, November 9, 2023, https://www.nationalreview.com/magazine/2023/12/the-consciousness -project/. Video of the speech on which this article was based is here: https: //jmp.princeton.edu/events/2023/consciousness-political-project-how -legacy-americas-great-universities-being-destroyed. To Will's observation I would add the self-evident qualification that most things—institutions, traditions, memories, families—last longer when people work to preserve them.

48   Beha, *The Index of Self-Destructive Acts*, 477.

Conclusion

1   George Eliot, *Middlemarch* [1871] (London: Oxford's World's Classics, 2019), 134.

2   Maria Edgeworth, *Belinda* [1801] (London: Oxford World's Classics, 2020), 207.

3   Jane Austen, *Pride and Prejudice* [1813] (London: Oxford World's Classics, 2020), 52.

4   J. K. Rowling, *Harry Potter and the Sorcerer's Stone* (New York: Scholastic Inc., 1998), 37–38.

5   Lionel Trilling, "Manners, Morals, and the Novel," in *The Liberal Imagination* (New York: New York Review of Books Classics, 1950), 222.

6   Peggy Noonan, "Signposts on the Wisdom Trail," *Wall Street Journal*, January 2, 2025, https://www.wsj.com/opinion/signposts-on-the-wisdom -trail-lincoln-david-foster-wallace-cs-lewis-advice-21334ef2.

7   Rod Dreher, "Story Lines, Not Party Lines," *American Conservative*, July 10, 2013, https://www.theamericanconservative.com/story-lines-not -party-lines/.

8   Mark Helprin, "Without Which Conservatism Is Stillborn," *National Review* December 19, 2005, 42.

9   Ibid.

10   For example, see Simon During, "The Conservative Turn in Literary Studies," *Chronicle of Higher Education*, January 6, 2025, https://www .chronicle.com/article/the-conservative-turn-in-literary-studies.

11 Calvin Coolidge, "Bunker Hill Day," June 17, 1918, https://coolidge foundation.org/resources/bunker-hill-day/. The expression has received broader attention thanks to its use by the Federalist website.

Appendix 1

1 Samuel Johnson, *The History of Rasselas, Prince of Abissinia* (London: Penguin Classics, 2007), 32.

2 Carla Kaplan, *Their Eyes Were Watching God* Audio Guide, National Endowment for the Arts, November 24, 2013, https://www.arts.gov/stories /other/their-eyes-were-watching-god-audio-guide#transcript.

Index

Note: Page numbers followed by 'n' with number refer to endnotes.

READING NOTES

READING NOTES

READING NOTES

READING NOTES

READING NOTES

READING NOTES

READING NOTES

READING NOTES

READING NOTES

READING NOTES

READING NOTES

READING NOTES